BID OUR JARRING CONFLICTS CEASE

A WESLEYAN THEOLOGY AND PRAXIS OF CHURCH UNITY

DAVID N. FIELD

"BID OUR JARRING CONFLICTS CEASE!"
A WESLEYAN THEOLOGY AND PRAXIS OF CHURCH UNITY

The General Board of Higher Education and Ministry leads and serves The United Methodist Church in the recruitment, preparation, nurture, education, and support of Christian leaders—lay and clergy—for the work of making disciples of Jesus Christ for the transformation of the world. The General Board of Higher Education and Ministry of The United Methodist Church serves as an advocate for the intellectual life of the church. The Board's mission embodies the Wesleyan tradition of commitment to the education of laypersons and ordained persons by providing access to higher education for all persons.

Foundery Books is named for the abandoned foundery that early followers of John Wesley transformed into a church, which became the cradle of London's Methodist movement.

HIGHER EDUCATION & MINISTRY
General Board of Higher Education and Ministry
THE UNITED METHODIST CHURCH

Dedicated to my mother, Joan Field, and in memory of my father, Nugent Field, in gratefulness for their encouragement and support for many years. While they never read John Wesley's "Catholic Spirit," they lived it.

CONTENTS

ACKNOWLEDGMENTS

It is appropriate that a book on the unity of the church in the context of theological diversity was not produced in isolation. Family members, friends, and colleagues made valuable contributions to the development of this book. I owe a major debt of gratitude to Bishop Patrick Streiff of the United Methodist Central Conference of Central and Southern Europe. About eleven years ago he took the risk of asking someone who did not know very much about Methodism to develop an Internet-based study program on Methodist Studies for people preparing for ministry in The United Methodist Church in Europe, out of which the Methodist e-Academy was born. Having agreed to take on this responsibility I engaged in an intensive research in Wesley and Methodist Studies and in doing so discovered my theological home. Patrick has taken time out of his very busy program to read part of the manuscript and to discuss aspects of it with me. I greatly appreciate his support and encouragement. My initial ideas for the book were prepared to be part of an online course on unity and diversity in the church offered by the e-Academy. Unfortunately, insufficient student numbers resulted in the course being canceled, but I did have the opportunity to discuss some of my initial ideas with Eva Michel and Neal Christie. Sections of the book were also presented and critiqued at an e-Academy block seminar on Methodist ethics.

Sam McBratney of the Queens Foundation for Ecumenical Theological Education read and critiqued sections of the manuscript. We discussed aspects of it over a memorable Mexican meal in Houston, Texas, during the World Methodist Conference. A number of his ideas were helpful in shaping the final chapter and conclusion. Michael Nausner of Reutlingen School of Theology reviewed the manuscript and provided an important critique of the earlier version. The final version is much improved as a consequence. Michael has also been a strong encourager for me to complete the work. I owe a particular thanks to Kathryn Armistead, publisher at GB-HEM. She was an enthusiastic supporter of the project from when I first approached her and has continued to encourage and support me along the way. She thoroughly reviewed various versions of the manuscript. She not only made the manuscript more readable but also provided substantial critique and proposals with regard to a number of significant issues. Thank you, Kathy!

The book was written in the context of the hurly-burly of family life. My wife, Caroline, is the pastor of a large church, and I take the major responsibility for the household. Writing a book meant that I tended to bury myself in my work, and the laundry was done even more irregularly than normal. Thank you, Caroline, Carlo, and Ernst, for putting up with it all and for supporting me throughout. The title of the book is the product of an intensive discussion with Caroline in which she subjected my very boring ideas to thorough critique.

My parents, Nugent and Joan Field, they have supported my theological work from the beginning of my studies. When I began to make professional contributions to theology they took the time to plow through some of the obscure academic language, discussed aspects of it with me, and kept me focused on its relevance for the life of the church. I would have loved to discuss major parts of this work with Dad, but he passed away while it was still in its initial stages. I know he would have provided both support and important critique if he had had the opportunity. Mom supported me all the way, constantly encouraging me and regularly asking whether the book was finally finished.

ABBREVIATIONS

- *Works of Wesley*

  The Works of John Wesley (begun as the Oxford Edition of *The Works of John Wesley* (Oxford: Clarendon Press, 1975–1983), continued as The Bicentennial Edition of *The Works of John Wesley*, vols. 1–27 (Nashville: Abingdon Press, 1984–).

- *Works* (Jackson)

  The Works of the Rev. John Wesley, M.A., ed. Thomas Jackson, 3rd ed., 14 vols. (London: Wesleyan Methodist Book Room, 1872; repr. Grand Rapids: Baker Book House, 1979).

- *Letters*

  The Letters of John Wesley, ed. John Telford, 8 vols. (London: Epworth, 1931).

- *OT Notes*

  John Wesley, *Explanatory Notes upon the Old Testament,* (Bristol: W. Pine, 1765; repr. Oxford: Benediction Classics, 2010). Cited by biblical reference.

- *NT Notes*

  John Wesley, *Explanatory Notes upon the New Testament* (Bristol: Graham and Pine, 1760–62; repr. London: Epworth, 1976). Cited by biblical reference.

INTRODUCTION

Jesu, Lord, we look to thee,
Let us in thy name agree;
Show thyself the Prince of peace,
Bid our jars forever cease.
By thy reconciling love
Every stumbling block remove,
Each to each unite, endear;
Come and spread thy banner here![1]

With hymns like this, Charles Wesley gave expression to the passion for the unity of the church that was integral to early Methodism. In the theology of both John and Charles Wesley, "jars"—or in modern English "strife," or better expressed in the modernized version of the line used for the title of this book: "jarring conflicts"[2]—between Christians was a contradiction of the love that ought to define the Christian life. The presence of such conflict was a destructive disturbance that severely compromised the identity of the church as a people called to embody the divine love. As another hymn expresses it:

Love, like death, hath all destroyed,
Rendered our distinctions void!
Names, and sects, and parties fall,
Thou, O Christ are all in all![3]

The singing of hymns such as these not only gave expression to a Wesleyan ideal but also deeply embedded within the ethos of Methodism a vision of the visible unity of the church.

Despite the prayer of Jesus, narrated in John's Gospel, that his disciples may be one, from its earliest history disunity seems to have been a constant feature of the life of the church. Diversity quickly gives way to division; movements for renewal become new denominations; differences over theology, ethics, or liturgy become barriers to communion; power struggles and personality conflicts bedevil the life

---

1 *A Collection of Hymns, for the Use of the People Called Methodists*, no. 495, *Works of Wesley,* 7:683.

2 This version is used in a number of contemporary sources. See for example *Singing the Faith* (London: The Methodist Church, 2011), no. 686.

3 *A Collection of Hymns, for the Use of the People Called Methodists*, no. 504, *Works of Wesley,* 7:694.

of congregations and denominations; racism, cultural imperialism, and nationalism have split churches. Methodism began as a renewal movement but soon became a separate church. The Wesleyan vision of a church that embodied love through its commitment to unity was suppressed as Methodism further split into numerous denominations.

Jesus' prayer and the vision of the visible unity of the church remains as a disturbing memory of God's intention for the church and is a constant challenge as we confront diversity, difference, and conflict within and between congregations and denominations. Even so, the vision of the visible unity was an inspiration for many church leaders in the twentieth century. It expressed itself in different ways, including the 1910 Edinburgh Missions Conference and the founding of the World Council of Churches (WCC) in 1948; the creation of various united and uniting churches; and the reunification of divided denominations. Given the oft-suppressed Wesleyan vision of love that transcends and overcomes divisions, it is perhaps to be expected that Methodists played a key role in these developments. John R. Mott, a Methodist layperson, was the key mover behind the Edinburgh Conference. Methodists have served as general secretaries of the WCC. Methodist churches have been part of church unions in Canada, India, and Australia. Different branches of the Methodist church came together in Britain in 1932 and in various unions in the United States, culminating in the formation of The United Methodist Church in 1968. These attempts were never complete; not all churches joined the ecumenical movement; the reunion of Methodist churches in the USA did not include historic African-American Methodist churches. Nevertheless, they were a significant witness to the vision of a unity in the midst of the diversity of the church and in small ways the embodiment of the Wesleyan ideal.

While the vision of visible unity remains, the dawning of the twenty-first century has raised new issues as a consequence of the radical shift in the geographical center of global Christianity from the north to the south; the growth of evangelical and Pentecostal churches particularly in the majority world; the emergence of new theological and ethical disagreements at a time when progress was being made in resolving old ones and of new divisions between and within east and west, north and south. Tensions and divisions exist not only between churches but also within churches and families of churches—a situation that has been exacerbated by the numerical, and with it the financial, decline of many churches in Western Europe and North America. Methodist churches have not escaped these challenges and tensions, and they have been particularly present within The United Methodist Church due to its international character.

The realities of theological diversity, disagreement, and even division within churches within the Wesleyan and Methodist tradition, and the new complexities and tensions within world Christianity, are a challenge and an opportunity for Methodists to recover the ecumenical dynamic deeply rooted within their tradition. This book seeks to contribute to such a recovery through an examination of John Wesley's theology of the unity of the church.

The book also reflects a personal ecumenical pilgrimage; in many ways I am an accidental Methodist. While members of my father's family have been Methodists since at least the early decades of the nineteenth century, my grandparents left the Methodist church soon after my father was born. I began my theological education at a Bible college deeply rooted in conservative Calvinism, and my master's and doctoral work entailed a deep engagement with the Reformed tradition though within an ecumenical context. For a number of years, I was a member of the Presbyterian Church. Equally formative for my theological formation was that this took place within the context of the oppression and political struggles of South Africa in the 1980s and early 90s. This context gave rise both to division and unity, as Christians responded to apartheid in contradictory ways. The postapartheid call to reconciliation provided new challenges for the churches.

As my academic career progressed, I taught in evangelical colleges, secular universities, an Anglican theological college, and a Methodist university. However, it was only when my wife took up a pastoral position in The United Methodist Church that I began to seriously engage with the Methodist and Wesleyan tradition. This was immensely fruitful for my own theological development, as I discovered within the Methodist and Wesleyan tradition resources for creative ways of responding to unresolved questions within my own theological understanding. One significant issue was the development of a theological basis for ecumenical relationships, which held together a commitment to unity and truth, particularly in the context of confronting social injustice. However, as I read various Methodist texts dealing with ecumenical relationships or tensions and divisions within Methodist denominations, I discovered that apart from standard citations usually from John Wesley's sermon "Catholic Spirit," and his "A Letter to a Roman Catholic," the theological depth of the Wesleyan heritage had not been mined in a significant way. This discovery occurred as I was engaged in preparing courses on Methodist studies for candidates for ordination in The United Methodist Church. The courses were designed to root students in the particularities of Methodist identity. Paradoxically I came to the conclusion that one of the distinctive particularities of John Wesley's theology was the vision of the unity of the church that in a particular way relativized denominational particularities. This vision was an integral part of his theology and a constitutive element of his ideal for the Methodist movement, meaning that an ecumenical dynamic is a constitutive aspect of Methodist and Wesleyan identity.

The issue of ecclesial identity is crucial to any discussion of the unity of the church. Within particular churches it is the question of the relationship between identity and diversity. How much diversity can be included within a church, denomination, or organization without compromising its particular identity? From an ecumenical perspective the question becomes: How can this particular identity become a gift to the universal church? If the ecumenical dynamic is a constitutive element of Methodist identity, then the Methodist ecumenical engagement is the natural fruit of the Methodist tradition. The divisions and separations within Methodism must then also be understood as a challenge to and in many cases a contradiction of Methodist identity even when they are pursued in the name of Methodist and Wesleyan identity.

So, what is it that constitutes our particular identity as Methodists? While denominations and traditions develop a dynamic of their own it is helpful to ask the question historically—what was the guiding vision of early Methodism and, in particular, of John Wesley? For Wesley it was clear: "To reform the nation, and in particular the Church, to spread scriptural holiness over the land."[4] In a letter to Joseph Benson in 1777, Wesley stated: "We are called to propagate Bible religion through the land—that is, faith working by love, holy tempers, and holy lives."[5] The identity of early Methodism was constituted by its mission of forming a holy people whose presence and lives would bring reformation to the church and society.[6] As Wesley argued in his pamphlet "The Character of a Methodist,"[7] the distinguishing feature of Methodism was not unique doctrinal affirmations but the holy character of its members. When Wesley addressed the theological dimensions of Methodist identity, he returned to the same theme. He stated: "Our main doctrines, which include all the rest, are three, that of repentance, of faith, and of holiness. The first of these we account, as it were, the porch of religion; the next, the door; the third, religion itself."[8]

We might well ask if Wesley's vision is still relevant for Methodism; after all, Methodism has developed and changed. It is now a family of denominations and not an association of religious societies with members from various denominations. It has spread across geographical, cultural, and national boundaries. It has developed a diversity of organizational structures, and its theological scholarship is carried out in vastly different intellectual contexts. Despite this, I argue that a recovery of holiness is central to Methodist identity, because it not only roots us in our historic tradition but also has the potential to make a significant contribution to the struggle over identity, unity, diversity, and disagreement in the contemporary

---

4   The Methodist Societies, The Minutes of Conference, "Minutes of Several Conversations between the Reverend Mr. John and Charles Wesley and Others," *Works of Wesley*, 10:845.

5   Letter to Joseph Benson December 8, 1777, *Letters*, 6:291

6   This basic understanding is described in Sermon 63, "The General Spread of the Gospel," *Works of Wesley*, 2:485-99.

7   "The Character of a Methodist," *Works of Wesley*, 9:31-46.

8   "The Principles of a Methodist Farther Explained," *Works of Wesley*, 9:227.

context. It is a recovery of this vision of our identity that can provide the necessary theological perspective from which we can address the structural, relational, and organizational issues of living with diversity within denominations and of engaging in ecumenical dialogue with other confessions and denominations. To advocate a recovery of "holiness" is not unproblematic given that there are diverse interpretations of holiness even within the Wesleyan and Methodist tradition. I will argue that at its core, holiness is the gracious work of God in human persons, which transforms us so that our lives are characterized by love for God and our fellow human beings.

The aim of this book is to develop a constructive approach to the issue of theological diversity rooted in Wesley's theology. It is, however, not an attempt to answer the questions: What would Wesley say to us today? Or what would Wesley do today? Such questions are open to two possible interpretations, neither of which is particularly helpful. The one would ask Wesley to speak directly from the eighteenth century to us in a normative way, ignoring the huge developments in human knowledge, including developments in our understanding of the Bible and Christian tradition. Given Wesley's deep interest in science and culture, this would be contrary to his own approach to issues. The second would be to try and discern how Wesley would respond to the developments and changes in human knowledge since the eighteenth century. We simply have no real basis for discerning this. We need to acknowledge that Wesley was a child of the eighteenth century, and we live in vastly different contexts. This does not mean that Wesley is irrelevant but rather that our approach must be different. Instead of asking what would Wesley say and do today, we need to ask what did he say and do then? This provides us with a basis for the constructive task of asking: "What should *we* say and do today in the light of what he said and did then?"

In doing this we are faced with the question of which Wesley? This question has two dimensions. The first is that of time; Wesley scholars generally divide his work into three periods—the early period 1733–1738, a middle period 1738–1765, and a late period 1765–1791. Wesley recognized the major shift in 1738 but tended to view the rest of his theology as being essentially consistent with some variations in expression, caused in part by his having to respond to a variety of attacks from different viewpoints.[9] From the standpoint of Methodist ecclesiology, the middle period has greater weight, as it was in this period that he wrote his *Explanatory Notes upon the New Testament* and

---

9   See "A Letter to the Rev. Dr. Rutherford," *Works of Wesley,* 9:375; and his letter to William Green October 25, 1789, *Letters,* 8:179.

the forty-four Standard Sermons,[10] which provide the standards of doctrine in most Methodist churches, although churches originating in the American Methodist tradition add another nine sermons from a slightly later date. Nevertheless, some scholars give priority to the late period as expressing his mature position. Though it could also be argued that some of the positions he adopted in the later writings are not so much a maturing of his thought as his application and development of his theology to address particular controversies. As the purpose of this work is not merely historical but also constructive, I will note the developments in his thought but seek to develop elements which, in my opinion, give the most satisfactory expression to the dynamic continuity of Wesley's central ideas. The book assumes that the reader has a basic knowledge of John Wesley's theology and develops its constructive proposals in the light of this.

The question's second dimension is, should one focus on Wesley's clearly presented theological ideas or his actual practice? While there is, as would be expected, continuity between his theology and his practice, at times there is dissonance between them. Again, given the constructive nature of this work, I will focus primarily on his theological ideas and illustrate this from his practice, while recognizing that in some contexts his praxis embodies an implied theology, which enriches and develops his explicit theology.

In seeking to discern what we should say and do today, the book focuses on the theme of holiness as the core of Wesley's vision and then explores how he relates this to the theme of theological diversity and disagreement. The first two chapters examine the theme of holiness. The third briefly sketches key elements of Wesley's context. This provides the context for examining two classic Wesleyan sermons, "Catholic Spirit" and "A Caution against Bigotry" in chapters 4 and 5. In the sixth and seventh chapters, I examine the theological roots that underlie these two sermons. Chapter 8

---

10 The title Standard Sermons is given to those sermons that are affirmed to be the standards of doctrine in Methodist churches. In 1763, John Wesley prepared the "Model Deed," which all Methodist societies in England were expected to accept. (See *Works of Wesley*, 10:869–70, "The 'Large' *Minutes*, 1763.") In this he set out the doctrinal standards for Methodism as being the doctrine contained in the *Explanatory Notes upon the New Testament* and the sermons in the first four volumes of his *Sermons on Several Occasions*. The *Sermons on Several Occasions* went through different editions in Wesley's lifetime with different numbers of sermons. At the time the Model Deed was written it contained forty-four sermons. The Methodist Church in Britain and Methodist churches that are the products of its mission work therefore accept these forty-four sermons as the Standard Sermons. When Wesley sermons were published in America in 1783, the first four volumes included nine more sermons. Hence when the Methodist Episcopal Church was founded, the reference to the first four volumes of sermons would probably have been taken to refer to this American edition and therefore to fifty-three sermons. As a consequence, American Methodist churches and churches founded by their missionaries accept these fifty-three sermons as the Standard Sermons. See the discussion in Scott J. Jones, *United Methodist Doctrine: The Extreme Center* (Nashville: Abingdon, 2002), 51–55.

relates to Wesley's understanding of the church, and chapter 9 sketches key elements of a Wesleyan praxis of seeking unity in the midst of diversity.

Writing this book was a journey of theological discovery. From my initial study of Wesley and various studies of Wesley's theology, I had developed some clear ideas as to what I thought Wesley's approach to diversity was. A careful reading of many of his writings led me to significant changes in my interpretation of Wesley, particularly in relation to the issues discussed in chapters 7 and 8. Some readers of this book will agree and others not. I welcome critique and correction. This book makes no claim to be definitive but is rather an invitation to join in this journey of discovery in order to gain insights from Wesley for our task of pursuing the unity of the church today. Given my own ecumenical pilgrimage, this journey has a personal character, as I seek to relate not only to friends and relatives who belong to different ecclesial traditions (my wife is now a pastor in a Reformed church) or hold to very different theological positions but also to my twenty-one-year-old self, who was a vigorous opponent of women preachers and Wesleyan Arminian theology.

CHAPTER 1

WHAT HAS HOLINESS GOT TO DO WITH IT?

If holiness is central to Methodist identity, we might well ask: How can a discussion of holiness contribute to a way forward for churches characterized by diverse and even contradictory theological perspectives? How does holiness contribute to ecumenical relationships? Holiness seems rather otherworldly, somewhat old fashioned, a bit esoteric and irrelevant to the often messy world of church politics. More problematic, it often conjures up images of self-righteousness, legalistic rule keeping, or the narcissistic pursuit of one's own spiritual purity at the expense of others and has often become a campaign slogan of particular theological parties, often in contrast to "love" used by opposing groups. On the face of it, holiness does not appear to be a helpful perspective from which this issue can be addressed. Is holiness of any use at all? To answer, I will explore key aspects of John Wesley's understanding of holiness and then make proposals for a contemporary Wesleyan theology of holiness.

WHAT DID WESLEY MEAN BY HOLINESS?[1]

In the broadest possible terms, the language of holiness is characteristically used to describe that which separates a religious community from the broader society and simultaneously describes its commitment to the divine or the sacred. John Wesley developed his understanding of holiness in relation to two contemporary perspectives. The first perspective understood holiness in terms of religious observance and moral behavior. The second understood it as a mystical relationship with God brought about through withdrawal from society. Wesley countered this with his dual emphasis that true holiness was holiness of heart and life or that it included inner and outer dimensions. His emphasis is not merely a combination of two opposites or an attempt to find a middle way that does justice to both; rather

---

1   For the purposes of this chapter, I will not provide a comprehensive analysis of Wesley's theology of holiness. More detailed discussions can be found in Harald Lindström, *Wesley and Sanctification: A Study in the Doctrine of Salvation* (Nappanee, IN: Francis Asbury, 1996); Christoph Klaiber, *Von Gottes Geist verändert: Ursprung und Wirkung wesleyanischer Pneumatologie* (Göttingen: Edition Ruprecht, 2013); and David B. McEwan, *The Life of God in the Soul: The Integration of Love, Holiness and Happiness in the Thought of John Wesley* (Milton Keynes, UK: Paternoster, 2015).

it is a radically different conceptualization of holiness in which the inner and outer dimensions are dynamically related to each other. And while Wesley emphasized holiness of the heart and life, he gives a particular priority to what he referred to as "religion of the heart," "heart" metaphorically referring to the center of our deepest motivations combining entrenched emotions, patterns of thinking, and characteristic values. In Wesley's terminology it includes the following:[2]

> **Affections:** These are the inclinations that motivate human action. As such they include both rational and emotional dimensions and are our responses to reality beyond us. This reality may be divine or creaturely. The affections are changeable and subject to development.

> **Tempers:** These are affections that have been strengthened and focused so that they become habitual or enduring inclinations to behave in a particular way. Thus the tempers lead to characteristic words and deeds. Sinful tempers lead to sinful actions, holy tempers to holy actions.

> **Passions:** These are emotional expressions characterized by less mental control than affections; they are more spontaneous and do not endure.

> **Will:** This is the combination of our various affections and tempers that act together to direct our behavior.

> **Liberty:** This is the capacity to act or to refuse to act in accordance with a particular passion, affection, or temper. It is the faculty of liberty that guarantees human responsibility and enables Wesley to avoid a deterministic understanding of the human person.

---

2   There is some debate in Wesley scholarship as to the relationship among these different dimensions of the heart, particularly whether affections and tempers can be distinguished. A discussion or resolution of this debate is not necessary for the purposes of my argument. For more detail see Kenneth J. Collins, "John Wesley's Topography of the Heart: Dispositions, Tempers and Affections," *Methodist History* 36, no. 3 (1998); Randy L. Maddox, *Responsible Grace: John Wesley's Practical Theology* (Nashville: Abingdon, 1994), 69–70; "Holiness of Heart and Life: Lessons from North American Methodism," *Asbury Theological Journal* 51, no. 1 (1996), 151–72; "Reconnecting the Means to the End: A Wesleyan Prescription for the Holiness Movement," *Wesleyan Theological Journal* 33, no. 2 (1998), 29–66; "The Change of Affections: The Development of John Wesley's 'Heart Religion,'" in Richard B. Steele, ed., *"Heart Religion" in the Methodist and Related Movements* (Metuchen: Scarecrow, 2001), 3–31; Anthony J. Headley, *Getting It Right: Christian Perfection and Wesley's Purposeful List* (Lexington: Emeth, 2013), 39–87; and Gregory Clapper, *The Renewal of the Heart Is the Mission of the Church: Wesley's Heart Religion in the Twenty-First Century* (Eugene, OR: Cascade, 2010), 17–30.

This is not a complete analysis of the human person, and Wesley supplements his pastoral advice with other considerations, particularly relating to the influence of biological and on occasions sociological factors. In more contemporary language Wesley is arguing that the human character is shaped by a complex of inner desires, attitudes, and attractions that combine emotional and rational components. These aspects vary in their intensity and in their endurance and are shaped by our behavior, experience, and habits. However strong, they do not deprive human beings of the capacity for responsible action. In other words, humans respond to objects, people, and situations in a variety of ways arising from the impressions that the object makes on the person's emotions, desires, and intellect. Yet the person retains the liberty to accept or reject this response and to act or not to act accordingly. Through the process of acceptance or rejection, persons shape their own character, or in Wesley's term, their affections and passions, turning them into tempers. Holiness for Wesley is the renewal and transformation of the heart; that is, this inner complex of desires, attitudes, and attractions that shapes and reshapes a person's character. This inner transformation is then manifested or expressed in the transformation of a person's outward behavior. There is no inner change that does not express itself in outer change.

It is this transformation of the person that was for Wesley the goal of Methodist mission. More important, transformation was the goal because, in his understanding, it is the core of genuine religion. He thus proposed that "true religion, in the very essence of it, is nothing short of holy tempers."[3] He provided a more expanded description in another context:

> What is religion then? It is easy to answer, if we consult the oracles of God. According to these it lies in one single point; it is neither more nor less than love; it is love which "is the fulfilling of the law, the end of the commandment." Religion is the love of God and our neighbour; that is, every man under heaven. This love ruling the whole life, animating all our tempers and passions, directing all our thoughts, words, and actions, is "pure religion and undefiled."[4]

These two quotations not only emphasize the centrality of inner transformation but also demonstrate a correlation of love and holiness, which we will explore later in this chapter.

In Wesley's understanding, the transformation involved both crises and gradual transformation. The initial crisis of new birth brought about a radical change of heart. This was followed by a process of gradual transformation, which could be

---

3   Sermon 91, "On Charity," *Works of Wesley,* 3:306.
4   Sermon 84, "The Important Question," *Works of Wesley,* 3:189.

shifted to a new level by the second crisis of entire sanctification or Christian perfection, which was followed by further gradual transformation. Wesley argued that while entire sanctification could take place at any time, in most people it occurred immediately prior to death.

There has been considerable debate within the Wesleyan and Methodist traditions as to the nature, extent, and manner of transformation. These debates relate both to the understanding of Wesley's writings and how his central ideas should be interpreted and applied in the contemporary context.[5] While these debates have significance, for the purpose of this discussion we will put them to one side and concentrate on the continuing process of transformation and on understanding Wesley's descriptions of Christian perfection as portraying a decisive intensification of this process. In the midst of the debate on the nature, extent, and manner of transformation, the issue of what the characteristic features of holiness are has often been lost from sight. What does a holy person look like?

WESLEY'S PORTRAITS OF HOLINESS

As is characteristic of Wesley, he did not present a single definition of holiness but rather provided numerous descriptions of holiness using lists of various phrases, images, and formulas; many, but not all, were quotations from the Bible. These lists are scattered throughout his writings, repeating a similar set of phrases but sometimes adding different ones. These were not random lists but an attempt to display the multifaceted character of holiness and its transforming impact on the human heart and life. In his sermon "The New Birth" he states:

> Gospel holiness is no less than the image of God stamped upon the heart; it is no other than the whole mind which was in Christ Jesus; it consists of all heavenly affections and tempers mingled together in one. It implies such a continual, thankful love to Him who hath not withheld from us his Son, his only son, as makes it natural, and in a manner necessary to us, to love every child of man; as fills us "with bowels of mercies, kindness, gentleness, long-suffering."[6]

Similarly, in the first sermon on the Sermon on the Mount he states:

> This is that kingdom of heaven, or of God, which is within us; even

---

5 See for example Theodore Runyon, *The New Creation: John Wesley's Theology Today* (Nashville: Abingdon, 1998), 82–101, 222–33; and Klaiber, *Von Gottes Geist verändert: Ursprung und Wirkung wesleyanischer Pneumatologie,* 184–223.

6 Sermon 45, "The New Birth," *Works of Wesley,* 2:194.

"righteousness, and peace, and joy in the Holy Ghost." And what is "righteousness," but the life of God in the soul; the mind which was in Christ Jesus; the image of God stamped upon the heart, now renewed after the likeness of Him that created it? What is it but the love of God, because he first loved us, and the love of all mankind for his sake?[7]

And in the eighth sermon on the Sermon on the Mount:

> The second thing which we may here understand by light, is holiness. While thou seekest God in all things thou shalt find him in all, the fountain of all holiness, continually filling thee with his own likeness, with justice, mercy, and truth. While thou lookest unto Jesus and Him alone thou shalt be filled with the mind that was in him. Thy soul shall be renewed day by day after the image of him that created it. If the eye of thy mind be not removed from him, if thou endurest "as seeing him that is invisible," and seeking nothing else in heaven or earth, then as thou beholdest the glory of the Lord thou shalt be transformed "into the same image, from glory to glory, by the Spirit of the Lord."[8]

After a similar list in his *A Plain Account of Christian Perfection*, he states that there is "no material difference"[9] between such descriptions—they are, as it were, portraits of the same reality looked at from different perspectives. Despite this multi-perspectival approach, Wesley does in places focus on the core of holiness. He said: "What is holiness? Is it not, essentially love? The love of God and of all mankind? Love producing 'bowels of mercies, humbleness of mind, meekness, gentleness, long suffering'? . . . Love is holiness wherever it exists."[10] In "On Patience" he wrote: "Love is the sum of Christian sanctification; it is the one kind of holiness, which is found . . . in various degrees."[11]

---

7   Sermon 21, "Upon our Lord's Sermon on the Mount, I," *Works of Wesley*, 1:481.

8   Sermon 28, "Upon our Lord's Sermon on the Mount, VIII," *Works of Wesley*, 1:614.

9   "A Plain Account of Christian Perfection," *Works of Wesley*, 13:190.

10   *The Doctrine of Original Sin: According to Scripture, Reason and Experience*, Part II, *Works of Wesley*, 12:277. Kenneth Collins has argued that for Wesley the essence of holiness is purity and not love (Kenneth J. Collins, *The Theology of John Wesley: Holy Love and the Shape of Grace* [Nashville: Abingdon, 2007], 7). He bases this on a letter to Miss Marsh where Wesley wrote that "the essence of Christian holiness is simplicity and purity" (Letter to Miss Marsh April 14, 1771, *Letters*, 5:238). Collins's argument not only fails to address the numerous passages where Wesley identifies holiness with love for God and neighbor but is also based on a partial quotation. Wesley goes on to define what he means by "simplicity and purity" as "one design, one desire—entire devotion to God"; given Wesley's tendency to use numerous synonyms, this is clearly another way of expressing love for God.

11   Sermon 83, "On Patience," *Works of Wesley*, 3:175.

Wesley summed up his understanding of Christian perfection thus: "Nothing higher and nothing lower than this the pure love of God and man—the loving God with all our heart and soul, and our neighbour as ourselves. It is love governing the heart and the life, running through all our tempers, words and actions."[12]

In his 1750 open letter to Mr. Baily of Cork, Wesley wrote: "From the true love of God and man directly flows every Christian grace, every holy and happy temper. And from these springs uniform holiness of conversation, in conformity to those great rules, Whether ye eat or drink, or whatever you do, do all to the glory of God; and, Whatsoever you would that men should do unto you, even so do unto them."[13]

Love is the essence of holiness because to be holy is to be transformed into the image of God who is love; as Wesley commented on 1 John 4:8: "God is often styled holy, righteous, wise but not holiness, righteousness, or wisdom in abstract, as he is said to be love: intimating that this is His darling, His reigning attribute, the attribute that sheds an amiable glory on all his other perfections."[14] We can picture Wesley's description of holiness as light passing through a prism, which is then split into a diversity of colors.

LOVE AND THE TRANSFORMATION OF THE HEART

Becoming holy is the process by which the Spirit of God transforms the inner complex of tempers, affections, and passions that make up the heart, so that its love becomes the controlling disposition. In his sermon "On Zeal," Wesley describes love as ruling at the center of the soul, such that when love reigns, it is manifested in holy tempers that give rise to works of mercy and piety.[15] Negatively, Wesley described love as purifying the heart from sin and evil:

> It is this Spirit which continually, "worketh in them, both to will and to do of his good pleasure." It is he that sheds the love of God abroad in their hearts, and the love of all mankind; thereby purifying their hearts from the love of world, from the lust of the flesh, the lust of the eye, and the pride of life. It is by him they are delivered from anger and pride, from all vile and inordinate affections. In consequence, they are delivered from evil words and works, from all unholiness of conversation; doing no evil to any child of man, and being zealous of all good works.[16]

---

12 "Thoughts on Christian Perfection," *Works of Wesley,* 13:63.
13 "A Letter to Rev. Mr. Baily of Cork," *Works of Wesley,* 9:309–10.
14 *NT Notes,* 1 John 4:8.
15 Sermon 92, "On Zeal," *Works of Wesley,* 3:313–14.
16 Sermon 9, "The Spirit of Bondage and of Adoption," *Works of Wesley,* 3:262–63.

The Spirit of God works in a person, drawing them to faith in Christ as savior. Faith is the deep-seated conviction that God loves me and has manifested that love in the crucifixion of Christ who has died for me, reconciling me to God by bearing my sins. While faith is a gift from God, it involves the free decision of the person; it is a response to the attractiveness of the gospel but it is not forced. Love never forces a decision—the person must decide to respond to God. In response to this faith, God justifies the sinner and the Spirit bears witness that the believer has been forgiven and is accepted as a child of God. Simultaneously, with justification the Spirit brings about the new birth of persons, which radically redirects their hearts toward God. This Spirit-induced consciousness of God's love combined with the transforming effect of the new birth enables, empowers, and motivates believers to love God and, in loving God, to love all their fellow human beings, who are also created and loved by God. This is the renewal of the image of God in the heart of believers that spreads out to transform their tempers, affections, and passions as their entire lives transform the world.

The consequence is that a person develops a new character whose dominating feature is love for God that gives rise to a love for our fellow human beings. As Wesley described it:

> And at the same time that we are justified, yea, in that very moment, sanctification begins. In that instant we are born again, born from above, born of the Spirit: there is a real as well as a relative change. We are inwardly renewed by the power of God. We feel "the love of God shed abroad in our heart by the Holy Ghost which is given unto us"; producing love to all mankind, and more especially to the children of God; expelling the love of the world, the love of pleasure, of ease, of honour, of money, together with pride, anger, self-will, and every other evil temper; in a word, changing the earthly, sensual, devilish mind, into "the mind which was in Christ Jesus."[17]

Holiness is thus the reorientation of the inner life of the person from being centered on oneself to being centered on God and directed toward the good of others. As noted above, in Wesley's understanding, this involves both crisis and development. The initial transformation brought about by the new birth leads to a process of further gradual transformation of the person's tempers, affections, and passions resulting in the transformation of their lives to express love for God and neighbor. Wesley further argued that the initial process of gradual sanctification reaches its consummation in the crisis of entire sanctification or perfection in love, which is then followed by further growth in love.

---

17   Sermon 43, "The Scripture Way of Salvation," *Works of Wesley,* 2:158.

From a Wesleyan perspective there can be no contrast between holiness and love, for holiness is love. In a world where the language of love is used and abused in multifaceted ways, it is important to describe more concretely what is meant by love.

OUTER HOLINESS AS EMBODIED LOVE

In his ninth sermon on the Sermon on the Mount, Wesley summarizes what it means to love God: "It is to desire God alone for his own sake, and nothing else, but with reference to him; to rejoice in God; to delight in the Lord; not only to seek, but find, happiness in him; to enjoy God as the chiefest among ten thousand; to rest in him, as our God and our all—in a word, to have such a possession of God as makes us always happy."[18]

To love God is to have God as the central focus of one's life, so that the whole of one's life is lived to the glory of God. Such devotion to God is embodied in constant prayer and thanksgiving, regular participation in communal worship and praise, obedience to God's commandments, contentment in life despite the circumstances, and a rejection of idolatry. Wesley described love for one's neighbor in his sermon "On Pleasing Men":

> See that your heart be filled at all times and on all occasions with real, undissembled benevolence; not to those only that love you, but to every soul of man. Let it pant in your heart; let it sparkle in your eyes, let it shine on all your actions. Whenever you open your lips, let it be with love; and let there be in your tongue the law of kindness. Your word will then distill as the rain, and as the dew upon the tender herb. Be not straitened or limited in your affection, but let it embrace every child of man. Everyone that is born of a woman has a claim to your good-will. You owe this, not to some, but to all. And let all men know that you desire both their temporal and eternal happiness, as sincerely as you do your own.[19]

The radical character of Wesley's understanding of love can be seen in relation to four features.

First, love for others is not merely outward actions; it is a set of attitudes and motivations, or in Wesley's terms, affections and tempers. For Wesley, 1 Corinthians 13 provided the fullest list of these tempers, though he adds further tempers in other contexts. His list of loving tempers includes: humility, patience, meekness, justice, mercy, truthfulness, benevolence, temperance, not envying and therefore rejoicing

---

18   Sermon 29, "Upon our Lord's Sermon on the Mount, IX," *Works of Wesley,* 1:635.
19   Sermon 100, "On Pleasing Men," *Works of Wesley,* 3:42–43.

in blessings of others, sincerity, not rejoicing in the failures of others, fidelity, hope, and trust.[20] This depth dimension is a vital corrective that prevents the message of holiness from descending into moralism, legalism, or nonreflective activism.

Second, love extends to all human beings; Wesley thus writes that love for one's neighbor is a "sincere, fervent, constant desire for the happiness of every man, good or bad, friend or enemy as for their own."[21] In another context he wrote: "Let your heart burn with love to all mankind, to friends and enemies, neighbours and strangers; to Christians, Heathens, Jews, Turks, Papists, heretics; to every soul which God hath made."[22] Elsewhere he stated that love cannot be confined to "his own family, or friends, or acquaintance, or party, or to those of his own opinions; . . . those who are partakers of like precious faith."[23] It includes the "*evil* and the *unthankful.*"[24] In other places he includes "the enemies of God."[25] While Wesley emphasizes that Christians have a particular responsibility toward their fellow Christians, a genuinely holy love extends to all even the most unworthy.[26] Such an extension is grounded in God's love for all human beings. The doctrine that all human beings have been created in the image of God and Christ's death for all is a corollary of Wesley's Arminian theology. God's prevenient grace extends to the unworthy and reprehensible, who are thus potential siblings in Christ.

Third, love is characterized by a deep compassion for and solidarity with those who are suffering. Writing to Lady Maxwell in 1788 Wesley stated: "I do not know . . . that we can have too great a sensitivity to human pain. Methinks I should be afraid of losing any degree of this sensibility."[27] Such compassion leads to self-denial in solidarity with and action on behalf of those who are suffering.[28] This characteristic has as its consequence the particular concern for and the commitment to being with the suffering,

---

20   See Sermon 22, "Upon our Lord's Sermon on the Mount, II," *Works of Wesley,* 1:499–509.

21   "Farther Thoughts upon Christian Perfection," Q.12, *Works of Wesley,* 13:101.

22   "A Word to a Protestant," *Works* (Jackson), 11:191.

23   "Upon our Lord's Sermon on the Mount, III," *Works of Wesley,* 1:519.

24   Sermon 4, "Scriptural Christianity," *Works of Wesley,* 1:163, emphasis in the original.

25   Sermon 2, "The Almost Christian," *Works of Wesley,* 1:138, 141; and Sermon 39, "Catholic Spirit," *Works of Wesley,* 2:89.

26   Wesley also distinguished between the love for those who are Christians or who are seeking salvation and love for all human beings by adding a further dimension to the love of the former, the dimension of delight or complacence. Christians delight in the relationship with and the presence of others who are striving to serve God. See Sermon 80, "On Friendship with the World," *Works of Wesley,* 3:132. See the discussion in Donald L Cubie, "Separation or Unity? Sanctification and Love in Wesley's Doctrine of the Church" in *The Church: An Inquiry into Ecclesiology from a Biblical Theological Perspective,* ed. Melvin E. Dieter and Daniel N. Berg, Wesleyan Theological Perspectives, vol. 4 (Anderson, IN: Warner Press, 1984), 333–80.

27   Letter to Lady Maxwell August 8, 1788, *Letters,* 8:83.

28   See Sermon 100, "On Pleasing All Men," *Works of Wesley,* 3:424.

the victims, the vulnerable, the poor, the voiceless, and the rejected, which was a characteristic of Wesley's ministry.[29] The inclusive character of love, described above, does not result in an undifferentiated response to all. On the contrary a response of love to the exploiters, the oppressors, and those who were indifferent to human suffering is to warn, to correct, and to oppose them as Wesley did in his response to slavery.[30]

Fourth, love is pervasive, transforming all aspects of a person's life. A person's family life, business practices, politics, and so on must all be transformed, so that everything can be directed toward the comprehensive good of others. A key concept that Wesley uses to describe the pervasive character of love is "stewardship." Stewardship means that all of who we are and all we have ultimately belongs to God and is to be used in accordance with the commands to love God and our fellows.[31] Stewardship provides a theocentric grounding for concern for our own comprehensive well-being (our belonging to God has as its corollary that we need to be concerned for our own well-being) and for a radical concern for the comprehensive well-being of others. Two examples of what this entails are illuminating.

- In regard to business, Wesley argued that business practices should not be rooted in a concern for profit but rather intended for the well-being of all involved. This meant, for example, a concern for the well-being of one's workers (who should be paid appropriate wages); of one's competitors (one should not seek to undermine their business, poach their workers, or undercut their prices); and one's customers (this included not only integrity in one's business practices but also charging just prices and not engaging in producing or selling products that were dangerous to the bodily and spiritual well-being of others). This does not exclude the significance of making a profit; Christians have a duty to make a profit, so that this can be used to meet the needs of others, but the manner in which the profit is made must conform to the dual love command. To us, some of Wesley's

---

29 See M. Douglas Meeks, ed., *The Portion of the Poor: Good News to the Poor in the Wesleyan Tradition* (Nashville: Kingswood, 1995); Richard P. Heitzenrater, *The Poor and the People Called Methodists* (Nashville: Kingswood, 2002); Theodore Jennings, *Good News to the Poor: John Wesley's Evangelical Economics* (Nashville: Abingdon, 1990); and Manfred Marquardt, *John Wesley's Social Ethics: Praxis and Principles* (Nashville: Abingdon, 1992).

30 See Sermon 65, "The Duty of Reproving our Neighbour," *Works of Wesley,* 2:511–20; and *Thoughts upon Slavery* in *Works* (Jackson), 11:59-79.

31 See Sermon 50, "The Good Steward," *Works of Wesley,* 2:266–98.

instructions appear to be totally impractical and reflect his eighteenth-century context, his rudimentary understanding of economics (which was in its infancy as an academic discipline), and his lack of business experience. Nevertheless, they provide an important challenge to rethink business in the light of stewardship and the commandments to love God and neighbor.

- Wesley's approach to political economy: Wesley made two significant interventions into the realm of political economy. The first was his opposition to slavery articulated in his booklet *Thoughts upon Slavery* and practically embodied in his support for the Society for the Abolition of Slavery.[32] Given that slavery was an integral component of the British economy, particularly for cities such as Bristol, Wesley's actions constituted a significant intervention into the political economy of Britain, which would impact not only positively on the lives of the slaves but also negatively on the lives of many people employed in the trades and industries that were dependent on the products and profits of slavery. His second intervention was through his pamphlet "Thoughts on the Present Scarcity of Provisions,"[33] which advocated radical government intervention in the economy to redirect it for the benefit of the poor. The details of Wesley's proposal are not as significant as his fundamental perspective that love for one's neighbor required that the economy must be directed toward the benefit of the poor, the suffering, and the exploited rather than toward the profit for those who have enough or more than enough.

For Wesley the great test case for people's love for God and for others was their use of money. Wesley argued that God gives human beings material resources to be used to meet their own needs, and what is not required for this is to be given back to God by providing for the needs of the poor. The pursuit of wealth for its own sake is a form of idolatry that contradicts the love for God. It is also a contradiction of love for one's neighbors, as love requires that we use any excess money that we have in meeting the needs of others and not for our own enrichment. All who use their

---

32   Iva A. Brendlinger, *Social Justice through the Eyes of Wesley: John Wesley's Theological Challenge to Slavery* (Ontario: Joshua, 2006); and Warren Thomas Smith, *John Wesley and Slavery* (Nashville: Abingdon, 1986)

33   "Thoughts on the Present Scarcity of Provisions," *Works* (Jackson), 11:53–59.

money on luxury goods or merely for making more money are robbing the poor. The communion of property practiced in the post-Pentecostal church was an act of obedience to the command to love one's neighbor and the natural consequence of deep love the early Christians had for each other.[34] Particularly toward the end of his life, Wesley returns again and again to this theme, emphasizing that the pursuit of wealth for its own sake is incompatible with holiness.[35]

Holiness is that which distinguishes the Christian community from the broader society. Paradoxically, when the core of holiness is love, then that which is to be the primary distinguishing marker of the Christian community is that which directs Christians, as individuals, and the church, as a community, away from themselves toward God and others.

LOVE AND LAW

In contemporary discussion many people draw a strong contrast between law and love; this would have been unthinkable for Wesley. For him, a central dimension of loving God was obedience to God's commandments. Further he equated loving others with obeying the moral law.[36] The moral law was for Wesley the revelation of the moral character of God. He described it comprehensively as follows:

> It prescribes exactly what is right, precisely what ought to be done, said, or thought, both with regard to the Author of our being, with regard to ourselves, and with regard to every creature which he has made. It is adapted, in all respects, to the nature of things, of the whole universe, and every individual. It is suited to all the circumstances of each, and to all their mutual relations, whether such as have existed from the beginning, or such as commenced in any following period. It is exactly agreeable to the fitnesses of things, whether essential or accidental. It clashes with none of these in any degree; nor is ever unconnected with them. If the word be taken in that sense, there is nothing arbitrary in the law of God.[37]

---

34 See *NT Notes,* Acts 15:29. See *NT Notes,* Acts 2:45, 4:32-34, and 5:1-12; Sermon 4, "Scriptural Christianity," *Works of Wesley,* 1:165; and Sermon 61, "The Mystery of Iniquity," *Works* (Jackson), 2:454–56.

35 See for example Sermon 28, "Upon our Lord's Sermon on the Mount, VIII, *Works of Wesley,* 1:612–31; Sermon 50, "The Use of Money" and Sermon 51, "The Good Steward," *Works of Wesley,* 2:266–80 and 282–98; and Sermon 87, "The Dangers of Riches," "On God's Vineyard," and "On Riches," *Works* (Jackson), 3:228–46, 503–17, and 519–28.

36 Wesley expounds his understanding of the law in four sermons. Sermon 25, "Upon our Lord's Sermon on the Mount, V," *Works of Wesley,* 1:550–71; Sermon 34, "The Original, Nature, Properties and Use of the Law," *Works of Wesley,* 2:4–19; Sermon 35, "The Law Established Through Faith, I," *Works of Wesley,* 2:20–32; Sermon 36, "The Law Established Through Faith, II," *Works of Wesley,* 2:33–43.

37 Sermon 34, "The Original, Nature, Properties and Use of the Law," *Works of Wesley,* 2:12.

The content of the moral law is love because God, whose moral character the moral law reveals, is "the great ocean of love,"[38] and human beings were created to love. Hence the moral law is "the great unchangeable law of love, the holy love of God and of neighbor."[39]

The center and goal of the moral law is love so that each commandment flows from, is centered in, and leads to love. Love fulfills the law so that Wesley can declare: "It is not only the first and great command, but it is all the commandments in one."[40] More than this, love is the goal of every moral commandment.[41] Hence in Wesley's understanding the moral law is the explication of what love means in all the diverse relationships and contexts in which human beings find themselves. Different relationships require different manifestations of love; what is appropriate in one context might be completely inappropriate in another context.

Wesley's discussion of the moral law provokes the question of how does this somewhat idealized portrait relate to the concrete commandments found in the Bible, particularly in the Old Testament. Wesley, in line with the Thirty-nine Articles of the Church of England, divided the Old Testament law into three categories: the moral law, the ceremonial (or ritual) law, and the civil (or judicial) law.[42] In this tradition, New Testament passages that speak negatively of the law or law, which are no longer valid, refer only to the ceremonial and civil law, and passages that speak positively and affirm its continuing validity refer to the moral law. Hence the ceremonial and civil law were specifically given to Israel under the Mosaic dispensation that has now been fulfilled in Christ. The moral law is reaffirmed by Christ and is binding on Christians. The hermeneutical challenge is then to discern among the various Old Testament laws which commandments belong in each category.

Wesley noted, for example, that much of Exodus and virtually all of Leviticus contain ceremonial law from which Christ has liberated Christians; yet he asserts that "many excellent moral precepts are interspersed among these ceremonial laws,"[43] without providing criteria for determining which were moral precepts. He recognized that any categorization of the laws was controversial. In his sermon "A Caution against Bigotry," he refers to debates about the ceremonial law and "the nature and use of the moral law" as significant points of contention amongst Christians.[44] In his

---

38 Sermon 35, "The Law Established Through Faith, I," *Works of Wesley,* 2:39.

39 Sermon 5, "Justification by Faith," *Works of Wesley,* 1:194.

40 Sermon 17, "The Circumcision of the Heart," *Works of Wesley,* 1:407.

41 See Letter to "John Smith" June 25, 1746, *Works of Wesley,* 26:203.

42 See Article 7 of the Thirty-nine Articles and repeated with minor variations in the articles Wesley prepared for the American Methodists (Article 6). This categorization is not unique to the Thirty-nine Articles but goes back to Thomas Aquinas (see *Summa Theologia,* Part 2a, Q. 99).

43 Sermon 65, "The Duty of Reproving your Neighbour," *Works of Wesley,* 2:512.

44 Sermon 38, "A Caution against Bigotry," *Works of Wesley,* 2:70.

journal of October 29, 1745, Wesley described an interesting example of this, refer-ring to a dispute as to whether Christians should eat blood or not. He argued for the continuing validity of this ban on eating blood, basing his argument on the fact that it was a command given to Moses, reaffirmed in Acts 15:29, and upheld in the early church.[45] More generally he argued that the content of the moral law was codified for the people of Israel in the Ten Commandments and then expounded fully by Jesus in the Sermon on the Mount. The ethical commands within the New Testament are also expressions of the moral law. The logic of Wesley's understanding of the core of the moral law as the dual love command suggests that the biblical commandments that belong to the moral law are those that explicate what love requires in the context of particular relationships.

Discerning which biblical commands belong to the moral law does not solve all the issues raised by Wesley's portrait of the law. He argued that the moral law addresses all issues in all contexts and relationships, yet there are moral issues that arise in different contexts that are not addressed in the Bible. While Wesley strongly rejected adding any commands to Scripture,[46] he could not avoid this problem if he was to provide guidance to his followers as to how they should live in their contexts. He did this most concretely in his General Rules, which set out what love required in the eighteenth century.[47] While he did not explicitly describe these rules as an expression of the moral law, they do suggest that new contexts and new challenges require Christians to discern what the moral law requires in a way that goes beyond the explicit commands of scripture.

A further challenge remains in that the attempt to relate the central command of love to a particular contemporary issue might result in questions being posed to the concrete commands in the Bible. Wesley's response to slavery provides a useful example of this. Despite the acceptance and regulation of slavery within the Bible, Wesley argued that all slavery was incompatible with the Golden Rule and hence the command to love one's neighbor. He went even further and affirmed the validity of the resistance of enslaved persons to their masters as a legitimate expression of a person's natural liberty despite biblical commands that slaves submit to their masters.[48] While he provided no biblical explanation for his assertions, it appears that the understand-ing of love as the essence of the moral law led him to a position that, at least, appears to run counter to express biblical commands. Hence Wesley's insistence that love is the center and goal of the moral law leaves a certain untidy open-endedness to the

---

45   See *Journal* October 29, 1745, *Works of Wesley*, 20:97–98, and compare his comment in *NT Notes*, Acts 15:29.

46   See for example Sermon 21, "Upon our Lord's Sermon on the Mount, I," *Works of Wesley*, 1:472, and *Journal* December 4, 1749, *Works of Wesley*, 20:315.

47   "The Nature, Design, and General Rules of the United Societies," *Works of Wesley*, 9:67–73.

48   See *Thoughts upon Slavery*, *Works* (Jackson), 11:59–79.

task of discerning what the moral law requires in particular contexts even where there are specific biblical commands. It is precisely this untidiness and the uncertainty to meaning and application of individual commandments that provides significant space for Christians to disagree with each other about the contents and requirements of the moral law even when they agree on its normative authority.

HOLINESS AND THEOLOGICAL CONTROVERSY

Returning to our central theme of holiness and diversity, we see that Wesley warned in numerous places that theological controversy is a danger to genuine holiness. As he noted in his sermon "A Caution against Bigotry":

> Nor are any animosities so deep and irreconcilable as those that spring from disagreement in religion. For this cause the bitterest enemies of a man are those of his own household. For this the father rises against his own children, and the children against the father; and perhaps persecute each other even to the death, thinking all the time they are doing God service. It is therefore nothing more than we may expect, if those who differ from us, either in religious opinions or practice, soon contract a sharpness, yea, bitterness towards us; if they are more and more prejudiced against us, till they conceive as ill an opinion of our persons as of our principles. An almost necessary consequence of this will be, they will speak in the same manner as they think of us. They will set themselves in opposition to us, and, as far as they are able, hinder our work; seeing it does not appear to them to be the work of God, but either of man or of the devil.[49]

In "The Principles of a Methodist" he expresses his reluctance to get involved in theological controversy, because such controversy often results in people seeking to win the argument by strategies that hurt one's opponents—exposing them, portraying them in the worst possible light, treating them with contempt, and using underhand tactics. [50]

Theological controversy, as the zealous promotion of particular theological positions, even when they are true and valid, poses a danger to holiness. It easily leads to the destruction of loving and holy tempers and the promotion of evil tempers. Despite his strong objection to predestination, Wesley wrote in 1768: "I do not believe it is necessarily subversive of all religion. I think hot disputes are much more so."[51] As Wesley commented on a group of Methodists in his journal of October 7, 1753,

---

49   Sermon 38, "A Caution against Bigotry," *Works of Wesley*, 2:72.
50   See for example "The Principles of a Methodist," *Works of Wesley*, 9:49.
51   Letter to Rev. Mr. Plenderlieth May 23, 1768, *Letters*, 5:90.

they had "disputed themselves out of the power, and well nigh the form, of religion."[52] When theological debate is not pursued out of true Christian zeal, which "is no other than *the flame of love*,"[53] the consequences are the ruin of holiness. The failure to truly love one's theological opponents is often combined with a failure to recognize one's own fallibility and the potential of sin to cling to and compromise one's best intentions. This is often combined with a tendency to see the worst in the intentions, motives, and expressions of one's opponents. This in turn leads to pride, prejudice, bitterness, anger, contempt, discontent, impatience, and other sinful tempers.[54] More positively, Wesley proposed in a letter to James Clark in 1756: "I would to God we could all agree both in opinions and outward worship. But if that cannot be, may we not agree in holiness?"[55]

WESLEY IN THE CONTEMPORARY CONTEXT

Even for Methodists, Wesley is not the final word on the subject of holiness. In relation to what has been discussed, there are four themes that need to be addressed in the contemporary context.

1. Is Wesley's Theology Outdated?

The first question that we might rightly ask is to what extent Wesley's theology of holiness is dependent upon his eighteenth-century moral psychology. And haven't new discoveries rendered it obsolete? Contemporary scientific thinking has moved away from the understanding of the central dynamic of the human person being a metaphysical entity distinct from the body—a spirit or soul—rather it understands the central dynamic of personhood as "an emergent property or function of the human brain, which is to say, of the body."[56] Hence our embodied nature shapes our identity and behavior—neuroscience has uncovered the biological roots of our thinking and decision-making processes; sociobiology has argued that our genetic heritage has a major influence on who we are; sociology has emphasized the influence of social structures on our knowledge and behavior; and epigenetics has shown how various factors alter a person's genetic heritage.

In contrast to this, Wesley's conceptual categories appear dated and irrelevant. However, despite his eighteenth-century categories, his analysis was also rooted

---

52 *Journal* October 7, 1753, *Works of Wesley*, 20:475.

53 Sermon 92, "On Zeal," *Works of Wesley*, 3:312, emphasis in the original.

54 See Sermon 92, "On Zeal," *Works of Wesley*, 3:15–17.

55 Letter to Rev. James Clark July 3, 1756, *Works of Wesley*, 27:39.

56 Michael Lodahl, "Was There Room in Wesley's Anthropology for *Anybody*, Particularly that the Lowly Jesus," in *This Is My Body: Philosophical Reflections on Embodiment in a Wesleyan Spirit*, ed. John Thomas Brittingham and Christina M. Smerick (Eugene, OR: Pickwick, 2016), 25.

in his own experience and the experience of those under his pastoral care. The concrete practices of early Methodists, particularly the use of small groups, their regular meetings for worship and teaching, and their active engagement in meeting the needs of others provided the environment for moral and spiritual renewal and transformation. Hence a number of Wesleyan scholars have argued that while contemporary science portrays a more complex picture of the human person than Wesley's and one that is rooted in its embodied nature, these points are not incompatible with key elements of Wesley's theology and praxis. Joel B. Green's summary of the key findings of contemporary neurological research that cohere with New Testament perspectives can be more broadly applied to the various developments in modern science, which emphasize the embodied character of our identity and behavior as they relate to Wesley's theology of holiness. He states:

- We do what we are. That is, our behaviors are generated out of, and so reflect, our character and dispositions.

- Who we are is both formed and continually being formed socioculturally, and especially relationally.

- "Choice" is contextually determined, especially vis-à-vis ongoing relational influences and self-reflexive contemplation on the basis and futures of past and prospective decisions.[57]

These contemporary developments can also contribute to an enriched and complex understanding of holiness. In particular, they provide a more integrated portrait of the relationship between what Wesley described as inner and outer holiness and suggest new ways of addressing some of the unresolved tensions and difficulties within Wesley's thought.

2. Discerning Moral Law from Biblical Commands

The second theme revolves around the attempt to discern the requirements of the moral law from the concrete biblical commands. As noted above, Wesley's praxis leaves a certain untidiness and room for debate. The threefold division of the law needs to be recognized for what it is. It is not a set of categories that we find within the biblical texts; rather, it is a hermeneutical perspective, which is brought from

---

57   Joel B. Green, *Body, Soul, and Human Life: The Nature of Humanity in the Bible* (Grand Rapids, MI: Baker Academic, 2008), 104. For other studies relating Wesleyan and contemporary scientific views see Clapper, *The Renewal of the Heart*, 33–88, Headley, *Getting it Right*, 171–78; and Mark H. Mann, *Perfecting Grace: Holiness, Human Being, and the Human Sciences* (New York: T&T Clark, 2006); Paul N. Markham, *Rewired: Exploring Religious Conversion* (Eugene, OR: Pickwick, 2007); and Matthew Nelson Hill, *Evolution and Holiness: Sociobiology, Altruism and the Quest for Wesleyan Perfection* (Downers Grove, IL: IVP Academic, 2016).

outside the text as a tool to deal with two issues. The first involves the diverse and, at least apparently, contradictory statements about the law that are found within the New Testament. The second is the challenge of relating the complex biblical material to the praxis of contemporary Christians. Like all hermeneutical models it cannot be subjected to an *a priori* justification, rather its justification lies in its exegetical and theological fruitfulness. Does the understanding or interpretation promote better readings of the biblical texts in their diversity? Does it enable us to move beyond the text to address the contemporary world? Does it equip Christians for faithful discipleship? The historical longevity and the use of this framework within a variety of theological traditions suggest that it has proved its fruitfulness, yet a number of contemporary challenges emphasize the complexity of the task of discerning divine moral law within the Bible. These include:

- Historical-critical scholarship has led to a greater emphasis on the diversity of and context embeddedness of the biblical legal and ethical material. The majority of scholars, even more conservative ones, propose that the biblical legal texts developed over time in relation to changing contexts and by different groups within Israelite society. Hence before one can determine what is ethical, civil, or ceremonial, greater attention must be given to the complex historical context and the role played by the given legal text in that context. Yet as we have little information about these contexts, scholarly opinion is often a matter of informed conjecture. Further, it is not always easy to discern how a law addressing a particular context relates to vastly different contemporary contexts.

- Comparative studies with other ancient Near Eastern legal codes show a complex pattern of similarities and differences between the biblical legal codes and those of Israel's neighbors. The theological and ethical significance of these similarities and differences is not always clear.

- Literary studies have emphasized that the law codes present the material as a unified whole in such a manner that ancient Israelites would not have discerned a division into separate categories. Many legal passages include ethical, ritual, and civil dimensions; and it is not a simple matter to determine or clearly distinguish the ethical principle from the ritual and/or civil dimensions.

- Cultural anthropological study has led to a new appreciation of the "ritual," "ethical," and "civil" laws as parts of coherent world views within particular sociocultural matrices. This means that the significance of particular laws, whether ritual or ethical, needs to be interpreted in context before questions of their continued relevance can be posed. A particular law might express an ethical value within a particular sociocultural matrix, while in another sociocultural matrix that law might have no meaning or even be deeply unethical.

- Various forms of socio-critical scholarship have given prominence to issues implied in Wesley's critique of slavery; that is, there are some biblical passages that condone, regulate, and even promote practices that not only do we find to be horrific but that run against the most profound ethical values found within the Bible. While Wesley did not address this issue, he commented that some psalms or parts of psalms were "highly improper for the mouths of a Christian congregation."[58]

The challenges do not mean that it is not possible to discern ethical norms within biblical laws, but rather they emphasize that the process is complex, and the further question of how these ethical norms can be related to contemporary contexts is not always clear. At the very least they emphasize the need for greater awareness of the complexity of the process and room for significant difference of opinion.

3. Holiness as Righteousness

A third theme is suggested by Wesley's own terminology. In developing a contemporary understanding of holiness, love, and law, a term frequently used by Wesley is perhaps helpful. This is the term *righteousness*, which Wesley tends to use as a synonym for holiness as obedience to the double love command.[59] An alternative way of understanding righteousness emerges when it is interpreted in relation to the Hebrew words *sedeq* and *sedeqah*, which are often translated as righteousness. This provides an illuminating way of drawing together some of Wesley's concerns in a more dynamic way. The words *sedeq* and *sedeqah* do not primarily refer to obedience to God's commands or to living in accordance with the traditional moral standards. Sometimes a righteous act goes contrary to what is expected by moral

---

58   The introduction to *John Wesley's Sunday Service of the Methodists in North America* (Nashville: United Methodist Publishing House, 1984), 2.

59   See for example Sermon 7, "The Way of the Kingdom," *Works of Wesley,* 1:221–22.

norms of a society (see the story of Tamar in Genesis 38). Rather, these words refer to an action in faithfulness to the requirements of a particular relationship; to action that seeks to maintain and preserve that relationship; to actions that put right what is wrong in that relationship; and to actions that demand that one is treated in accordance with that relationship.[60]

Holiness as righteousness, so understood, emphasizes the circumstantial and contextual character of what love requires in particular situations and certain power relationships. Appropriate responses to perpetrators, victims, and bystanders will be different from each other. Attempts must be made to discern what an appropriate response to complex situations is where such categorization is not clear. Interpreted in a Wesleyan manner, it is the manifestation of love in a way that is appropriate to a particular relationship. The moral law contained within the biblical command-ments is then to be understood as concrete exemplars, describing what righteous-ness requires in particular relationships. As culture and society change, so do our relationships and what righteousness concretely requires in our relationships. Some relationships, such as that between master and slave, need to be rejected as con-trary to righteousness. Further, as the biblical narratives unfold and culminate in the ministry, crucifixion, and resurrection of Christ and the outpouring of the Spirit, so the understanding of God's righteousness deepens and widens. The task today is to discern how we embody the fullness of this righteousness in our relationships with God and our fellow human beings.

4. Love Counters Perversions of Holiness

The fourth theme is that understanding holiness as love counters the dangers of self-righteousness, spiritual narcissism, and legalism. Unfortunately, Wesley's de-scendants have not always escaped these dangers. One can find within Wesley's ideas that when abstracted from the context of the whole can become seeds of such perversions of holiness. The danger of self-righteousness is often hidden in the language of purity and separation from the world.

For Wesley, purity was primarily to be understood as single-minded devotion to God that gives rise to self-giving love for one's neighbor; this love for God and neighbor drives out sin.[61] Nevertheless, in a number of passages, Wesley struggles with articulating the relationship between loving one's neighbors and separation from the world.[62] In places, the fear of contamination by the unholy seems to

---

60 Bruce C. Birch, *Let Justice Roll Down: The Old Testament, Ethics, and the Christian Life,* (Louisville: Westminster/John Knox, 1991), 153–57.

61 See Joseph E. Cunningham, "Purity in the Wesleyan Tradition," in *Purity: Essays in Bible and Theology,* ed. Andrew Brower Latz and Arseny Ermakov (Eugene: Pickwick, 2014), 233–49.

62 See for example Sermon 80, "On Friendship with the World," *Works of Wesley,* 3:127–40.

overcome the priority of love.[63] While the centrality of holiness as love means that individual salvation is inseparable from a concrete, self-sacrificing concern for the holistic good of others, Wesley's individualism, in places, leads him to prioritize saving oneself as if it could be separable from loving others.[64] The danger of legalism lurks whenever lists of rules lose their connection to the love commands and become in themselves marks of purity as ends in and of themselves. Wesley strongly critiques the Quakers' insistence on plainness in dress in this regard.[65] Later Methodists fell into a similar trap in relation to Wesley's instructions. Hence there is a need to emphasize love as the center of holiness, which must qualify and shape the theory and practices of holy living.

The pursuit of holiness, as the transformation of persons so that they love God and their neighbors, lies at the heart of Methodist identity; faithfulness to that identity summons Methodists to embody love in all their relationships, particularly within Methodist churches. As Wesley emphasized, love is "the life, the soul, the spirit of religion, the river that makes glad the city of God, the living water continually springing up into everlasting life."[66] The challenge before us is how this love can be embodied in contexts where people have contradictory theological and ethical positions, given the danger to genuinely loving relationships posed by negative emotions and attitudes that are often associated with theological controversy.

---

63   Examples of this can be found in Sermon 52, "The Reformation of Manners," *Works of Wesley*, 2:301–23; and his "A Word to a Drunkard" and "A Word to an Unhappy Woman," *Works* (Jackson), 11:169–73.

64   Compare Sermon 22, "Upon our Lord's Sermon on the Mount, II," *Works of Wesley*, 1:502, and his definition of the church in Sermon 52, "The Reformation of Manners," *Works of Wesley*, 2:302.

65   See A *Farther Appeal to Men of Reason and Religion*, Part II, *Works of Wesley*,11:255–56.

66   "A Short Address to the Inhabitants of Ireland," *Works of Wesley*, 9:285.

CHAPTER 2

PARTICIPATION IN A DIVERSE COMMUNITY AS A MEANS OF GRACE

In the previous chapter, I argued that the core of Wesley's understanding of holiness is the transformation of the human heart by the grace of God so that love of God and human beings became the controlling disposition. Integral to this transformation was the concrete embodiment of holiness in a life of love in obedience to the moral law. While this is central to Wesley's thought, it is only a partial and hence inadequate description of his theology of holiness. Fundamental to Wesley's theology is that God's grace always empowers and provokes a response from human beings, and God responds in turn to that response.[1] The practical embodiment of God's love in outward action leads, in turn, to the growth in transformation of the heart. Two concepts used by Wesley provide an illuminating way of exploring his understanding of the human response to God's sanctifying presence. The first is the means of grace, and the second is social holiness. In this chapter we will examine both of these in relation to contexts of theological diversity and contention.

THE MEANS OF GRACE[2]

God's work of transformation in the human heart provokes a diversity of possible positive responses, whereby we seek to grow in grace. In a number of places Wesley refers to these responses as means of grace.[3] In doing this, he further developed an existing tradition that interpreted the sacraments and certain other devotional practices referred to in scripture as the means of grace. In line with this tradition, Wesley defined the

---

1   See Sermon 43, "The Scripture Way of Salvation," *Works of Wesley,* 2:160; and Sermon 85, "On Working Out Your Own Salvation," *Works of Wesley,* 3:199–209.

2   For detailed analysis of Wesley's understanding of the means of grace see Henry H. Knight, *The Presence of God in the Christian Life: John Wesley and the Means of Grace* (Lanham: Scarecrow, 1992); Randy L. Maddox, *Responsible Grace: John Wesley's Practical Theology,* (Nashville: Abingdon, 1994), 192–229; and Andrew Carl Thompson, "John Wesley and the Means of Grace: Historical and Theological Context" (PhD diss., Duke University, 2012).

3   See Sermon 16, "The Means of Grace," *Works of Wesley,* 1:378–97; Sermon 92, "On Zeal," *Works of Wesley,* 3:308–21; and "The 'Large' *Minutes,* 1763" *Works of Wesley,* 10:855–58.

means of grace as "outward signs, words, or actions, ordained of God, and appointed for this end, to be the ordinary channels whereby he might convey to men, preventing, justifying, or sanctifying grace."[4] He also sometimes used the term "ordinances of God" and "works of piety" to refer to these practices. These practices included searching the scriptures, participating in Holy Communion, prayer, fasting, and Christian fellowship or conversation. Wesley's particular contribution was to expand the understanding of the means of grace beyond the "ordinances of God."

The first way that he expanded it was to add "works of mercy" to the means of grace. Works of mercy are a wide variety of practices aimed at meeting the spiritual and physical needs of others, including: "feeding the hungry, clothing the naked, entertaining the stranger, visiting those that are in prison, or sick, or variously afflicted; such as the endeavouring to instruct the ignorant, to awaken the stupid sinner, to quicken the lukewarm, to confirm the wavering, to comfort the feeble-minded, to succour the tempted, or contribute in any manner to the saving of souls from death."[5]

His second expansion was to add a list of "prudential" means of grace.[6] These included the particular practices of Methodism such as classes, watch night services, and love feasts as well as other practices that Christians have historically found helpful in promoting growth in grace. As such, they are practices that are "prudential helps, grounded on reason and experience given in order to apply the general rules given in scripture according to particular circumstances."[7]

A third category that Wesley refers to is the general means of grace, which include "watching, denying ourselves, taking up our cross, exercise of the presence of God."[8] The means of grace share a number of important common features.

- They are human responses to the Holy Spirit's transforming presence and activity in a person's life. As such, they are expressions of love to God or one's fellow human beings. Wesley emphasizes that they are things we do; thus *searching* the scriptures is a means of grace and not "scripture" and *receiving* Communion and not "Communion."

---

4   Sermon 16, "The Means of Grace," *Works of Wesley,* 1:381.

5   Sermon 43, "The Scripture Way of Salvation," *Works of Wesley,* 2:166.

6   Wesley's concept of prudential works of grace is based on John Norris, *A Treatise Concerning Christian Prudence, or The Principles of Practical Wisdom, fitted to the Use of Human Life and Designed for the Better Regulation of It* (London, 1710). See Thompson, "John Wesley," 73–89.

7   "A Plain Account of the People called Methodists," *Works of Wesley,* 9:268.

8   "The 'Large' *Minutes,* 1763," *Works of Wesley,* 10:870.

- The goal of the means of grace is love—that is, that we might grow in love for God and our fellows. Wesley thus proposed that "the whole value of the means depends on their actual subservience to the end of religion; that consequently all these means, when separate from the end, are less than nothing, and vanity; that if they do not actually conduce to the knowledge and love of God they are not acceptable in his sight."[9]

- God graciously uses these practices to engage with human beings in order to further transform us. Hence the practices become a means by which we become more loving. As we express loving affections to God or our fellow humans through the means of grace, our affections are transformed into tempers, and as we exercise loving tempers they grow and develop.

- The means of grace do not operate automatically. On the one hand, they are means that God uses, and hence we are dependent on the presence and activity of the Spirit of God. On the other, they are dependent upon the attitude and intention of the human participant.

One means of grace that transcends the categories described above is what Wesley variously describes as Christian fellowship, Christian conversation, or Christian conference.[10] Wesley's category is fairly broad but refers primarily to times of intense fellowship and conversation about spiritual things. Wesley viewed it as an instituted means of grace and a work of piety expressing our love for God; yet at the same time it was directed toward encouraging the spiritual needs of people and thus is a work of mercy. Further, the various Methodist organizational structures, as prudential means of grace, provided the opportunity for such fellowship. Engaging in such activity often entailed denying one's self and a communal seeking of the presence of God.

SOCIAL HOLINESS

In many Methodist contexts, "social holiness" is regarded as a typically Wesleyan way of describing social activism, often with the imperative that social holiness must be added to personal holiness. This usage is highly problematic, not only

---

9   Sermon 16, "The Means of Grace," *Works of Wesley,* 1:381.
10   See Richard P. Heitzenrater, "The Exercise of the Presence of God: Holy Conferencing as a Means of Grace," in Robert Webster, *Perfecting Perfection: Essays in Honor of Henry Rack* (Eugene, OR: Pickwick, 2015), 61–80.

because the term only occurs once in Wesley's writings, although there are other related terms, but more important, the one reference that Wesley makes to social holiness is the assertion that all holiness is social holiness.[11] This reference is in his preface to the 1739 edition of *Hymns and Sacred Poems*[12] and forms part of a critique of the "mystic divines."

In Wesley's perspective the theology and praxis of the mystic divines had three fundamental problems. The first is in relation to the "foundation" of the Christian religion; they "suppose we are to be justified for the sake of our inward righteousness" (ibid., 13:36–37). They thus denied the genuine foundation, which is that we are justified by faith on the basis of "the righteous death of Christ" (ibid., 13:37). The second is that "the manner of building thereon which they advise is quite opposite to that prescribed by Christ" (ibid., 13:37). The mystics argued that the soul is purified by "entire seclusion from men" (ibid., 13:37). Wesley in contrast argued that holiness is achieved through active participation with our fellow Christians in the life of the Christian community. Intimate Christian fellowship provides the context through which God's grace works to enable Christians to grow in holiness.

The third problem that Wesley identifies is the "superstructure" that is being built; that is, religion itself as contrasted with the "foundation" and the "manner of building." The religion of the "mystic divines" is "solitary religion" (ibid., 13:38). This "solitary religion" entails not troubling "thyself with outward works" (ibid., 13:38). He further stated: "For contemplation is with them the fulfilling of the law, even a contemplation that 'consists in the cessation of all works'" (ibid., 13:38). It is in contrast to this understanding of holiness that Wesley wrote: "Directly opposite to this is the Gospel of Christ. Solitary religion is not to be found there. 'Holy solitaries' is a phrase no more consistent with the Gospel than holy adulterers. The Gospel of Christ knows of no religion, but social; no holiness, but social holiness" (ibid., 13:39).

Wesley goes on to describe what he means by social religion or social holiness as follows:

> Faith working by love is the length and breadth and depth and height of Christian perfection. This commandment have we from Christ, that he who loves God, love his brother also; and that we manifest our love by doing good unto all men, especially to them that are of the household of faith. And, in truth, whosoever loveth his brethren not in word only, but as Christ loved

---

11   Andrew C. Thompson provides an important critique of this usage in "From Societies to Society: the Shift from Holiness to Justice in the Wesleyan Tradition," *Methodist Review* 3 (2011), 141–72, http://www.methodistreview.org/index.php/mr/article/view/56/80. However, his alternative interpretation that "social holiness" refers to the environmental context of holiness is not convincing.

12   "Prefaces to *Hymns and Sacred Poems* (1739)," *Works of Wesley,* 13:36–40.

him, cannot but be zealous of good works. He feels in his soul a burning, restless desire of spending and being spent for them. My Father, will he say, worketh hitherto, and I work and, at all possible opportunities, he is, like his Master, going about doing good. (Ibid., 13:39)

Wesley expanded his understanding of "social holiness" in his fourth discourse on the Sermon on the Mount.[13] Here again is a critique of mysticism, and here he refers to "social religion" and not "social holiness." However, given the equivalence of religion and holiness in the "Prefaces to *Hymns and Sacred Poems*," one can attribute no substantial difference to the meaning of the phrases "social religion" and "social holiness."[14]

Wesley's sermon expounds the significance of the description of Christians as the salt of the earth and the light of the world (Matt 5:13-16). He begins the sermon with a discussion of the beauty and desirability of holiness that is the renewal of the heart in the image of God but then immediately rejects an exclusive focus on this inward renewal as a perversion of the religion that is described in the Beatitudes. If Christians are the salt of the earth and the light of the world, it follows that "Christianity is essentially a social religion, and to turn it into a solitary one is to destroy it."[15] He then defines society as "living and conversing with other men."[16]

Wesley proceeded to argue that the significant dispositions, referred to in the Beatitudes, are the essential components of "true religion," and they are only present when there is "intercourse with the world."[17] Thus meekness "cannot possibly have a being . . . without intercourse with other men."[18] Likewise "peace making, or the doing of good" is a "fundamental branch of the religion of Jesus Christ" and "cannot possibly subsist without society, without living and conversing with other men."[19] The social character of religion is not confined to interaction with fellow Christians, rather without "commerce with the world" "we cannot be Christians at

---

13 Sermon 24, "Upon our Lord's Sermon on the Mount, IV," *Works of Wesley,* 1:531–49. This was published in 1746 as part of the first volume of *Sermons on Several Occasions.* As Albert Outler notes, the material on which these sermons were based was developed by Wesley from about 1725 (*Works of Wesley,* 1:466–69).

14 Wesley also describes Christ's intention in giving the Sermon on the Mount as: "to lay down the whole plan of his religion, . . . to describe at large the nature of that holiness without which no man shall see the Lord," Sermon 24, "Upon our Lord's Sermon on the Mount, I," *Works of Wesley,* 1:473.

15 Sermon 24, "Upon our Lord's Sermon on the Mount, IV, *Works of Wesley,* 1:533.

16 Ibid., 1:534.

17 Wesley had earlier proposed that in the Beatitudes Christ "lays down the sum of all true religion in eight particulars," Sermon 21, "Upon our Lord's Sermon on the Mount, I, *Works of Wesley,* 1:475.

18 Sermon 24, "Upon our Lord's Sermon on the Mount, IV," *Works of Wesley,* 1:534.

19 Ibid., 1:534–35.

all." He argues that "some intercourse . . . with ungodly and unholy men is absolutely needful in order to the full exertion of every temper which [Christ] has described as the way of the kingdom."[20] Further, he argued that "Christians 'are the light of the world,' with regard both to tempers and actions."[21] Holiness makes them conspicuous in the world for: "Love cannot be hid . . . least of all when it shines forth in action, when ye exercise yourselves in the labour of love, in beneficence of every kind."[22] It is God's purpose that Christians give visible expression to the religion revealed by Christ through works of piety and mercy.

In this sermon, the social character of religion and holiness arises out of the centrality of love that is manifested in the relationships between people. Social holiness refers to the essential manifestation of holiness in the Christian's relationships with others; however, it is through the active expression of love in the world that the holy tempers and affections are formed and grow. We can only be and grow in holiness in the complexity of our living in diverse relationships with other people, for it is these relationships, both negative and positive, that facilitate the development of holy tempers. From this perspective "sanctification . . . is a continued course of good works, springing from holiness of heart."[23]

Wesley's description of society as "living and conversing with other men"[24] is suggestive in that he refers in other writings to "holiness of conversation," quoting 1 Peter 1:15. An examination of these passages suggests not only that there are similarities between his descriptions of social holiness/religion and the "holiness of conversation" but also that these references can deepen the understanding of social holiness/religion. The word *conversation* in the eighteenth century referred not only to verbal communication but also more broadly to people's patterns of behavior when they interact with each other.[25] Wesley at times uses the word *conversation* to refer to verbal communication. But he refers to "holiness of conversation" to refer to this broader interaction with others as in his sermon "The First Fruits of the Spirit."

> They who "walk after the Spirit," are also led by him into all holiness of conversation. Their "speech is always in grace, seasoned with salt"; with the love and fear of God. "No corrupt communication comes out of their mouth; but only that which is good," that which is "to the use of edifying," which is "meet

---

20   Ibid., 1:536.
21   Ibid., 1:539.
22   Ibid.
23   A Letter to the Rev. Mr. Horne, *Works of Wesley*, 11:444.
24   Sermon 24, "Upon our Lord's Sermon on the Mount, IV," *Works of Wesley*, 1:535.
25   Samuel Johnson provided four definitions of conversation: (1) Familiar discourse; chat; easy talk: opposed to a formal conference; (2) A particular art of discoursing upon any subject; (3) Commerce; intercourse; familiarity; (4) Behaviour; manner of acting in common life; (5) Practical habits; knowledge by long acquaintance (Samuel Johnson, *Dictionary of the English Language*, 6th ed. [London, 1785]).

to minister grace to the hearers." And herein likewise do they exercise themselves day and night, to do only the things which please God; in all their outward behaviour to follow him "who left us an example that we might tread in his steps"; in all their intercourse with their neighbour, to walk in justice, mercy, and truth; and "whatsoever they do," in every circumstances of life, to "do all to the glory of God."[26]

In *An Earnest Appeal to Men of Reason and Religion,* Wesley refers to "that holiness of conversation which is the image of God visibly expressed."[27] Holiness of conversation is thus the visible expression of the transformed heart with an emphasis on the interaction between people that includes but goes beyond verbal communication.

Relating the concepts of social holiness and holiness of conversation together provides a portrait of outward holiness as a way of living and interacting with others that manifests a deep love for God and for others. Further, this expression of love in our interaction with our neighbors leads to further transformation of the heart through the development of appropriate, loving tempers. Hence, holiness can only exist and grow in the context of relationships with other people. The encounter with people in physical need provides us with an opportunity to meet their needs and thus grow in love for them. Living and working with people who are difficult to get on with enables us to develop patience with and love toward them. Interacting with people we categorize as sinful or evil provides new opportunities to show love for them despite our problems with their behavior. Hence, we can only grow in holiness as we interact with diverse people. Holiness from a Wesleyan perspective is not merely negative, the overcoming of sin, but is inherently positive. It is the development of new ways of embodying love, the growth of already developed tempers, and the emergence of new tempers in response to new situations and new people. These new situations and people provide new opportunities to embody love in new ways and thus to develop new holy tempers. Hence, entire sanctification does not end the process of growth; as entirely sanctified people encounter new situations they have the opportunity to develop new ways of embodying love.

The outward manifestation of love is not merely a consequence and a means of growth in holiness, it is an essential component of it. Thus Wesley states: "It is true that the root of religion lies in the heart . . . but if this root be really in the heart it cannot but put forth branches. And these are several instances of outward obedience, which partake of the same nature of the root, and consequently are not only marks or signs but substantial parts of religion."[28]

---

26 Sermon 8, "The First Fruits of the Spirit," *Works of Wesley,* 1:236.
27 *An Earnest Appeal to Men of Reason and Religion, Works of Wesley,* 11:54.
28 Sermon 24, "Upon our Lord's Sermon on the Mount, IV," *Works of Wesley,* 1:541–42.

Hence from a Wesleyan perspective, the outer and the inner, and hence ethics and theology, are integrally and inseparably linked.

Contemporary understandings of the inherently embodied character of human identity and existence complement and enrich this Wesleyan theology. First, the affirmation of human embodiment emphasizes the locations, boundaries, and potentials of our existence. The diversity of locations and limits provides multiple opportunities for growth in love so that people in different locations, within different boundaries, and with different potentials will come to experience and express love in a variety of different ways. Hence not only is there no one manifestation of holiness, but people from different contexts can learn from each other how holiness can be embodied. Second, the affirmation of our inherent embodiment places a greater emphasis on the integration of inner and outer holiness. How we embody love in concrete contexts shapes the human brain and hence our inner attitudes and motivations.

THEOLOGICAL DIVERSITY, SOCIAL HOLINESS, AND THE MEANS OF GRACE

Wesley's theology of the means of grace and social holiness together provides an integrated understanding of the significance of the human response to God's grace, which is simultaneously an expression of inner transformation and a means to inner transformation and which occurs in and through our interaction with God and with other people. Moreover, this is not something automatic. We are required to engage in responsible action, to participate in appropriate practices, and to develop new patterns of behavior inspired, empowered, and directed by the Spirit of God.

Wesley identified Christian fellowship or conferencing as a means of grace and this is best understood as a particularly focused expression of social/conversational holiness. Here holiness is expressed and pursued in interaction with real people in all their complexity. This is intensified when we are interacting with people with whom we disagree and are promoting what we believe to be true and right in the context of diverse and even contradictory opinions. Participating in such community can become a means of expressing and growing in holiness as we adopt loving patterns of behavior in our interaction with those with whom we disagree. The possibilities for this are seen in Wesley's discussion of Christianity as a social religion in his fourth sermon on the Sermon on the Mount. This sermon presupposes his first three sermons on the Sermon on the Mount, in which he expounded the Beatitudes as the summary of what it means to be a Christian and hence as describing the key features of Christian holiness. A number of these are relevant to the issue of theological and ethical diversity.

- Poverty in spirit—this is for Wesley the starting point of the way of holiness. To be poor in spirit is to have a deep knowledge of one's own sins and failures. This knowledge grows as we grow in the knowledge of God.

• Meekness—patience or contentedness. It "is mildness to the good and gentleness to the evil."[29] This does not mean one is not zealous for that which is good and right, but one expresses this zeal in a self-controlled, gentle, and loving manner. Meekness is contrary to an attitude of contempt for others. Legitimate anger at that which is evil must not lead to contempt for or the degrading of those who perform evil deeds.

• Hungering and thirsting after righteousness is a hungering and thirsting after love for God and our fellows.

• Mercy—compassion and tenderheartedness that leads one to grieve for others, including those who fail to love God and others. It is patient enduring the failures, ignorance, mistakes, and sinfulness of others—responding to them in love. It is contrary to harshness but is rather mild and tender.

• Peacemaker—those who detest strife and argument and therefore work to prevent conflict from breaking out and to reconcile warring parties. One who seeks to do good to all regardless of whether they belong to their party or whether they agree with them.

• Self-denial may also be added; Wesley in his *Journal* described himself as taking up his cross when he engaged in a conversation with someone he disagreed with.[30]

A comparison between Wesley's exposition of the Beatitudes and the way in which theological disagreements are frequently dealt with within the church and in the social media exposes a gaping cleft between Wesley's ideal of holiness as the manifestation of love and the realities of the life of the church. Many of the ways in which Christians deal with their theological and ethical differences are the opposite of what Wesley regarded as holiness. They display a pride that assumes the correctness of one's own opinions, contempt of and condemnation of one's opponents, a quickness to assume the worst of one's opponents, and an unwillingness to seek peaceful resolutions

---

29   Sermon 22, "Upon our Lord's Sermon on the Mount, II," *Works of Wesley,* 1:490.
30   See *Journal* August 27, 1739 and October 4, 1746, *Works of Wesley,* 19:89 and 20:143.

to conflicts. Hence the challenge posed by this reality is not merely what does it mean to pursue holiness in this context, but also how can the reality of theological and ethical diversity and disagreement be approached from a completely different perspective.

In his sermon "On Working Out Your Own Salvation" Wesley urged his readers to approach issues of theological contention from the perspective of zeal for love and not zeal for truth.[31] This approach to theological diversity and conflict transforms the goal from that of winning arguments in order to establish the rightness of one's own opinion to the goal of growing in love and enabling others—including those with whom we disagree—to grow in love. By adopting this approach, it is possible that participating in a theologically and ethically diverse church can become a means of grace—a means God uses to encounter and transform us, a way of both manifesting and growing in holiness.

If holiness is constitutive of Methodist identity, then participation in theologically diverse community is not contrary to but can become an important component of Methodist identity, because it provides a very particular context in which we can grow in holiness, allowing us to find new ways of embodying and expressing God's love to others. This approach gives rise to further questions about the extent of diversity. Are there contexts where diversity becomes a hindrance to the pursuit of holiness? These are questions that we will address later on in the book; for now, I want to emphasize the basic proposition that participation in theological and ethical discussion and debate with people of diverse and even contradictory convictions can be a means of grace through which we can come to new and fuller expressions of what it means to be holy.

However, the means of grace are not magically an automatic means of sanctification, rather they are the instruments that God uses to encounter and transform us. Their transformative potential is in part dependent on our use and response to the means. Theological and ethical diversity provides an opportunity for us to grow in holiness, but there is no automatic connection between the existence of diversity and our growth in holiness, just as there is no automatic connection between our general interaction with other people and our growth in holiness. For participation in a diverse community to achieve its sanctifying potential, it must be approached and responded to as a means of grace with the goal of embodying and growing in love.

CONCLUSION

Approaching the issue of theological diversity and disagreement from the perspective of a Wesleyan theology of holiness highlights the danger that diversity and disagreement have both destructive and constructive potential. When diversity and

---

31   See Sermon 85, "On Working Out Your Own Salvation," *Works of Wesley,* 3:199–209.

disagreement lead to controversy, they can demolish our love for each other, thus destroying holiness. When participation in a diverse community containing contradictory opinions is approached as an opportunity to learn and embody love, it can become a means of growing in holiness. If the latter is to happen, our approach to difference needs a deeper theological grounding and a gracious praxis. The rest of this book will explore these themes in relation to key writings and concepts from John Wesley's writings.

CHAPTER 3

WESLEY IN HIS HISTORICAL CONTEXT

In discussing how Methodists should deal with theological diversity and difference, an appeal is often made to Wesley and particularly his sermon "Catholic Spirit." In what follows I will argue that Wesley has important insights that have the potential to make a significant contribution to the development of an appropriate theological and practical response to theological diversity. This potential, however, can only be realized when we understand Wesley in his own context. This chapter will provide a brief description of aspects of Wesley's context and describe Wesley's theological critique of four significant theological parties—the Moravians, the Roman Catholics, the Calvinists, and the Quakers. First, it will locate Wesley's contribution in the context of the political debates over tolerance of religious diversity. Second, it will give a negative critique of other theological positions as a background for interpreting his positive response to many people who represented these positions.

HISTORICAL AND POLITICAL CONTEXT

Wesley's approach to theological conflict and diversity emerged within a multifaceted religio-political context. Over two hundred years earlier, Henry VIII's break with the Roman Catholic Church had set in motion a complex combination of political developments in which theological contentions played an integral role. The separation from the Papacy led to the legal establishment of the Church of England with the king as its head. The Church of England was established as the state religion subject to the authority of the monarch and Parliament. The rejection of papal interference in the political affairs of England was accompanied by the rejection of papal authority in the church. As this separation was not on theological grounds, the newly established church did not directly adopt the continental Protestant theology of a Reformed or Lutheran type. However, there was a gradual movement toward a more Protestant formulation of Christianity. During the short reign of Henry's young son, Edward VI, the church came under the influence of continental Reformed theology leading to the adoption of the Protestant-orientated Forty-Two Articles. Edward reigned only six years and was succeeded by his sister, Mary, who initiated the return of the church to Roman Catholic communion accompanied by the persecution of Protestant leaders. Many Protestants fled, and those who did not faced imprisonment, torture, and death.

Mary was succeeded by Elizabeth I, who had practiced Catholicism while Mary was queen but adopted Protestant beliefs and practices on her ascension to the throne, though her personal convictions remain obscure. In establishing her religious policy, Elizabeth was confronted with two conflicting movements. On the one hand, there was a strong party of Catholics and Catholic sympathizers among the nobility and, on the other, the returned Protestant exiles who had been deeply influenced by Continental Reformed theology and wanted to remove all vestiges of Catholicism from the theology and practice of the Church of England. The Elizabethan settlement attempted to develop a middle way, which was essentially Protestant in theology but maintained aspects of Catholic practice and church order and tolerated some diversity of opinion. Under the Act of Uniformity (1559), all clergy were required to subscribe to the new order. The Act of Supremacy declared Elizabeth to be the head of state and supreme governor of the church. This was later reinforced by the Crown Act of 1562, which made refusal to take the oath of loyalty to her as supreme governor of the church an act of treason. All people taking public or church office were required to take an oath of loyalty to her in both offices. Further laws were added, criminalizing various aspects of Catholic worship and life.

Pope Pius V responded by excommunicating Elizabeth; he declared that she was not a rightful queen and called on Catholics to depose her. A number of Catholics were executed for committing treason, some for being involved in uprisings against Elizabeth and others because their Catholic practices were deemed treasonable. Elizabeth's long reign resulted in the integration of Protestantism into the English national identity. Catholic-inspired rebellions and wars with Catholic nations led to Catholicism being identified as a major threat to English national freedom. Memories of the sufferings of Protestants under Mary recorded by John Foxe in his *Book of Martyrs* intensified anti-Catholic sentiment.

A new chapter in British history was opened when James VI (of the house of Stuart) of Scotland became King James I of England, thus beginning a process of union between Scotland and England. Conflicts between those who advocated a more Reformed theology and church (the Puritans) and the Anglican establishment continued. James attempted to address this by sponsoring a common translation of the Bible. He provoked opposition from the Puritans by his relatively tolerant attitude to Catholics as long as they did not cause disturbances. He was a strong advocate of the divine right of a king to rule and came into increasing conflict with Parliament, where Puritans had significant power. This was to be fatal for his son, Charles, who further alienated himself from Parliament and people by marrying a Roman Catholic. The resultant civil war culminated in Charles's execution and the establishment of a republican government dominated by Puritans.

The establishment of the Commonwealth under Oliver Cromwell included the further reformation of the Church of England; the episcopacy was abolished and the use of the Book of Common Prayer forbidden. A presbyterian system of church government was established but never became fully functional, and there was considerable toleration for divergence of opinion within the church, although many priests remained loyal to the Anglican liturgy and practices. Outside of the established church there was considerable religious freedom for a wide variety of Protestant groups, and some of the restrictions on Roman Catholics were lifted. The restoration of the monarchy under Charles II led to a return to the order of the Church of England as it had existed before the Civil War. The Act of Uniformity of 1662 required the use of the liturgy and ceremonies of the Book of Common Prayer, and the Conventicle Act of 1664 prohibited gatherings of more than five people for religious purposes that did not fall under the authorization of the Church of England. Clergy who were not prepared to accept this new order were thrown out of their jobs and houses. Those who did not accept and continued to preach were subjected to imprisonment. Both of John Wesley's grandfathers were "ejected" from their ministry as a result of their refusal to conform to the new order, and his paternal grandfather John Westley [sic] was imprisoned a number of times. Wesley's parents, as young people, rejected their parents' position and returned to the Church of England. This family heritage must have impacted John Wesley's response to a number of issues. These include his emphasis on religious liberty and his rejection of religious persecution, his strong attachment to the Church of England as the church chosen by his parents in opposition to their parents, and possibly his respect for and caution in dealing with civil authorities, being mindful of the consequences in opposing them.

Charles II was succeeded by his brother James II, who was a Roman Catholic. He sought to promote greater freedom for Roman Catholics and appointed them to major political offices; he ordered the persecution of Presbyterians in Scotland. At the end of his three-year reign he tried to win the support of non-Anglican Protestants in a move to end the legal privileges of Anglicans. Before he could achieve this he was deposed in 1688 by the Glorious Revolution that established Dutch Prince William of Orange and Mary (James II's daughter) as joint monarchs. In the following years there were a number of Jacobite uprisings; these were attempts by the supporters of James II and his sons to restore the House of Stuart to the throne, often with the support of France. In many cases these uprisings were supported by English Roman Catholics and were perceived to be attempts to restore Catholicism as the religion of England. The most significant uprising was in 1745, when the English army was in continental Europe fighting the French.

One of the consequences of the Glorious Revolution was the Act of Toleration passed in 1689, which permitted non-Anglican Protestants who were Trinitarian in theology and who took oaths of allegiance to the king to register as Dissenters. This allowed them to worship freely and to establish their own congregations. However, as the offices of state, senior ranks in the military, as well as the opportunity to study at the universities of Cambridge and Oxford were limited to members of the Church of England, registration confined Dissenters to a second-class status. Catholics were not included in the Act of Toleration. While it was not forbidden to be a member of the Roman Catholic Church, the church was not permitted to operate, and Catholics were excluded from all influential offices.

Catholicism was generally regarded as politically subversive; this was in part a consequence of their association with foreign enemies and the Jacobite cause. It was also argued that the pope could grant Catholics permission to break oaths made to Protestants and they thus could not be trusted. It was widely believed that if the Roman Catholic Church was allowed to organize itself it would seek to reestablish its dominance in society, and this would result in the persecution of Protestants. John Wesley opposed the lifting of the restrictions on the Roman Catholic Church, not on theological grounds, but because he saw the Catholic Church as a political threat, as inherently disloyal to the British king, and as opposed to religious liberty.

When we seek to understand what Wesley said, we need to be aware of this highly charged political context. The issues of theological opinion and church practice were not merely internal issues for churches; they were significant political issues. Differences in belief and practice could have a major effect on one's life and position in society.

METHODIST CONTEXT

Quotations from John Wesley's writings have often been used to address contemporary theological diversity within Methodism and its ecumenical relationships in a way that does not grapple sufficiently with the differences between Wesley's Methodism and contemporary Methodist churches. While Methodism became a separate church in America during Wesley's lifetime, its identity in Britain was very different. Its structure was modeled not on the Church of England but on the variety of religious societies that emerged in England at the end of the seventeenth century. The religious societies were a response to the decline in the religious life and commitment within the Church of England and growing departure from traditional morals that accompanied the restoration of the monarchy. The societies were usually made up of members of the Church of England who met regularly to promote their own spiritual growth and in some cases to address broader social issues. They did not constitute themselves as dissenting churches and retained a formal relationship with the church through the leadership or patronage of a member of the Anglican clergy. Samuel Wesley, father to John and Charles, organized such a society in his parish. Some of the societies expanded beyond the local level to establish national networks, such as the Society for the Promotion of the

Propagation of the Gospel and the Society for Promoting Christian Knowledge. Moravian-influenced societies were established when Moravian missionaries, on the way to the Americas and the West Indies, passed through London and established contact with devout Anglicans.

It was at such a Moravian-influenced society in Aldersgate Street that John Wesley had his heartwarming experience. As the religious revival developed he co-founded another such society in Fetter Lane. When Wesley and his associates began to expand their work, they established similar societies. Early Methodism emerged as a network of religious societies scattered through different parts of Britain that were related to each other by their relationship to Wesley. In the language of the time, they were part of Mr. Wesley's connection. There were other Methodist groups who were in connection with other leaders such as George Whitefield, the Countess of Huntingdon, and Howell Harris.

The organizational structures of these various connections varied. Wesley implemented a relatively authoritarian structure at both a local and a national level with membership in a society and participation as a traveling preacher being dependent upon conformity to the rules that he established. At a national level he invited key preachers to a Conference in 1744 to discuss the teaching and organization of the emerging movement. Yet he clearly understood this to be an advisory body with him having the final authority. Preachers who propagated views contrary to the established theology of the connection or who did not submit to Wesley's authority were excluded from the connection. At a local level membership of the societies was open to all who wished to "flee the wrath to come," but it was expected that their behavior would conform to such a desire by following the standards of behavior set out in the General Rules of the Society.

The majority of the members of Wesley's societies were members of the Church of England, and Wesley deliberately organized the life of the societies so that it did not compete with the services of the local Church of England, where the members of the societies were encouraged to worship and take Communion. Wesley's aim was to renew the Church of England and not to establish another dissenting denomination. However, a particular feature of Wesley's connection was that its membership was explicitly open to members of dissenting churches. The expectation was that the members were free to have their own opinions on a variety of theological and liturgical issues but that they would not make these an issue within the society. Here a common commitment to the core emphases of justification, the new birth, and sanctification was all that was required. In most societies the society meetings did not include sacramental worship. Members of the society were encouraged to attend their local church and to receive Communion there. On occasions where John Wesley or other ordained priests of the Church of England were present, they would also celebrate Communion. As a consequence of the regular presence of such clergy in the London and Bristol societies, Communion was held more regularly there.

As Methodism developed, the relationship between the new movement and the established church was fraught with problems.[1] From the beginning there was considerable opposition to Wesley's theology, and local clergy often objected to Methodist preachers holding services in their parishes. Wesley strongly maintained his theological conformity to the doctrinal standards of the Church of England and argued that Methodism was restoring the Church of England to its original theology. However, his preaching in other parishes, his preaching in the outdoors, and most significantly his use of lay preachers brought him into conflict with the church hierarchy and the rules of the church.

The tension did not emerge only from outside the church; there was a developing resistance to continuing participation in the Church of England from within Methodism. Members of the societies complained about the spiritual lives, theology, and lifestyles of the local clergy as well as the quality of their preaching. Further, there was growing pressure from the preachers to be permitted to administer Communion. Wesley gradually developed ecclesiological ideas that were opposed to the traditional understandings of the Church of England. He came to reject the idea of an unbroken succession of bishops from the apostolic era. He further came to understand that presbyters and bishops were of the same order of ministry and drew from this the conclusion that he as a presbyter had the right to ordain others to ministry.

Despite his disagreement with these major components of the polity of the Church of England, he remained a member of the Church and resisted any attempt to turn Methodism into an independent church. While he was convinced of his right to ordain, he saw no need to implement this right and recognized that such an implementation would constitute a break with the Church of England. The new political situation in America after the Revolution led him to ordain two preachers to serve in America in 1784; and in 1785, he ordained preachers to serve in Scotland, arguing that this was outside the territorial boundaries of the Church of England. In 1788 and 1789 he ordained preachers to serve in England but still affirmed his loyalty to the Church of England.

Wesley's ordination of the preachers to serve in America was one of a number of steps he took to provide for the Methodist movement in America. Among other things, he provided a revised version of the Anglican Thirty-nine Articles of Religion, which not only changed the content of some articles but also excluded some articles.

---

1   For full details of this relationship see Frank Baker, *John Wesley and the Church of England* (London: Epworth, 2000); Gwang Seok Oh, *John Wesley's Ecclesiology: A Study of Its Development and Sources* (Lanham: Scarecrow, 2008); and Ryan Nicholas Danker, *Wesley and the Anglicans: Political Division in Early Evangelicalism* (Downers Grove, IL: InterVarsity, 2016).

WESLEY'S CRITIQUE OF OTHER TRADITIONS

Wesley's relationships with people holding different theological perspectives from his own often appears to swing between rejection and welcome. In an ecumenical age there has been a tendency to emphasize the welcoming and accommodating aspects of his thought and to hold this up as an example for contemporary inter-church relationships. While recognizing that Wesley is not always consistent in his theology and practice, it is problematic to contrast the rejecting and welcoming aspects of his theology and then favor only the welcoming aspects. On the contrary, Wesley's particular contribution to the understanding and practice of the unity of the church is dependent on taking both aspects equally serious. The significance of the welcoming dimension can be seen only in the context of Wesley's radical, if not always just and accurate, theological critique of those with whom he disagreed. The remaining part of this chapter will briefly sketch Wesley's theological critique of the Moravians, Calvinists, Roman Catholics, and Quakers as the necessary context for understanding his approach to the unity of the church in the context of diverse and even contradictory theological perspectives.

Wesley and the Moravians

Wesley's relationship with the Moravians was deeply personal, and his disagreements with them clearly combined issues of theology with a variety of personal factors. He first encountered the Moravians when sailing to America, where they impressed him with their calmness in the face of the deadly threat of storms at sea. In contrast to Wesley, they had no fear of death and a calm assurance of their salvation. Wesley continued to engage them during his time in Georgia and when he returned to London. It was the Moravian leader Peter Böhler who led Wesley to an understanding of salvation by faith and the instantaneous character of conversion that provided the backdrop to Wesley's Aldersgate experience.

In the aftermath of Aldersgate, Wesley visited the Moravian community at Herrnhut and met the Moravian leader Count Nicolas von Zinzendorf. While he did not agree with all that the Moravians taught, Wesley continued to work with them in London. Tension arose in 1740 when Philip Henry Molther arrived from Germany and began to teach what Wesley described as the "stillness." Molther taught that until a person experienced the new birth, they must be still and wait for God to give them faith. While they were still they should not take Communion or use the means of grace, whether works of mercy or piety, for Christ was the only means of grace. Further, Zinzendorf taught that the moment persons were justified they were sanctified. For Wesley both of these views struck fundamentally at his understanding of holiness, and he rejected them as unscriptural mysticism. The disagreement was particularly sharp due to personal factors and eventually led to Wesley leaving the Fetter Lane Society that he had cofounded and setting up the society at the Foundery, which became the base for his connection. Wesley tried on a number of occasions to reconcile with the Moravians but both theological and personal factors prevented it.

Wesley and Calvinism

In a similar way to his debate with the Moravians, Wesley's disagreement with the Calvinists had personal as well as theological dimensions, perhaps best portrayed in his relationship with George Whitefield. Whitefield had been a member of the early Methodist group in Oxford; he had an evangelical conversion experience before Wesley's Aldersgate experience, and it was Whitefield who encouraged Wesley to begin preaching in the open air at Bristol. Wesley's relationship with Whitefield went through ups and downs and included both sharp attacks and heartfelt reconciliation. After Whitefield's death, Wesley's interaction with the Calvinist wing of the revival movement continued to be a major source of conflict, which varied in intensity. Despite this, Wesley welcomed Calvinists into his societies as long as they did not promote a Calvinist understanding of predestination, and he had a long and good relationship with Howell Harris, the leader of the Welsh Calvinistic Methodists. The major points of Wesley's critique of the Calvinist doctrine of predestination were as follows:[2]

- It makes preaching "vain," because it is useless to save the nonelect, and the elect will be saved even if there is no preaching. It thus introduces a contradiction within God, who has ordained the preaching of the gospel.

- It undermines holiness by taking away a key motive for holiness, the hope of heaven and the fear of hell. Further it encourages attitudes that are contrary to meekness and promotes the despising of those whom one considers rejected by God.

- It destroys assurance of faith and creates hopelessness in those who believe they are rejected by God.

- It destroys a zeal for good works, for there is no point in promoting the spiritual and material welfare of those God has rejected.

- It "tends to overthrow the whole Christian revelation,"[3] by making it contradict itself. Fundamental to the Christian

---

2   Wesley sets them out in a number of writings, notably Sermon 110, "Free Grace," *Works of Wesley*, 4:544–63; and *Predestination Calmly Considered* (1752), *Works of Wesley*, 13:261–320.
3   Sermon 110, "Free Grace," *Works of Wesley*, 4:552.

revelation is the proclamation that God is love and loves all human beings—this cannot be reconciled with a proposition that God chooses some to salvation and others for damnation without any conditions.[4]

- It is a "doctrine full of blasphemy"[5] because it represents Christ as deceiver, because the Bible clearly portrays Christ as offering salvation to all and being willing to save all. Further, it overturns God's "justice, mercy, and truth. Yes, it represents the most Holy God as worse than the devil; as both more false, more cruel, and more unjust."[6] For Wesley, "justice, mercy, and truth" summarize the moral character of God revealed in scripture, so Calvinism presents a picture of God that is not the God of the Bible.[7]

- It is "utterly irreconcilable to the whole scope and tenor both of the Old and the New Testament."[8] Scripture constantly presents human beings with challenges to make the choice of obeying God. Such challenges only make sense if human beings have a genuine choice in the matter. Biblical passages teach that God is willing to save all and that Christ died for all.

He summarizes his objections as follows: "Because if this were true the whole of scripture must be false. But it is not only this, because it is an error of so pernicious consequence to the souls of men, because it directly and naturally tends to hinder the inward work of God in every stage of it.[9] At the end of his life Wesley still regarded Calvinism as the "direct antidote to Methodism."[10]

Wesley and Roman Catholicism

Wesley's interaction with Roman Catholicism lacked the deeply personal dimension of his engagement with the Moravians and Calvinists. His positive encounters with Catholicism were largely through their writings rather than personal meetings. When he did encounter Catholics, it was primarily as potential converts or as organizers of opposition to his mission work in Ireland. Ironically, opponents

---

4   *Predestination Calmly Considered* (1752), *Works of Wesley,* 13:284–87.
5   Sermon 110, "Free Grace," *Works of Wesley,* 4:554.
6   Ibid., 4:555.
7   He works this out in detail in *Predestination Calmly Considered, Works of Wesley,* 13:272–84
8   Ibid., 13:269.
9   Ibid., 13:317.
10   Letter to Robert Dall January 19, 1791, *Letters,* 8:256.

of Methodism often accused it of promoting "popery" and supporting the Jacobite uprisings. This probably contributed to the mob violence against Methodism in the 1740s. Wesley combined a strenuous critique of Catholicism with a deep appreciation of certain Catholics and their writings. In particular Thomas à Kempis's *The Imitation of Christ* had a major impact on Wesley's understanding of holiness. From a contemporary perspective we can see that Wesley's strong anti-Catholicism was in some cases based on misconception, misunderstanding, and Protestant propaganda. Nevertheless, in order to appreciate his perspective on theological diversity, we need to begin with his stark and thorough rejection of Catholic theology and practice.[11] Let us note the following points.

- Catholic theology and practice is idolatrous—Wesley accepted the typical early Protestant rejection of Catholic theology and practice in relation to the veneration of the saints, Mariology, and the transubstantiation as idolatrous worship of the creature in place of the Creator. In his understanding there was no place for the distinction drawn in Catholic theology between veneration and worship. Further, Catholics (and Lutherans) numbered the Ten Commandments differently than did the Reformed and Anglican traditions. In the Reformed and Anglican traditions, the first commandment is: "You shall have no other gods before Me [the Lord]." And the second commandment is: "You shall not make images and worship them." In the Catholic tradition these two commandments are interpreted as one command rejecting the worship of other gods and hence not applying to the veneration of images. Wesley accuses Catholics not only of idolatry but also of making one of the Ten Commandments disappear in order to justify their practices.

- Catholic theology and practice denied justification by faith. Wesley, like most Protestants, held that the Catholic theology taught justification by faith and works and that the

---

11 For contemporary assessments of Wesley's views on Catholicism, see David Butler, *Methodists and Papists: John Wesley and the Catholic Church in the Eighteenth Century* (London: Darton, Longman and Todd, 1995); and David Chapman, *In Search of the Catholic Spirit: Methodists and Roman Catholics in Dialogue* (London: Epworth, 2004), 6–43. Wesley's most significant writings against Catholicism are "A Roman Catechism, Faithfully Drawn Out of the Allowed Writings of the Church of Rome: With a Reply Thereto"; "The Advantage of the Members of the Church of England over Those of the Church of Rome"; and *Popery Calmly Considered, Works* (Jackson), 10:86–128, 133–58.

practices of confession and indulgences were an expression of this.

- The Catholic Church had added doctrines, practices, and traditions to Christianity that were not taught in the New Testament.

- The Catholic Church supported and justified the persecution, imprisonment, and killing of non-Catholics.

- Catholic theology and practice undermined the authority of the political order by providing that the pope could depose rulers by affirming that there was no need to keep faith with heretics and hence oaths of loyalty were not binding, and by providing a way of forgiveness through confession for those who rebelled against the political authorities.

The last point led Wesley not only to reject Catholic theology but also to oppose the repeal of laws that suppressed the establishment of Catholic churches in Britain.

Wesley and the Quakers

Wesley's relationship with the Quakers was never a major theme in his ministry or writings, but some Quakers did become members of Wesley's societies and he did interact with them. Quakerism also represents a more radical group on the left of the Reformation. He sets out his views in a letter in response to the inquiries of a Quaker who asked: "Is there any difference between Quakerism and Christianity?"[12] Wesley describes commonalities and differences; here we will note the major differences.

- The Quakers subordinated scripture to further revelations from the Spirit.

- Quakers taught justification by works. They believed that justification is the process of making a person just rather than the declaration that a person is just; thus they confused justification and sanctification.

- They did not regard it as unlawful for women to preach in their assemblies.

---

12 "A Letter to a Person Lately Joined with the People Called Quakers," *Works* (Jackson), 10:177–88.

- They limited the moving of the Spirit to a strong inner impulse and hence did not act until this was felt.

- They did not recognize that God directs in other ways that require obedience.

- There is no basis in scripture for silent worship, which characterized Quaker assemblies.

- They rejected the sacraments of baptism and Holy Communion.

CONCLUSION

Wesley's approach to people with differing and even contradictory theological viewpoints arose out of a context of religious conflict. Like other thinkers of his age, he argued for greater tolerance of difference. But in a particular way, he combined this with strenuous critique of certain religious and theological positions. In what follows I will argue that Wesley's remarkable openness to people who held different religious convictions was deeply rooted in his theology of holiness. However, his passion for holiness meant that he was not uncritical of theological ideas that he believed were detrimental to growth in holiness. Openness was not the uncritical inclusion of or indifference to theological issues.

CHAPTER 4

CATHOLIC SPIRIT — BEING ONE IN HEART

John Wesley's sermon "Catholic Spirit"[1] is often regarded as a classic statement of his views on the relationship between theological diversity and the unity of the church. The sermon was written and first published in 1750, though Wesley did preach on the same text in 1749. The context of this sermon and "A Caution against Bigotry," which we will examine in the next chapter, is threefold:

First, there were the tensions between different groups within the revival movement, notably between Arminians and Calvinists, between Anglicans and Dissenters, and between stricter members of the Church of England and the Wesleyan societies.

Second, while the majority of Methodists in Wesley's connection were members of the Church of England, there were members who were nonconformists; this raised issues as to how people from different denominations should relate to each other within Wesley's movement.

Third, Wesley had visited Ireland where the majority of the population was Roman Catholic and experienced tension with Roman Catholic priests. It is important to note therefore that these sermons are not directly addressing the issue of unity within a given institutional church or denomination or the relationship between denominations and churches. The focus is on the form that relationships between people from different churches, denominations, and theological traditions should take within the context of the revival in general and in Wesley's connection in particular.

These sermons, however, do not stand alone; Wesley set out his views on these and related issues in other writings. There are important precedents in his earlier writings, notably in "The Character of a Methodist" (1742)[2] and *A Farther Appeal to Men of Reason and Religion* (1745).[3] He addressed the relationship with Roman Catholicism more particularly in his "A Letter to a Roman Catholic" published in 1749.[4] References to similar themes recur in a wide variety of other writings throughout his

---

1   Sermon 39, "Catholic Spirit," *Works of Wesley,* 2:81–95.
2   See "The Character of a Methodist," *Works of Wesley,* 9:42. Wesley here quotes 2 Kings 10:15, the text of his sermon "Catholic Spirit," as the basis for his argument eight years before the sermon was published.
3   See *A Farther Appeal to Men of Reason and Religion,* Part III, *Works of Wesley,* 11:320–21.
4   Albert Outler, ed. *John Wesley,* "A Letter to a Roman Catholic" (New York: Oxford University Press, 1980), 493–99.

career. If we are to understand the significance of Wesley's contribution, we need to see this sermon in relation to his other contributions. This chapter will provide an analysis of the sermon in relation to holiness as the central integrating theme of Wesley's theology, relate it to other passages in his writings, and identify key concepts, which will be explored in later chapters.

CATHOLIC SPIRIT

Wesley's sermon is built on three basic theses:

1. We have a duty to love all human beings. Further, Christians have a particular calling to show deeper love for their fellow Christians.

2. While this is agreed to in theory, in practice it does not happen because Christians cannot "all think alike"; and in proportion to their disagreements in thinking, they differ in their practices. They do not "all walk alike." These differences often lead to conflicts.

3. These differences might prevent organizational or institutional unity, but they ought not to prevent a genuine love for each other. Christians can be of one heart even when they are not united in thought and practice.

We might summarize this by saying that the "catholic spirit" that the sermon expounds may be described as the expression of holiness in the context of theological and ecclesiological diversity.

The text (2 Kgs 10:15) that Wesley chose for this sermon is, in its original context, a very strange source for developing his ideas. It portrays two very different people—Jehu and Jehonadab—with different ideas and practices, who despite this, recognize a kindred heart. Wesley began by exploring their differences. First, he noted that they would have had very different ideas. He described some of the particularities of Jehonadab's ideas referred to in Jeremiah 33 and emphasizes that Jehu, who is a person of strong opinions, does not address these ideas but lets them be. Wesley then explained this by arguing that all human beings are limited in their knowledge, and this will remain so until the return of Christ. He went further to propose that, while we believe all our opinions are true, we also know that because of our human finitude some of them are false. Our difficulty is that we do not know which ones are false and which are true. It is possible that we cannot know this in the present life, for we do not know how far "invincible ignorance" or "invincible prejudice" extends. The concept of invincible ignorance and prejudice refers to ignorance and prejudice for which we are not responsible.

Wesley noted further that prejudice, here probably meaning opinions formed without proper examination, is often formed at a very early age and is extremely difficult to change afterward.[5] In other places he suggested a sociological origin for differences of opinion. He noted in his journal entry of July 25, 1756, that some differences are the product of a person's upbringing,[6] and in a number of places he refers to people's opinions being shaped by their education.[7] The new birth does not free people from ingrained prejudice. Commenting on Acts 15:5 Wesley noted: "For even believers are apt to retrain their former turn of mind, and the prejudices derived there from."[8] However, "invincible ignorance" or "invincible prejudice" is compatible with holiness. In his journal of December 21, 1747, Wesley described how he had been reading an account of the deaths of some Trappist monks and stated: "I am amazed at the allowance which God makes for invincible ignorance. Notwithstanding the mixture of superstition that appears in every one of these, yet what a strong vein of piety runs through all! What deep experience of the inward work of God: of righteousness, peace, and joy in the Holy Ghost!"[9]

In summary, Wesley argued that while we believe all our opinions to be true, we must also affirm that some of them are not—and we do not know which are true and which are not. This is a consequence of human finitude and the shaping of our attitudes in our childhood and youth, over which we have no control and that are difficult to change. He concluded by emphasizing that, because of this, we must grant others the liberty to hold opinions that we believe to be false and should not insist on them adopting our opinions. This is not because Wesley thinks truth does not matter—quite the opposite, truth does matter—but we are finite and make mistakes. Hence, we must allow others the right to advocate and live by their opinions, which might be correct even if we regard them as wrong because our opinions might be wrong. In his "A Letter to a Roman Catholic" written about the same time, he went further and stated that he was not asking Catholics to change their religion or their opinions but asking them to pursue the "fear and love of God."[10]

---

5   In his comment on Luke 5:39, *NT Notes*, he noted that "men are not wont to be immediately freed from old prejudices."

6   *Journal* July 25, 1756, *Works of Wesley*, 21:71.

7   See for example Sermon 20, "The Lord Our Righteousness," *Works of Wesley*, 1:454–55, and "Thoughts on Christian Perfection," Q. 3., *Works of Wesley*, 13:59.

8   *NT Notes*, Acts 15:5.

9   *Journal* December 21, 1747, *Works of Wesley*, 20:200.

10   Outler, ed., *John Wesley*, "A Letter to a Roman Catholic," 496.

Second, he refers to modes of worship arguing that Jehonadab would have worshiped God at Jerusalem, whereas Jehu worshiped God through the golden calves set up by Jeroboam. This is a fairly radical difference given the strong condemnation of golden calves in the book of Kings. Different opinions will lead to different practices, not the least than in our worship. Here, too, nobody can prescribe a mode of worship for others, rather everyone must be fully convinced before God what he or she believes to be correct and then follow his or her conscience. Every Christian is obliged to be a member of a particular congregation, and particular congregations have their own modes of worship. No power on earth has the right to compel one to belong to a congregation against one's conscience. This extends not only to the manner in which we worship and celebrate the sacraments, but whether we have sacraments at all. Here Wesley is embracing not only Catholics but also Baptists and Quakers. In his journal of August 10, 1739, he commented: "I had the satisfaction of conversing with a Quaker and . . . an Anabaptist who, I trust had a large measure of the love of God shed abroad in their hearts."[11] He went on to argue in the sermon that the "right of private judgment"[12] was fundamental to the Reformation. Different denominations and church structures are the consequence of this, for they provide the possibility of people who share the same opinions and practices to worship in a way that is consistent with their convictions.

Wesley's reference to the worship of golden calves demonstrates a considerable level of tolerance, and given his context and other writings, he probably had in mind the use of images in Roman Catholic worship, which he and other Protestants rigorously condemned as idolatry. This, in Wesley's understanding, was a clear violation of the moral law of God set out in the Ten Commandments. Hence he is dealing not simply with what might be considered indifferent humanly devised practices but issues of interpreting and obeying the moral law. Yet he could argue in "A Letter to a Roman Catholic":

> All worship is an abomination to the Lord, unless you worship him in spirit and in truth, with your heart as well as your lips, with your spirit and with your understanding also. Be your form of worship what it will, but in everything give him thanks, else it is all but lost labour. Use whatever outward observance you please; but put your whole trust in him, but honour his holy name and his word, and serve him truly all the days of your life.[13]

We see something similar in a case referred to in chapter 1. In his journal entry of October 29, 1745, Wesley refers to a person who was excluded from a religious

---

11 *Journal* August 10, 1739, *Works of Wesley,* 19:88. See also *Journal* September 22, 1743, *Works of Wesley,* 19:341.
12 Sermon 39, "Catholic Spirit," *Works of Wesley,* 2:86.
13 Outler, ed., *John Wesley,* "A Letter to a Roman Catholic," 496.

society (not a Methodist society) in Scotland because he disagreed with the position of the society that Christians are not permitted to eat blood. Wesley firmly asserted that the command not to eat blood was still binding on Christians, but he stated: "O that *we* may never make anything, more or less, the term of union with *us* but having the mind which was in Christ and the walking as he walked."[14]

Given this state of affairs, Wesley argued that despite differences of opinion and practice, which may and do lead to different denominations and church structures, Christians can still experience genuine unity. The core of this unity was having the "same heart." In the first chapter, I described Wesley's understanding of the heart as the center of our deepest motivations, combining entrenched emotions, patterns of thinking, and characteristic values. To have the same heart is to have the same fundamental commitment and life orientation. For Wesley, to be a Christian was to have our heart transformed so that the fundamental orientation was shaped by the love for God and a love for all human beings. Hence to have the same heart is to recognize in other Christians this same fundamental orientation or commitment despite differences of opinion and practices. In a letter to James Clark commenting on this sermon, he asked even if they (Wesley and Clark) could not agree on opinions and worship, could they agree in being holy in heart and conversation?[15] In a similar way, he stated in "A Letter to a Roman Catholic": "If we cannot as yet think alike in all things, at least we may love alike. Herein we cannot possibly do amiss. For of one point none can doubt a moment: God is love; and he that dwelleth in love, dwelleth in God, and God in him."[16] Interestingly in his earlier comments in *A Farther Appeal to Men of Reason and Religion,* written primarily for members of the Church of England, he had affirmed his agreement with them with regard to opinions received from the Anglican reformers but responds to further critique on the basis of differing opinions:

> Only see that your heart be right toward God; and you know and love the Lord Jesus Christ; that you love your neighbour, and walk as your master walked; I desire no more. I am sick of opinions. I am weary to bear them. My Soul hates this frothy food. Give me solid and substantial religion. Give me an humble, gentle lover of God and man; a man of mercy and good fruits, without partiality, and without hypocrisy; a man laying himself out in the work of faith, the patience of hope, the labour of love. Let my soul be with these Christians wheresoever they are, and whatever opinion they are of.[17]

Love for God, Wesley went on to argue in the sermon, entails believing certain

---

14 *Journal* October 29, 1745, *Works of Wesley*, 20:98. The emphasis is Wesley's.
15 Letter to Rev. James Clark July 3, 1756, *Works of Wesley*, 27:39.
16 Outler, ed., *John Wesley,* "A Letter to a Roman Catholic," 498.
17 *A Farther Appeal to Men of Reason and Religion*, Part III, *Works of Wesley*, 11:321.

theological affirmations about the being, character, and reign of God in the world. Yet even here the focus is not so much on the affirmation of certain theological propositions but rather on a living faith in the God described by these propositions. He thus concludes this paragraph by asking "Dost thou 'walk by faith, not by sight'? 'Looking not at temporal things, but things eternal'?"[18] Even in these theological affirmations, Wesley would have been aware of differences of understanding and interpretation notable between his views and those of the Calvinists. He stated that loving God means that one affirms God's justice, mercy, and truth, yet these were precisely the attributes that he claimed Calvinism contradicted.

Wesley further affirmed that loving God entails affirming the deity of Christ, his crucifixion, and the salvation that comes through him. While there is again a quick move from theological affirmation to experiential faith with a focus on the experience of justification by faith, the theological affirmations are important. In his letter to James Clark, he explicitly stated that this affirmation of the deity of Christ excluded Arians, semi-Arians and Socinians.[19] The detailed focus on the experience of justification by faith raises significant questions, as it is formulated in typically Protestant terms as is his argument that Roman Catholic doctrine denied justification by faith. In other contexts, notably in "A Letter to a Roman Catholic," Wesley explicitly affirms Roman Catholics as having the same heart, and in parts of this sermon implicitly does so too.

"A Letter to a Roman Catholic" contains a lengthy statement on sanctification as a common opinion but only briefly refers to justification in a quotation from Romans 5:1.[20] Later in his life Wesley raised significant questions about the necessity of affirming the doctrine of justification by faith, arguing that a person may deny the doctrine and still experience salvation and thus be of the same heart.[21] Hence, Wesley's list of core doctrines remains open to question, not from a contemporary perspective but from the context of his own writings.

He then turns once more to expound what it means to love God and one's neighbor, using the language that I referred to in the first chapter. In other words, the common heart refers primarily to a holy heart, a heart transformed by the love of God and humanity that gives rise to concrete acts of piety and mercy in the world. We can give each other a hand when we see, because of our character and actions, that despite our differences in opinion and practice, we all love God and our neighbor. A catholic spirit is the recognition and affirmation of the holiness of those with whom we have significant disagreements.

---

18   Sermon 39, "Catholic Spirit," *Works of Wesley*, 2:87.
19   Letter to Rev. James Clark July 3, 1756, *Works of Wesley*, 27:38.
20   Outler, ed., *John Wesley*, "A Letter to a Roman Catholic," 498.
21   *Journal* November 23, 1767, *Works of Wesley*, 22:114.

What does it mean for someone to give me a hand?

Wesley argues that first it means to "love me with a very tender affection, as a friend that is closer than a brother, as a brother in Christ . . . as a companion in the kingdom and patience of Jesus."[22] Such a love ought to shape our actions, our words, and our attitudes in relation to each other. It rejects anything that would harm the other.[23] It bears with all the other's faults, mistakes, and brokenness; it always thinks the best of the other, interpreting the others behavior, action, and words in the best possible way, affirming that despite a person's faults they were acting with good intentions in complex circumstances, or when they failed, it was due to a particular stress or temptation. For Wesley such an approach is rooted in the example of Christ. Commenting on Mark 9:39 he said: "Christ here gives us a lovely example of candour and moderation. He was willing to put the best consideration on doubtful cases, and to treat as friends those who were not avowed enemies."[24] In some, but not all, cases Wesley expressed this in his relationships with his theological opponents, arguing, for example, that the Moravians with whom he had fundamental disagreements displayed greater levels of holiness than he did.[25]

Second, to give someone your hand means to make this person the continual subject of one's prayers—praying for this person's growth in grace and love, which will lead to a fuller knowledge of the truth.

Third, it means to encourage this person in a spiritual life and a growth in holiness.

Finally, it means where at all possible join with other people in God's work in the world.

Wesley continued with the emphasis that the catholic spirit does not mean indifference with regard to doctrinal or practical issues. It is not the attitude that theological, ethical, and liturgical differences do not matter, that different opinions are equally valid, or that one can blend contrary opinions into a unity. On the contrary, a person of catholic spirit is deeply convinced before God of the correctness of his or her opinions and is not someone who constantly runs after new or different ideas. A person with a catholic spirit "is fixed as the sun in his judgment concerning the main branches of Christian doctrine."[26] It is important to note here that Wesley does not contrast "the main branches of Christian doctrine" with "opinions." Rather he refers

---

22 Sermon 39, "Catholic Spirit," *Works of Wesley,* 2:90.
23 See Outler, ed., *John Wesley,* "A Letter to a Roman Catholic," 498–99.
24 *NT Notes,* Mark 9:39.
25 *Journal* August 21, 1740, *Works of Wesley,* 19:165.
26 Sermon 39, "Catholic Spirit," *Works of Wesley,* 2:93.

to them in the context of "indifference to all opinions,"[27] and the implication of the argument is that Christians may disagree on these "main branches," but they must hold to their convictions with regard to them. Nor does Wesley contrast modes of worship with the "the main branches of Christian doctrine." Persons with a catholic spirit have and should have deep convictions about modes of worship. Thus Wesley is not drawing a distinction between "the main branches of Christian doctrine," which should be held with greater conviction, and opinions and modes of worship where there is room for disagreement. Persons of catholic spirit combine deep convictions with the recognition of their own fallibility. They recognize the right of others to disagree with them and also to hold their views with deep conviction. More than that they deeply love those who disagree with them and desire to work with them in the midst of the diversity and contradictions.

This provides the context for understanding what is often perceived as Wesley's contradictory response to his theological opponents—that his strong critique of their views and his conciliatory approach still recognizes a common faith in and love for God. In a letter to James Hutton on December 26, 1771, Wesley goes further and comments: "We are sick of strife and contention. If we do not yet think alike, we may at least love alike. And indeed, unity of affection is a good step toward unity of judgement."[28] In other cases, he was not so hopeful. Writing to Gilbert Boyce, he commented: "I love you no less, not only though you do not think as I do, but even though I have no expectation of your thinking otherwise till our eyes are opened in eternity."[29]

Wesley provides a striking example of the catholic spirit in some comments on the Moravians. He stated:

> I love them . . . even because I believe (not withstanding all their faults) they "love the Lord Jesus in sincerity" and have a measure of "the mind that was in him". And I am "in" great "earnest when I declare" once more that I have a deep abiding conviction, by how many degrees the good which is among them overbalances the evil; that I cannot speak of them but with "tender affection", were it not only for the benefits I have received from them; and that at this hour "I desire union with them" (were those stumbling-blocks once put away which have hitherto made that desire ineffectual) "above all things under heaven."[30]

---

27 Ibid., 2:92

28 Letter to James Hutton December 26, 1771, *Letters*, 5:294.

29 Letter to Rev. Gilbert Boyce May 1, 1750, *Works of Wesley*, 26:419.

30 "An Answer to the Rev. Mr. Church's Remarks," *Works of Wesley*, 9:94; see also his comments on a meeting with a group of Quakers in *Journal* September 22, 1743, *Works of Wesley*, 19:341.

THE CATHOLIC SPIRIT IN "ON THE DEATH OF GEORGE WHITEFIELD"

There are numerous places in Wesley's journals and letters, some of which I have referred to above, where he expresses similar ideas to those found in the sermon "Catholic Spirit." One such place is his sermon "On the Death of George Whitefield"[31] preached in 1770. After describing key aspects of Whitefield's life, Wesley affirms their common theological convictions about justification by faith and the new birth. Wesley distinguishes between these "grand scriptural doctrines" and "doctrines of a less essential nature" where Christians have and may disagree with each other, thinking and letting think.[32] He then described Whitefield as a person of catholic spirit.

> One who loves as friends, as brethren in the Lord, as joint partakers of the present kingdom of heaven, and fellow heirs of His eternal kingdom, all, of whatever opinion, mode of worship, or congregation, who believe in the Lord Jesus; who love God and man; who, rejoicing to please and fearing to offend God, are careful to abstain from evil, and zealous of good works. He is a man of a truly catholic spirit, who bears all these continually upon his heart; who, having an unspeakable tenderness for their persons, and an earnest desire of their welfare, does not cease to commend them to God in prayer, as well as to plead their case before men; who speaks comfortably to them, and labors, by all his words, to strengthen their hands in God. He assists them to the uttermost of his power, in all things, spiritual and temporal; he is ready to "spend and be spent" for them; yea, "to lay down his life for his brethren."[33]

He goes on to note that such a catholic spirit is rare because many Christians, submitting to satanic persuasion, refuse to acknowledge that persons can be children of God if they belong to a "*vile congregation,*" hold "*detestable opinions,*" or "join in such senseless and superstitious, if not idolatrous worship."[34] Wesley argues that such an attitude involves justifying our sinful rejection of someone by adding the further sin of blaming others for our lack of love. On a number of occasions in his journal, Wesley notes that he responded to theological divisions in particular Methodist societies by preaching on Acts 10:15: "What God hath cleansed, that call not thou common." While he does not give any details of the sermons, one could deduce that the content would have been that persons who have been accepted by God should not be rejected as unclean because of their theological opinions or modes of worship.[35]

---

31   Sermon 53, "On the Death of George Whitefield," *Works of Wesley,* 2:330–47.
32   Sermon 53, "On the Death of George Whitefield," *Works of Wesley,* 2:341.
33   Ibid., 2:344.
34   Ibid., 2:345—emphasis in the original.
35   See for example *Journal* September 17, 1769, *Works of Wesley,* 22:205.

Persons of a catholic spirit do not quickly judge those they disagree with, nor do they think evil of them, but rather hoping the best of them, they make allowances for others in the same way that they would want others to make allowances for them. According to Wesley, it is the failure to love each other in this way that discredits Christianity.

METHODISM AS AN EMBODIMENT OF THE CATHOLIC SPIRIT

A catholic spirit is a manifestation of holiness of heart and life; and as such, it would be expected that Wesley would argue that this should be characteristic of Methodists. Wesley, however, goes beyond this and argues that paradoxically one of the primary distinctive characteristics of the early Methodist movement was that it did not seek to distinguish itself from other Christians.[36] Its goal was "to unite together all the children of God scattered abroad."[37] In contrast to other Christian churches or societies, it embodied a catholic spirit requiring no doctrinal commitment from its members, nor did it require them to belong to a particular denomination or practice a particular form of worship. In all these issues they would think and let think, allowing liberty of conscience to all members. The only condition for membership was a desire to save one's soul.[38] At the age of 78, he looked back over the development of Methodism and wrote:

> We all aim to spread . . . that truly rational religion which is taught and prescribed in the Old and New Testament; namely, the love of God and neighbor, filling the heart with humility, meekness, contentedness. . . . We leave every man to enjoy his own opinion, and to use his own mode of worship, desiring only that the love of God and his neighbor be the ruling principle in his heart, and show itself in his life by a uniform practice justice, mercy, and truth. And accordingly we give the right hand of fellowship to every lover of God and man, whatever his opinion or mode of worship be; of which he is to give an account to God.[39]

Wesley's picture is clearly idealized; while in theory Methodism was open to all, there were restrictions on what a person might teach within the society and rules for how they should worship. Calvinists might join a society in Wesley's connection; he even on occasion explicitly invited members of George Whitefield's society to attend a love feast.[40] However, they would not have been permitted to teach a Calvinistic

---

36 "The Character of a Methodist," *Works of Wesley*, 9:42.

37 *Journal* April 14, 1789, *Works of Wesley*, 24:129.

38 See "Advice to the People called Methodists," *Works of Wesley*, 9:129–130; "Thoughts upon a Late Phenomenon," *Works of Wesley*, 9:536–37, and *Journal* May 18, 1788 and August 26, 1789, *Works of Wesley*, 24:85 and 24:152.

39 "A Short History of the People called Methodists," *Works of Wesley*, 9:502.

40 See *Journal* October 8, 1769, *Works of Wesley*, 22:206.

understanding of predestination or to oppose Wesley's theology of Christian perfection, nor were his lay preachers permitted to administer Communion.[41] The understanding of Methodism as an embodiment of the catholic spirit should not be confused with an open inclusivism that embraced all people. Inherent to early Methodism was a system of discipline; members were subjected to regular examination by the preachers and Wesley himself, and those who were judged not to be living in accordance with behavior expected of members of the society were excluded. A visit by Mr. Wesley could result in a significant decrease in society membership as a consequence of Wesley excluding members who failed his examination. However, it is clear from Wesley's records that while no one was excluded for his or her theological opinions alone, he or she could have been for causing conflict by strongly contending for those opinions. Hence in his journal of April 26, 1753, he commented: "I can have no connexion with those who *will* be contentious. These I reject, not for their opinion, but for their sin; for their unchristian temper and unchristian practice; for being haters of reproof, haters of peace, haters of their brethren, and consequently, of God."[42]

Somewhat more vividly Wesley is recorded as stating at the end of a debate in the Irish Methodist Conference: "I have no more right to object to a man for holding a different opinion from me, than I have to differ with him because he wears a wig and I wear my own hair; but, if he takes his wig off, and begins to shake the powder about my eyes, I shall consider it my duty to get quit of him as soon as possible."[43]

The idea of Methodism as an embodiment of the catholic spirit was an ideal that was only partially manifested. Wesley often recounted stories of internal conflict in his journal. On one occasion after meeting with a peaceful and united society, he commented: "And what can hurt Methodists, so called, but Methodists? Only let them not fight one another, let not brother lift up sword against brother and 'no weapon formed against them shall prosper.'"[44]

CONCLUSION

A fitting conclusion to this chapter is provided by Wesley's statement in the preface to his *Explanatory Notes upon the New Testament* written in 1754:

> But my own conscience acquits me of having designedly misrepresented any single passage of Scripture, or of having written one line with a purpose of inflaming the hearts of Christians against each other. God forbid that I should make the words of the most gentle and benevolent Jesus a

---

41   See Letter to Nicholas Norton September 3, 1756, *Works of Wesley,* 27:45–50.

42   *Journal* April 26, 1753, *Works of Wesley,* 20:456.

43   Quoted in *The Centenary of Methodism* (Dublin: Primitive Wesleyan Methodist Book-Room, 1839), 232.

44   *Journal* April 29, 1754, *Works of Wesley,* 21:463.

vehicle to convey such poison. Would to God that all the party names, and unscriptural phrases and forms, which have divided the Christian world, were forgot: and that we might all agree to sit down together, as humble, loving disciples, at the feet of our common Master, to hear his word, to imbibe his Spirit, and to transcribe his life in our own![45]

In his journal entry of August 29, 1762, Wesley described a service at Exeter Cathedral where the bishop had been a staunch critic of Methodism. Wesley wrote: "I was pleased to partake of the Lord's Supper with my old opponent, Bishop Lavington. Oh may we sit down together in the kingdom of our Father!"[46]

A catholic spirit is both a manifestation of holiness and the recognition of the holiness of others, despite their different and even severely problematic theological and ethical opinions or their forms of worship and ways of concretely expressing their love for God. Christians ought to have a catholic love, that is the "sincere and tender affection for which is due to all those who, we have reason to believe, are children of God by faith . . . all those in every persuasion who 'fear God and work righteousness.'"[47] We are to love them as brothers and sisters in Christ and to delight in them even when we regard their practices and opinions as vile and detestable. However, Wesley's discussion raises a number of key issues which require further clarification. These include:

- What does Wesley mean by an "opinion"?

- If different opinions lead to different practices, does it mean that what some Christians regard as sinful others can regard as holy?

- What is the relationship between error and sin? He affirms that a person may die in error and still be saved but one "who lives and dies in sin must perish."[48]

- How can the idea of invincible ignorance and invincible prejudice and the resultant mistaken practices be compatible with the call to live a life of holiness?

---

45 *NT Notes*, Preface.

46 *Journal* August 29, 1762, *Works of Wesley*, 21:387. George Lavington was the author of *The Enthusiasm of Methodists and Papists Compared*. See Wesley's response to Lavington *A Letter to the Author of* The Enthusiasm of Methodists and Papists Compared, and *A Second Letter to the Author of* The Enthusiasm of Methodists and Papists Compared, *Works of Wesley*, 11:361–429.

47 Sermon 53, "On the Death of George Whitefield," *Works of Wesley*, 2:344.

48 Letter to Rev. James Clark July 3, 1756, *Works of Wesley*, 27:39.

- Wesley distinguishes between doctrines that are more essential than others and those that are less essential. How can these be discerned?

- What is the consequence of such a distinction? Does it mean that there are core doctrinal beliefs that all Christians need to hold in order to recognize each other as being of one heart?

- Are there limits to what can be considered legitimate opinions and practices, and how can we set such limits?

- The context of "Catholic Spirit" is that of the relationships within the Evangelical revival and his connection; what form does a catholic spirit take in church relationships and structures, and in relationships between churches and denominations?

CHAPTER 5

A CAUTION AGAINST BIGOTRY—A COMMON MISSION

Wesley proposed that the opposite of the catholic spirit was bigotry, which he defined as the "too strong an attachment to, or fondness for, our own party, opinion, Church and religion."[1] He set out his understanding of an opposition to bigotry in his sermon "A Caution against Bigotry" (published in 1750). While this is not as well known as "Catholic Spirit," its content is potentially more revolutionary. As in our previous discussion of "Catholic Spirit," we will provide a brief analysis of the sermon in relation to other writings from Wesley and then note significant issues that we will explore later in the book.

A CAUTION AGAINST BIGOTRY

The text that Wesley chose for the sermon was Mark 9:38 and 39: "And John answered him, saying, 'Master, we saw one casting out devils in thy name, and he followeth not us: and we forbad him, because he followeth not us.' But Jesus said, 'Forbid him not: for there is no man which shall do a miracle in my name, that can lightly speak evil of me'" (KJV). Wesley started by putting the passage in its context; Jesus had just declared that whoever receives a child in his name receives him and in receiving him receives the One who sent him. So Wesley argued that the heart of the question is more than the issue of casting out devils in Jesus' name. It is the question of whether the disciples ought to receive this exorcist as a fellow disciple of Jesus, even if the exorcist has not been in the company of Jesus. Wesley sets out to answer three questions in relation to his own context. First, what does it mean to cast out devils? Second, what does it mean that he (the one casting out devils) "followed not us"? And third, what does it mean to "forbid him not"?

1. Casting out Devils
In response to the first question, Wesley argued that there is a fundamental division in humanity between those within whom God dwells and those within whom the devil lives. He proposed that all human cultures, whether they acknowledge the existence of a personal devil or not, are deeply influenced by evil. He argued that

---

1 Sermon 38, "A Caution against Bigotry," *Works of Wesley*, 2:76. See also his "*Hymns and Spiritual Songs*, 1753: The Preface," *Works of Wesley*, 7:736.

this equally applies to what in his time were regarded as developed, sophisticated cultures (Ancient Rome) and those that were regarded as primitive cultures (Native Americans and Laplanders). It also applied equally to the so-called Christian cultures of Europe, including Britain, whom he accused of butchering thousands in their colonial conquests.

Some of Wesley's examples portray the typical prejudices and stereotypes of eighteenth-century Europeans in relation to other cultures, reflecting the problem of "invincible prejudice" that Wesley referred to in "Catholic Spirit" and his own tendency to use accounts of others that suited his theological and rhetorical purposes.[2] However, this must be balanced with his equally sharp critique of European countries. The point he was making is that evil permeated "sophisticated" skeptical cultures as much as those that were written off as primitive.

God's mission in the world, initiated in Jesus Christ and carried out through the work of the Spirit, is "casting out devils," or as Wesley puts it in another sermon, destroying "the works of the devil."[3] God is at work to overcome the power of evil in the world. Wesley described God's mission positively in his *Explanatory Notes upon the New Testament*: "To spread the fire of heavenly love over all the earth"[4] and elsewhere: "Love is the end, the sole end, of every dispensation of God."[5] God carries out this mission through people by bringing them into a relationship with God, resulting in their personal transformation, so that they become inwardly and outwardly holy—that is, their lives are dominated by love for God and their fellow human beings. Hence, while it is God's work in the world to overcome evil and spread love throughout the earth, God chooses human beings to participate in God's mission in that God takes and uses their actions to bring about transformation in persons and societies.

2. *"He followeth not us."*

Wesley expounds this phrase in relation to his context, identifying groups that were antagonistic to each other in eighteenth-century England.

- Those who are not in "outward connection with us" probably referred to those who were not part of Wesley's Methodist connection. Hence, other members of the Church of England who were not Methodists and also other groups who were part of the religious revival but not directly linked to Wesley.

---

2   The opposite, positive use of biased reports can be found in *Thoughts upon Slavery, Works* (Jackson), 11:59–79.

3   Sermon 62, "The End of Christ's Coming," *Works of Wesley*, 2:471–84.

4   *NT Notes*, Luke 12:49.

5   Sermon 36, "The Law Established through Faith, II," *Works of Wesley*, 2:38.

- "Not of our party"—here Wesley referred to divisions over issues that had nothing to do with religion. It is possible, as Albert Outler suggests in his notes on this sermon, that this refers to political parties and groupings. During Wesley's time there were two main political parties in Britain— the Whigs and the Tories—which were further divided into various groups and factions. The issues that divided them related to issues of internal politics and foreign policy. There were also divisions between rural and urban interests and various persons vying for their own power and wealth. In general, the Tories held to a stronger view of the authority of the monarch, with some conservative Tories having Jacobite sympathies. The Whigs emphasized the power of Parliament as representative of the people. Wesley regarded himself as a lifelong Tory although the Whigs had been in power for a long time. It is interesting to note, however, that on one occasion Wesley encouraged support for a Whig candidate in an election in Bristol.[6]

- Those of different religious opinions—Wesley took as his primary example the Antinomians and the Calvinists, whose views Wesley regarded as related and as deeply detrimental to Christian faith. Wesley mentions the Antinomians first as those who saw no necessity for Christians to keep the moral law. Then there are the Calvinists, and as I described in the third chapter, Wesley did not see his differences with them as merely minor theological problems.

- The fourth group Wesley describes as differing with him are the Nonconformists, who disagreed with the Church of England in relation to liturgy, sacraments, and church government. While we might regard these as minor issues, in Wesley's time there were still vivid memories of the role these differences played in the English Civil War and still played in everyday life. As we noted in chapter 3, Wesley's grandfathers (John Westley [sic] and Samuel Annesley) both considered these to be such serious issues that they sacrificed their jobs, houses, and income—and in the case

---

6   Letter to Ebenezer Blackwell March 4, 1756, *Works of Wesley*, 27:17.

of John Westley, his freedom—rather than conform in these matters. Being a member of a nonconformist church still involved deciding to accept discrimination in society.

- The fifth group he refers to are the Roman Catholics. It is sometimes suggested that Wesley's views of Roman Catholicism are inconsistent, with him being sometimes more tolerant and sometimes aggressively anti-Catholic. In my opinion there is no inconsistency. Wesley, like most Protestants of his time, regarded Roman Catholicism as "antiscriptural and antichristian: a Church which we believe to be utterly false and erroneous in her doctrines, as well as very dangerously wrong in her practice; guilty of gross superstition as well as idolatry." Wesley concluded: "Now most certainly 'he followeth not us' who stands at so great a distance from us."[7] The revolutionary dynamic of his positive view of some Catholics, their piety and their writings, is not to say he did not reject and condemn Roman Catholicism, but that he could be positive toward some Catholics despite and with a full recognition of his rejection of aspects of Roman Catholic theology and practice. In some of his writings, such as "A Letter to a Roman Catholic," he focused on commonalities; but in others, he focused on differences. Hence in a letter to Samuel Bradburn in 1779, Wesley recommended the distribution of both the conciliatory "A Letter to a Roman Catholic" and the critical "The Advantage of the Members of the Church of England over those of the Church of Rome."[8]

In concluding this section, Wesley emphasizes that the great divides are not merely theological differences but rather the deep personal animosity, bitter arguments, and spitefulness that often accompanies theological differences. It is not only the difference in content, but the way that Christians disagree with each other that causes significant problems. In these disagreements people think that they are serving God by arguing against the views and practices of others. Interestingly, he concludes this section by saying: "I purposely put the case in the strongest light, adding

---

7   Sermon 38, "A Caution against Bigotry," *Works of Wesley*, 2:71.
8   Letter to Samuel Bradburn August 5, 1779, *Letters*, 6:352. See Outler, ed., *John Wesley*, "A Letter to a Roman Catholic," 493–99; and "The Advantage of the Members of the Church of England over those of the Church of Rome," *Works* (Jackson), 10:133–40.

all the circumstances which can well be conceived, that, being forewarned of the temptation in its full strength, we may in no case yield to it, and fight against God."[9] When the work of such people is obviously "casting out devils," that is, bringing about personal transformation so that people love God and their fellow human beings, then to reject those people and the work they do is to fight against God.

3. "Forbid him not."

In the third major section of the sermon, Wesley expounded the phrase "forbid him not." First, he returned to the concept of casting out devils, which he defines as those whose ministry is clearly being used by God to bring about the transformation of persons. We are not to forbid those who do not belong to our groups but who are obviously being used by God in the fulfillment of God's mission. The evidence is the practical consequence of the person's mission, given, as Wesley noted, there is always the temptation to deny the positive work of those who "followeth not us." Wesley picks as his major example the practice of lay preaching, which had aroused considerable opposition from the Church of England clergy. While Wesley argued that to forbid lay preaching is to fight against God, he developed the concept of forbidding further. It is not merely the direct forbidding of the layperson to preach; it is also a whole range of indirect ways this is done. These include: denying or despising what God is doing through them, disputing with them, showing unkindness and contempt toward them in language and behavior, and/or representing their work in a bad light. This example is particularly striking given that the appointment of lay preachers was one of the areas where Wesley was accused of going against the order of the Church of England. He is accusing the opponents of lay preaching of fighting against God for acting in accordance with the established order of the Church of England.

The instruction not to forbid those who cast out devils is not merely negative, for: "He that is not with me is against me" (Luke 11:23 KJV). Rather, not forbidding requires the positive support of those who cast out devils even if we disagree with them. We see this as Wesley addressed his audience:

> Then you will not only not forbid any man that "casts out devils", but you will labour to the uttermost of your power to forward him in the work. You will readily acknowledge the work of God, and confess the greatness of it. You will remove all difficulties and objections, as far as may be, out of his way. You will strengthen his hands by speaking honourably of him before all men, and avowing the things which you have seen and heard. You will encourage others to attend upon his word, to hear him whom God hath sent. And you will omit no actual proof of tender love which God gives you an opportunity of showing him.[10]

---

9   Sermon 38, "A Caution against Bigotry," *Works of Wesley,* 2:72.
10   Sermon 38, "A Caution against Bigotry," *Works of Wesley,* 2:76.

In a similar way in his "A Letter to a Roman Catholic," Wesley encouraged Protestants and Catholics: "Let us . . . endeavour to help each other on in whatever we are agreed leads to the Kingdom. So far as we can, let us always rejoice to strengthen each other's hands in God. Above all, let us each take heed to himself (since each must give an account of himself to God) that he fall not short of the religion of love, that he be not condemned in that he himself approveth."[11]

BIGOTRY

The final section of the sermon focuses on the subject of bigotry, which Wesley defines as a "too strong attachment to, or fondness for, our own party, opinion, Church or religion." Bigotry occurs when we are not ready to believe that those who disagree with us can be God's instruments in carrying out God's mission in the world. But important for Wesley, it is not only about directly opposing others. He rather notes ways in which we can be bigoted.

- Various ways in which we discourage those who disagree with us, by attitudes of unkindness and anger, by spreading stories about their faults whether they are true or not, and by stopping others from listening to them.

- Another way is perhaps the most radical, in that Wesley argued that it is possible that "a Papist," an Arian (recall here Wesley's strong affirmation of the deity of Christ in "Catholic Spirit"), and a Socinian could cast out devils, and if so they are not to be forbidden. Hence in his "A Letter to a Roman Catholic," he proposed: "Let us . . . help each other on in whatever we are agreed leads to the Kingdom . . . let us always rejoice to strengthen each other's hand in God."[12] He then went further to affirm that it is bigotry to exclude the possibility that a Jew, a deist, or a Turk (a Muslim) could cast out devils. When we see people with whom we fundamentally disagree "cast out devils," we have an obligation to acknowledge God's work through them, to encourage them, to defend them and their mission, to show love and kindness to them, and to pray for them and their work.

He finishes the sermon with an expression of his own rejection of bigotry by paraphrasing a statement from John Calvin about Martin Luther.

---

11   Outler, ed., *John Wesley*, "A Letter to a Roman Catholic," 499.
12   Ibid.

BIGOTRY IN THE *EXPLANATORY NOTES*

In a number of his comments in his biblical notes, Wesley drew out implications for responding to divisions among Christians. And in so doing he further developed his understanding of bigotry.

In his notes on the story of Abraham and Abimelech, Wesley quoted Matthew Henry's comments: "There are many places and persons that have more of the fear of God in them than we think they have; perhaps they are not called by our name, they do not wear our badges, they do not tie themselves to that which we have an opinion of; and therefore we conclude they have not the fear of God in their hearts!"[13] While this line of thinking is not original to Wesley, it clearly resonates with his perspectives on bigotry. Further, given the highly selective character of Wesley's notes, it is suggestive of the importance of the concept of bigotry, that he included these comments on a passage that deals with an incident in the relationship between Abraham and a heathen king, which does not have obvious implications for relationships between different Christian groupings.

Turning to the New Testament, we see a similar pattern of Wesley developing insights from passages that have no direct reference to the relationships between different Christian groupings to address the issue of bigotry, indicating the importance he attached to it. Commenting on Matthew 5:47, he interpreted Jesus' words: "And if you greet only your brothers and sisters" as drawing a contrast between the prejudices that existed between different sects (it appears as if Wesley means Jewish parties) and his intention for his own disciples. Thus Wesley proposed that they "should not imbibe that narrow spirit," in contrast to Christians who should "cordially . . . embrace our brethren in Christ, of whatever party or denomination they are!"[14] Wesley's comments on verse 48 also demonstrate that he viewed the rejection of bigotry as an integral dimension of holiness.

In his comments on the parable of the good Samaritan, Wesley commented on the command, "Go and do likewise": "Let us renounce that bigotry and party zeal which would contract our hearts into an insensibility for all the human race, but a small number whose sentiments and practices are so much our own." To this he significantly adds: when we do this our love for those with whom we agree is merely the reflection of "self love."[15] In a similar fashion he commented on 1 John 4:21 that "he who loveth God love his brother also." For Wesley this means that those who truly love God will love "every one, whatever his opinions or mode of worship be, purely because he is the child, and bears the image, of God. Bigotry is properly the want

---

13   *OT Notes*, Genesis 20:11.
14   *NT Notes*, Matthew 5:47.
15   *NT Notes*, Luke 10:37.

of this pure and universal love. A bigot only loves those who embrace his opinions, and receive his way of worship; and he loves them for that, and not for Christ's sake."

Wesley strikingly argued that bigots not only do not love those who disagree with them but also do not truly love those who agree with them. Their love for those who agree with them is a form of self-love that arises from common opinions and not from the love of Christ, which was for Wesley the root of all genuine Christian love. Hence Wesley can argue that "the Spirit of God allows no party zeal."[16]

BIGOTRY AND ZEAL

In his preface to the 1753 edition of *Hymns and Spiritual Songs*, Wesley stated: "O when will [bigotry] be banished from the face of the earth! When will all who sincerely fear God employ their zeal, not for ceremonies and notions, but for justice, mercy, and the love of God!"[17] He developed the relationship between zeal and bigotry in his later sermon "On Zeal" (published in 1781—though he had preached on the same text, Gal 4:18, as early as 1758).

Wesley affirms that zeal is an important part of religion; however, misplaced zeal has been a source of great evil. He goes on to propose that "it is a certain truth, (although little understood in the world) that Christian zeal is all love. It is nothing else. The love of God and man fills up its whole nature."[18] Further: "But it is, properly, love in a higher degree. It is fervent love. True Christian zeal is no other than the flame of love. This is the nature, the inmost essence, of it."[19] In his earlier sermon "The Wilderness State" (published in 1760) he warned: "Indeed all zeal which is any other than the flame of love is 'earthly, animal, devilish'. It is the flame of wrath. It is flat, sinful anger, neither better nor worse. And nothing is a greater enemy to the mild, gentle love of God than this. They never did, they never can, subsist together in one breast. In the same proportion as this prevails, love and joy in the Holy Ghost decrease."[20]

Wesley identified four properties of true zeal: humility, meekness, patience, and the seeking after what is good in the sight of God—these constitute true religion. This zeal is contrary to hatred, bitterness, prejudice, bigotry, persecution, pride, anger, discontent, impatience, and murmuring. More particularly, if the object of true Christian zeal is that which is good in the sight of God, then fervor for any evil thing is not Christian zeal. Wesley named idolatry as an evil that he then related to Roman Catholic worship and belief, which is contrary to true Christian zeal, as demonstrated by Catholics in their persecution of Protestants that took place in the aftermath of the Reformation.

---

16   *NT Notes*, 1 Corinthians 3:4.
17   "*Hymns and Spiritual Songs*, 1753: The Preface," *Works of Wesley*, 7:736.
18   Sermon 92, "On Zeal," *Works of Wesley*, 3:92.
19   Ibid.
20   Sermon 46, "The Wilderness State," *Works of Wesley*, 2:210.

Wesley goes on to argue that the fervor for "indifferent things" is not true Christian zeal. Here his example is strife over liturgical vestments, which was debated in the Church of England between the moderate Protestants and the Puritans. Finally, Wesley argued that zeal for opinions is not true Christian zeal. The rest of the sermon argues that true zeal expresses itself in zeal for the church, greater zeal for the ordinances of God, a greater zeal for works of mercy, and a greater zeal for holy tempers; however, the most intense zeal is reserved for love.

EARLY METHODISM, BIGOTRY, AND A COMMON MISSION

The relationships between Methodists in the Wesleyan connection and other evangelicals were often fraught with tension and controversy. Theological differences were often exacerbated by interpersonal complexities, power struggles, misunderstandings, misinterpretation of opponents, and a failure to genuinely listen to each other. While Wesley often protested his desire to cooperate with others and overcome divisions, he seemed to be unaware of or unwilling to acknowledge the extent to which his own actions contributed to the controversies.[21] A classic case of this is found in his decision to publish his sermon "Free Grace" after casting lots to discern God's will, resulting in an outbreak of controversy with George Whitefield and other Calvinists. Despite this, and particularly in the latter part of his life, Wesley's own ministry displayed remarkable catholicity for its time, notwithstanding the tensions over the doctrines of election and Christian perfection that he often debated with George Whitefield and Howell Harris. In his journal of August 14, 1753, Wesley commented: "I willingly accepted the offer of preaching in the house lately built for Mr. Whitefield at Plymouth Dock. Thus it behoveth us to trample on bigotry and party zeal. Ought not all who love God to love one another?"[22]

While Wesley initially confined himself to preaching in Church of England churches during his visits to Scotland, he was invited to preach in Church of Scotland churches and also participated in Communion services. In his journal of April 20, 1753, he commented: "Who would have believed, five and twenty years ago, either that a minister would have desired it, or that I would have consented to preach in a Scotch Kirk."[23] In his entry for the next day he commented that "I explained (without touching on controversy) 'Who shall lay anything to charge God's elect.'"[24] In Ireland he was invited to Presbyterian churches, and toward the end of his life he accepted

21   This is a key theme running through W. Stephen Gunter, *The Limits of "Love Divine": John Wesley's Response to Antinomianism and Enthusiasm* (Nashville: Kingswood: 1989).
22   *Journal* August 14, 1753, *Works of Wesley,* 20:472.
23   *Journal* April 20, 1753, *Works of Wesley,* 20:454.
24   Ibid.

invitations to preach in Dissenting chapels in England. In 1757 Wesley attempted to develop a closer relationship with and cooperation among clergy who shared a common commitment to what Wesley saw as three central doctrines—original sin, justification by faith, and inner and outer holiness. However, he received very little response and eventually gave up.[25]

A particularly interesting example of common mission was Wesley's involvement in the Society for the Reformation of Manners. The aim of the society was reform by combating various social vices, particularly conducting business on the Lord's Day, ending exploitation by professional gamblers, and stopping public profanity and prostitution.[26] As all these were illegal, the members of the Society warned people, and when this had little effect, they laid charges against them. In the case of prostitutes, they sought to help those who wanted to leave the sex trade find alternative ways of earning a living. While many Methodists today might find it difficult to identify with the activities of the society, Wesley saw it as an expression of love for one's neighbors—friends and enemies. For the purposes of this chapter, two aspects of Wesley's involvement are significant. First, as Wesley noted in his sermon "The Reformation of Manners," he preached for the Society in 1763, whose members included people who were followers of Wesley and of Whitefield and Anglicans, and were not connected to either, and Dissenters. In his journal of February 28, 1779, Wesley recorded preaching for the Society again and commented: "This I trust will be a means of uniting together the hearts of the children of God of various denominations."[27]

A second significant point is that in his sermon "The Reformation of Manners," Wesley provided a description of the church and its mission, which resonated with but also was different from what he said in "A Caution against Bigotry." He describes the mission of the church as "to oppose the works of darkness, to spread the knowledge of God their Saviour, and to promote his kingdom upon earth."[28] He goes on to state that the purpose for which God joined people together into one body was "to destroy the works of the devil."[29] This includes saving people from "present and future misery."[30] What is significant is that Wesley widens his concept of overcoming evil, and thus the mission of the church goes beyond the promotion of personal spiritual transformation to include a broader overcoming of the impact of evil on persons and society.

---

25   Full details of this can be found in Baker, *John Wesley and the Church of England*, 180–96.
26   Details of the society and its activities can be found in Wesley's sermon "The Reformation of Manners," which he preached before the society, and Albert Outler's introduction to the sermon. Sermon 52, *Works of Wesley*, 2:300–23.
27   *Journal* February 28, 1779, *Works of Wesley*, 23.
28   Sermon 52, "The Reformation of Manners," *Works of Wesley*, 2:301.
29   Ibid., 2:302.
30   Ibid.

A further example of cooperation in common mission was Wesley's opposition to slavery. His pamphlet *Thoughts upon Slavery* not only made use of the work of Anthony Benezet, a Quaker, and Granville Sharp, an Evangelical Anglican layperson, but was part of a greater cooperation between Benezet, Sharp, and Wesley. This culminated in Wesley's becoming a supporter of the Society for Abolition of the Slave Trade when it was founded in 1787.[31] The original membership of the society included Anglicans, but the majority were Quakers. Further, Wesley used the *Arminian Magazine*, which he published as a means of instructing and encouraging his followers, to persuade Methodists to oppose slavery, to support the Society for Abolition of the Slave Trade, and to petition Parliament to end slavery. In his journal of March 3, 1788, he describes a strange noise that interrupted the sermon he was preaching against slavery, which he interpreted as Satan fighting to maintain his kingdom.[32] What exactly occurred is difficult to discern from his journal, but what is clear is that Wesley interpreted his work against slavery as part of God's mission to overcome the works of the devil.

CONCLUSION

Wesley's reflection on bigotry, zeal, and the mission of the church raises a number of issues that we will pursue in the following chapters. These include:

1. Wesley's evaluation of the validity of other groups is a practical test—having defined God's mission in the world as overcoming the power of the devil, the question then becomes: Are different groups being used by God in carrying out God's mission? The way to evaluate this is to see whether their work brings about the transformation of lives so that people come to love God and their fellow human beings. In "Reformation of Manners," he opens the possibility of a broader understanding of overcoming evil to include overcoming the impact of evil on society. His interpretation of the struggle against slavery deepens this to include the struggle against social injustice. In

---

31 Details of Wesley's continuing involvement in the struggle can be found in Iva A. Brendlinger, *Social Justice through the Eyes of Wesley: John Wesley's Theological Challenge to Slavery* (Ontario: Joshua, 2006); and Warren Thomas Smith, *John Wesley and Slavery* (Nashville: Abingdon, 1986), 104–12.
32 *Journal* March 3, 1788, *Works of Wesley,* 24:69–70.

addition, Wesley viewed poverty as consequence of human sin and proposed relatively radical structural measures to counter it.[33] It is thus possible to argue that God is present and at work when we see persons and societies overcome evil, even when these changes do not explicitly involve the church and its evangelism.

2. Recognizing that God is at work through people who through their actions overcome evil or help others overcome evil requires that we accept and affirm these people whom God is using, even when we have major and fundamental disagreements with them with regard to theological and doctrinal opinions. Rejecting such people involves rejecting God.

3. God uses people who hold beliefs and practices that we believe violate clear biblical teaching or the moral law of God. For example, Catholics continued, in Wesley's opinion, to violate the second commandment, and Calvinists continued to teach predestination. Wesley does not explain this—the logic of his argument from "Catholic Spirit" is that people can truly love God and their fellows and still be mistaken in their beliefs. Therefore their practices might contradict key aspects of the biblical message and even cause harm to others. Yet God can still use them, and we ought to recognize them as spiritual siblings.

4. Bigotry is a denial of love not only for those with whom we disagree with but also for those we agree with. Bigotry is incompatible with holiness.

5. It is interesting to note that while Wesley speaks of religious zeal, he contrasts zeal for opinions with zeal for love. He does not refer to zeal for truth. Yet those whom Wesley is critiquing would have regarded themselves as being zealous for truth and not zealous for opinions. This raises the question of the relationship

---

33   See "Thoughts on the Present Scarcity of Provisions," *Works* (Jackson), 11:53–59.

between opinions and truth. In other words, whose opinion is true and how can we distinguish truth from error? Further, if zeal for opinions is not true religious zeal, should we be zealous for truth and how might this manifest itself?

6. Wesley's understanding of the church and its mission is grounded in an understanding of the mission of God in the world. In the twentieth century, such a grounding of the mission of the church in the mission of God (*Missio Dei*) was regarded as a significant new development in missiological thinking. Wesley's concepts are thus an important foreshadowing of these developments. While he focuses on the transformation of the individual, there are a number of undeveloped themes in his writings that suggest the broader engagement in the transformation of society. Twenty- and twenty-first-century understandings of the *Missio Dei* invoke a broader and more comprehensive portrayal of God's mission in the context and a wider concept of what God is doing and whom God is using in the world.

Reviewing what Wesley says in his "A Plain Account of the People called Methodists," sums up the thinking of this chapter:

> The thing which I was greatly afraid of all this time, and which I resolved to use every possible method of preventing, was a narrowness of spirit, a party zeal, a being straitened in our own bowels; that miserable bigotry which makes many so unready to believe that there is any work of God but among themselves. I thought it might help to read, to all who are willing to hear, the accounts I received from time to time of the work which God is carrying on in the earth, both in our own and other countries, not among us alone, but among those of various opinions and denominations. It is generally a time . . . of breaking down the partition walls which either craft of the devil or the folly of men has built up; and of encouraging every child of God to say (O when shall it once be?), "Whosoever doth the will of my Father which is in heaven, the same is my brother and sister and mother."[34]

---

34 "A Plain Account of the People called Methodists," *Works of Wesley*, 9:265–66.

CHAPTER 6

THEOLOGICAL ROOTS— ANTHROPOLOGY

Wesley's approach to dealing with theological and ethical diversity is not uniform, but by 1750 he developed an identifiable approach set out in his sermons "Catholic Spirit" and "A Caution against Bigotry," which affirmed the importance of theological and ethical opinions. However, at the same time Wesley refused to see these opinions as fundamentally dividing Christians. On the contrary, Wesley argued that there are people who have a deep relationship with God that is expressed in love for God and neighbor; yet despite their actions, they may hold to opinions and Christian practices that he thought were not only mistaken but also contrary to the moral law and detrimental to Christian holiness. As he wrote in his sermon "Of Former Things": "By religion I mean the love of God and man, filling the heart and governing the life. The sure effect of this is the uniform practice of justice, mercy, and truth. This is the very essence of it, the height and depth of religion, detached from this or that opinion, and from all particular modes of worship."[1]

The key example can be found in his approach to Roman Catholicism. Wesley combined a strenuous critique of Catholicism with a deep appreciation of certain Catholics and their writings. One can see Wesley's position as rising out of his own experience. Thomas à Kempis's *The Imitation of Christ* had a major impact on Wesley's spiritual life while he was a student at Oxford. It continued to influence his understanding of holiness, such that he published an edited version of it and widely recommended it to his followers.

Nevertheless, Wesley's approach to the issue of diversity is not merely a product of his experience; it is rooted in key aspects of his theology. In this chapter we will examine how his idea of diversity is rooted in his understanding of humanity and his theological anthropology. In the next chapter we will examine its relationship to his understanding of human knowing, his epistemology. We will examine three fundamental theological concepts that underlie his approach to theological diversity.

1. Human finitude and "sin properly so called";

2. The law of love; and

3. Liberty and responsibility before God.

---

1 Sermon 102, "Of Former Times," *Works of Wesley,* 3:448. See also "A Short Address to the Inhabitants of Ireland," *Works of Wesley*, 9:281.

HUMAN FINITUDE AND "SIN PROPERLY SO CALLED"

The core question posed by theological diversity and the conflict it kindles among Christians is found in the different ways they understand the relationship between human limitations, as a consequence of being fallen creatures, ignorance and mistakes, and human sin. Wesley argued that ignorance and mistakes, even in relation to important theological and ethical issues, were not sinful.

The context for Wesley's theological reflection on these issues was his doctrine of Christian perfection. Wesley stressed that while Christian perfection entailed the overcoming of sin, it did not entail the overcoming of ignorance and its associated theoretical and practical errors. For Wesley the question revolved around the implications of human existence as a fallen and an embodied existence and the impact of salvation on this existence.

Wesley speculated that the unfallen Adam would have had perfect but limited knowledge, and therefore all his opinions would have been true, and all his behavior would have confirmed completely to God's will. The Fall fundamentally changed this. Underlying Wesley's argument is his somewhat speculative and dualistic interpretation of the relationship between the body and the soul. Wesley understood the human person to be an embodied spirit or soul. The essential person is the soul, as he stated in the "Preface" to *Sermons on Several Occasions*: "I am a spirit come from God and returning to God."[2] However this soul exists in a body, and there is an interdependent relationship between them. The soul is dependent upon the body for its interaction with created reality. It is affected by what happens to and within the body. The corruption of the body, brought about by the Fall, impacts and limits the capacities of the soul, resulting in ignorance, error, and confusion. The new birth and sanctification are a transformation of the heart or soul, not the body; and hence they do not fundamentally alter this situation.[3] The soul can be delivered from sin, but while it is still in the body, it is affected by the fallen condition of the body. Hence even mature Christians and those who are entirely sanctified have a weak, limited, confused, and inaccurate apprehension and understanding of reality.[4] Commenting on Acts 21:20, Wesley notes with astonishment that even some of the apostles were ignorant of the fact that the Mosaic dispensation had been abolished in Christ.[5]

---

2   "Preface" to *Sermons on Several Occasions*, 1746, *Works of Wesley,* 1:104–5. See also Sermon 116, "What is Man?" *Works of Wesley,* 3:20–27.

3   Wesley commented in *NT Notes*, Acts 15:5: "Even believers are apt to retain their former turn of mind, and the prejudices derived therefrom."

4   See Sermon 55, "On the Trinity," *Works of Wesley,* 2:382–83; Sermon 82, "On Temptation," *Works of Wesley,* 3:160; Sermon 129, "Heavenly Treasure in Earthen Vessels," *Works of Wesley,* 4:164–66; and *Journal* July 24, 1761, *Works of Wesley,* 21:337.

5   *NT Notes*, Acts 21:20.

Christian fallibility includes, first, ignorance about God's character, purposes, and acts. This arises from human fallenness and finitude and from the limited character of God's revelation, which does not fully describe who God is, what God does, and why God acts or does not act in a particular way.[6]

Second, our understanding of the world around us, of the facts of nature and history, and of human persons is also flawed. Thus Wesley argued in his sermon "Christian Perfection":

> The best and wisest of men are frequently mistaken even with regard to facts; believing those things not to have been which really were, or those to have been done which were not. Or, suppose they are not mistaken as to the fact itself, they may be with regard to its circumstances; believing them, or many of them, to have been quite different from what in truth, they were. And hence cannot but arise many farther mistakes. Hence they may believe either past or present actions which were or are evil, to be good; and such as were or are good, to be evil. Hence also they may judge not according to truth with regard to the characters of men; and that, not only by supposing good men to be better, or wicked men to be worse, than they are, but by believing them to have been or to be good men who were or are very wicked; or perhaps those to have been or to be wicked men, who were or are holy and unreprovable.[7]

Similarly, he argued in "On Temptation":

> See those who have tasted that the Lord is gracious. Yet still how weak is their understanding! How limited its extent! How confused, how inaccurate, are our apprehensions of even the things that are round about us. How liable are the wisest of men to mistake! To inform false judgments! To take falsehood for truth, and truth for falsehood; evil for good, and good for evil![8]

Third, mistakes will also be made in the interpretation and understanding of the Bible, so that "as careful as they are to avoid it even the best of men are liable to mistake and do mistake day by day."[9]

While we are under an obligation to pursue the truth, we are not under any obligation to make perfect judgments. God does not require us to do what is impossible for us to do.[10] Mistakes, confusion, and ignorance in our knowledge and understanding lead to mistakes in our words, actions, and behavior. Such words, actions, and behavior may appear to others to be wrong or even sinful.[11] It is not only from the

---

6   See Sermon 69, "The Imperfection of Human Knowledge," *Works of Wesley,* 2:568–86.

7   Sermon 40, "Christian Perfection," *Works of Wesley,* 2:101–2.

8   Sermon 82, "On Temptation," *Works of Wesley,* 3:160.

9   Sermon 40, "Christian Perfection," *Works of Wesley,* 2:102.

10 See Letter to Rev. Samuel Furley June 19, 1760, *Works of Wesley,* 27:198–99.

11 See Letter to Sarah Ryan November 30, 1757, *Works of Wesley,* 27:106–7.

perspectives of others that such opinions are mistaken; they may also be mistaken in God's perspective and thus lead to behavior that violates the moral law. "Every child of man is in a thousand mistakes, and is liable to fresh mistakes every moment. And a mistake in judgment may occasion a mistake in practice; yea, naturally leads thereto." [12] However, Wesley argued that such errors are not sins. He defined sin as: "By sin, I here understand outward sin, according to the plain, common acceptation of the word; an actual, voluntary transgression of the law; of the revealed, written law of God; of any commandment of God, acknowledged to be such at the time that it is transgressed." [13]

Hence, if we act in a manner that from God's perspective is objectively a violation of the moral law, it is not a sin when we have not fully understood or correctly interpreted the moral law in this respect. It is not a sin when we have misunderstood the human and social realities to which our behavior applies. If we are genuinely convinced that our actions are not contrary to the moral law, then they are not sin. It is thus possible and likely that people will hold and act according to different and even contradictory understandings of what God requires; thus according to Wesley, they have not sinned.

Wesley introduced a distinction between "sin properly so called," which is a direct violation of what a person knows to be God's will, and "sin improperly so called," which is an involuntary violation of God's will caused by ignorance, errors, misinterpretation, or confusion. [14] Wesley argued that both require God's forgiveness through the atonement brought about by Christ's death, but we are not responsible before God for the sin improperly so called.

The human capacity is limited, making ignorance, confusion, and mistakes inevitable, and God does not require us not to make mistakes. However, holiness and ignorance are interrelated in two ways. First, Wesley argued that our ignorance can, when approached correctly, lead to growth in holiness. When ignorance is considered in a right manner, it leads to the recognition of our own limitations before God and in relation to other human beings. Thus an awareness of ignorance becomes a means of grace through which we develop the temper of humility. Wesley argued God "entrusts us with only an exceeding small share of knowledge, in our present state; lest our knowledge should interfere with our humility, and we should again affect to be as gods." [15] Second, an awareness of our ignorance and mistakes should lead us to a more careful study of the Bible in order to bring our lives into conformity

---

12 Sermon 57, "The Fall of Man," *Works of Wesley,* 2:406.

13 Sermon 19, "The Great Privilege of Those Who Are Born of God," *Works of Wesley,* 1:436.

14 "Thoughts on Christian Perfection," Q. 6, *Works of Wesley,* 13:61–62; see also Sermon 8, "The First Fruits of the Spirit," *Works of Wesley,* 1:241.

15 Sermon 62, "The End of Christ's Coming," *Works of Wesley,* 2:482.

with the biblical message. When combined with humility, it results in a willingness to recognize that we may be in error and an openness to learning from others that we can grow together into a fuller understanding of God and God's purposes.[16]

THE LAW OF LOVE

Wesley's division of sin into "sin properly so called" and "sin improperly so called" opens up new possibilities for interpreting the complexities raised by Christians with contradictory opinions and practices. However, on its own it does not provide an entirely satisfactory response to the issues. Wesley developed this distinction by complementing it with another set of ideas related to the law of love. The fundamental question for Wesley was: What does God require of us in our contemporary context?

Wesley again uses a distinction between the situation of Adam before the Fall and the condition of humanity after the Fall. Before the Fall, God entered into a covenant with Adam that required that Adam be completely obedient to the perfect law of God, and as a reward for this perfect obedience he would receive eternal life.[17] Adam, before the Fall, was capable of such obedience. However, after the Fall no human "is able to *perform* the service which the Adamic Law requires."[18] The death of Christ is the end of the Adamic law, so that no one after the Fall is bound to observe it. While Wesley does not state this, it clearly appears that the death of Christ has a retrospective effect on all humanity after the Fall. This does not mean that we are not under any law—rather we are under the new law of faith, which is the law of love. The requirement of this law is faith working through love. We are required in our contemporary context to love God and our neighbors; however, unlike the pre-Fall Adam, we do this in the context of our being fallen creatures.[19]

The law of love requires that all our behavior is directed by the twofold love commandment. This requires that in all our thinking, acting, and speaking, we should be motivated and directed by love for God and our fellow humans. When we love God,

---

16   See Letter to Rev. William Dodd March 12, 1756, *Works of Wesley*, 27:19; the "Preface" to *Sermons on Several Occasions*, *Works of Wesley*, 1:107; and "Disciplinary *Minutes* of 1749," Q. 4, *Works of Wesley*, 10:823.

17   Wesley's argument is rooted in the tradition of covenant theology, which was influential within the Reformed tradition including British Puritanism. See Stanley J. Rodes, *From Faith to Faith: John Wesley's Covenant Theology and the Way of Salvation* (Eugene, OR: Pickwick Publications, 2013).

18   "Farther Thoughts upon Christian Perfection," Q.1, *Works of Wesley*, 13:96—emphasis in the original.

19   See "Farther Thoughts on Christian Perfection," Q. 1–12 in *Works of Wesley*, 13:95–101; and Letter to John Hosmer, *Works of Wesley*, 27:259–60.

then God is the object of our deepest desires, the source of our joy, and the one in whom we delight. This love is expressed in prayer, worship, loyalty, obedience, and praise. Love for one's neighbor is a "sincere, fervent, constant desire for the happiness of every man, good or bad, friend or enemy as for their own."[20] Such love expresses itself in self-sacrificial action in the service of others. Again, defects in our knowledge will lead to mistakes in actions, words, thoughts, and even in tempers. Such defects will lead to actions that negatively affect others, despite the person's genuine love for them. Wesley commented: "O what mischief may be done by one that means well."[21] Paradoxically, because love leads to a deep empathy with other human beings, to thinking the best of others, and to believing what they say, it can, as consequence, mean that one is more likely to make false judgments about people and their opinions. Love can lead one into error and hence into mistakes in behavior, thought, and speech. Perfection in knowledge is not possible, and God does not require it. God calls us to love in the midst of ignorance, confusion, and error. Hence for Wesley love with false opinions is to be preferred to truth without love.[22] People who are motivated by a deep love for God and their fellow human beings might come to contradictory convictions about what this love requires due to ignorance, confusion, and error.

Three important qualifications need to be made.

- First, the emphasis on love does not excuse us from pursuing truth in our understanding of God and God's will, of creation, and of human beings; rather, it ought to motivate us to a deeper and fuller pursuit with the goal of acting in a way that reflects God's character and genuinely promotes the good of the other.

- Second, the recognition of our capacity for ignorance, confusion, and mistakes leads to the recognition that, even with the best intentions, we may be acting contrary to God's perfect will and against the well-being of others. Hence even when we have the best intentions, we can join with all Christians in praying: "Forgive us our sins as we forgive the sins of others."

- Third, as humility is integral to love, so is considering others more than ourselves; thus love requires us to recognize that our views, no matter how strongly held, might be in error.

---

20   "Farther Thoughts upon Christian Perfection," Q.12, Works of Wesley, 13:101.
21   Journal October 16, 1760, Works of Wesley, 21:283.
22   See "Preface" to Sermons on Several Occasions, Works of Wesley, 1:107.

LIBERTY AND RESPONSIBILITY BEFORE GOD

Love leads to respect for other people's liberty to hold their own opinions. Wesley says: "And if you love God, you will love your brother also; you will be ready to lay down your life for his sake; . . . you will no more think of forcing him into your own opinions, as neither can he force you to judge by his conscience. But each shall 'give an account of himself to God.'"[23]

The affirmation that all human beings have liberty was fundamental to Wesley's theology. All human beings are accountable before God for their lives, and such accountability is only possible if human beings have the power of self-determination. Hence all human beings must have a genuine, if limited, ability to choose to act or not to act and choose to act in one way and not in another way. Wesley designated this ability as the faculty of liberty.[24] This faculty is a component of the image of God in which human beings were created, and as such it is an essential aspect of what it means to be human and is fundamental to the relationship between God and human beings.[25] Wesley developed this line of thinking in detail in his argument with the Calvinists. His argument had three components.

- First, he argued that biblical passages that portray people as being challenged to obey God and warned of God's judgment when they were disobedient required that human beings have the ability to make genuine choices that were not predetermined by God.[26]

- Second, God is just; and it would be unjust for God to condemn people for actions that they had not freely and responsibly chosen to do.[27]

- Third, God is love; and love does not coerce people to act in particular ways.[28] Hence he concludes that God always relates to human beings as responsible agents with a power of self-determination.

---

23   "A Word to a Protestant," *Works* (Jackson), 11:191.
24   See Sermon 116, "What Is Man," *Works of Wesley*, 4:23–24.
25   See the discussion in Young Taek Kim, "John Wesley's Anthropology: The Restoration of the *Imago Dei* as a Framework for Wesley's Theology" (PhD diss., Drew University, 2006), 34–39.
26   These passages include, for example, Deuteronomy 7:9, 12; 11:26–38; and 30:15–19. See *Predestination Calmly Considered, Works of Wesley*, 13:268–72.
27   *Predestination Calmly Considered, Works of Wesley*, 13:281; and "Thoughts upon Necessity, III," *Works of Wesley*, 13:535–46.
28   "Thoughts upon Necessity," *Works of Wesley*, 13:546.

For Wesley, God does not coerce humans nor overrule their free choices; on the contrary, it is God's prevenient grace that enables sinful human beings to make responsible choices. If God respects the human right to make responsible religious choices and holds them accountable for these choices, then human beings do not have the right to impose their religious views on others. Hence, the right to religious liberty, which Wesley defined as "liberty to choose our own religion, to worship God according to our own conscience according to the best light we have,"[29] is a fundamental, natural right of all human beings. He stated that "this is an indefeasible right; it is inseparable from humanity." It also has primary theological significance, "because every man must give an account of himself to God."[30] People "must not act contrary to their conscience even if it is an erroneous one."[31] And neither the state nor the church has the right to force people to act against their conscience, particularly in matters of religion. Wesley argued:

> Beware you are not a fiery, persecuting enthusiast. Do not imagine that God has called you (just contrary to the spirit of Him you style your Master) to destroy men's lives, and not to save them. Never dream of forcing men into the ways of God. Think yourself, and let think. Use no constraint in matters of religion. Even those who are farthest out of the way never compel to come in by any other means than reason, truth, and love.[32]

In contrast, Methodists "hold the right every man has to judge for himself to be sacred and inviolable."[33] He thus encouraged Methodists: "Condemn no man for not thinking as you think. Let everyone enjoy the full and free liberty of thinking for himself. Let every man use his own judgment, since every man must give an account of himself to God."[34]

Wesley's emphasis on freedom of conscience before God coheres with his decision to exclude Article 8 of the Church of England's Thirty-nine Articles (which affirmed the Nicene Creed, the Athanasian Creed, and the Apostles' Creed ought to be "received and believed") from his revision of the Articles for Methodists in America. The articles themselves are theological propositions that can be agreed with or not; but the creeds put creedal affirmations into the mouths of believers, thus depriving them of the liberty to disagree. The Athanasian Creed goes further and makes salvation dependent upon believing its propositions. Wesley demonstrated considerable freedom with regard to the Thirty-nine Articles, not only explicitly disagreeing with

---

29   "Thoughts upon Liberty," *Works* (Jackson), 11:37.
30   "Some Observations on Liberty," *Works* (Jackson), 11:92.
31   *Journal* June 3, 1776, *Works of Wesley*, 23:20.
32   Sermon 37, "The Nature of Enthusiasm," *Works of Wesley*, 2:59.
33   *A Farther Appeal to Men of Reason and Religion*, Part III, *Works of Wesley*, 11:279.
34   "Advice to the People called Methodists," *Works of Wesley*, 9:130.

them as we will see in the next two chapters, but also in critically revising them for use by the Methodists in America.

The protection of liberty of conscience within Methodism was not an abstract freedom allowing everyone to believe what they willed. It was rather the freedom that created the space for its members to pursue truth, in theory and practice, in the presence of God for the good of others. It is carried out in the recognition that we are responsible before God for our beliefs and the consequences of our beliefs on the comprehensive well-being of others.

CRITICAL REFLECTIONS

The logic of Wesley's position can be summarized as follows.

- As a consequence of the soul's dependence on the body, fallen human beings are subjected to ignorance, mistakes, and errors in knowledge leading to mistakes and errors in practice.

- These mistakes and errors are not sin "properly so called," even when they objectively violate the moral law.

- What God requires of post-Fall humanity, including re-deemed humanity, is not an absolute abstract perfection but perfection in love. Such love is compatible with ignorance, mistakes, and errors and may in fact lead to them.

- Humility, as a temper of a heart directed by love, leads to the recognition and affirmation that we are subjected to igno-rance, mistakes, and errors.

- All human beings have been given the liberty to come to their own conclusions before God as to what is true and false, right and wrong.

- Human responsibility before God requires that human be-ings act out of love in accordance with their understanding of the truth.

- Human responsibility before God requires that human be-ings seek to overcome ignorance and mistakes and act in accordance with the truth as they perceive it.

- People are under obligation before God to act in accordance with their conscience, and no one has the right to require them to act against their conscience.

Hence theological diversity and contradiction is an inherent part of our human existence in this world and is compatible with holiness as love for God and neighbor.

While the theological concepts described above provide significant roots for the theology that Wesley developed in "Catholic Spirit" and "Caution against Bigotry," there are two significant difficulties. The first is the adequacy of the distinction between "sin properly so called" and "sin improperly so called." The distinction problematically emphasizes sin as behavior, in contrast to sin as inner motivation and alienation from God. It is dependent on a legalist understanding of the relationship between God and humanity, shaped by understandings of law that developed in the course of Western European history. Sin is defined in terms of abstract obedience to absolute standards. While such an understanding of law has become deeply rooted in Western theology, particularly since the Reformation, it is in considerable tension with the more relational and personal aspects of Wesley's theology, notably his emphasis on love. The development of the concept of the "law of love" to some extent obviates the problems by focusing on inner motivation, and thus the depth dimension of sin, but it still works in legalistic categories. Further, this distinction, rooted as it is in an understanding of human bodies, raises significant christological problems. If we commit "sin improperly so called" because we are embodied creatures, how are we to understand the sinlessness of Christ? Either his embodiment, understood in relation to the nature of his body and/or the relationship between the body and the soul, must be significantly different from that of other humans, or the understanding of sin must be revised. Wesley appears to have chosen the latter as can be seen in his tendency to downplay Christ's human embodiment.[35]

The second problem arises from a contemporary perspective in that "sin properly so called" and "sin improperly so called" are based on a dichotomous understanding of the human person. As I noted in the first chapter, contemporary science and biblical scholarship points to an integrated holistic understanding of the human person, in which the central dynamics of human personhood are understood to be rooted in our embodied nature. Human limitation, ignorance, and potential for errors and mistakes are not the product of the impact of the body on the essence of the human person—the soul. Rather the central dynamic of the human person arises from the body, and hence these realities are much more integral to what it means to be human than Wesley conceived them to be. As embodied creatures we live in a particular historical context, cultural matrix, and social system. The knowledge we

---

35   See for example his comments on Matthew 27:50, Luke 4:30, John 8:59, and John 11:33 in *NT Notes*.

have is limited and shaped by these contexts. Our ability to process and understand knowledge is also shaped by biological and psychological factors. It is vital that we have the humility to recognize our own fallibility and limitations.

The conceptualization of holiness as righteousness, in the sense of the Hebrew *sedeq* and *sedeqah,* has significant potential to address both the concerns raised above. In this framework, the relationships between humanity and God and between human beings is personal and covenantal rather than legalistic. This does not mean that there are no laws but means that the laws are subjected to the personal and covenantal relationship. Hence righteousness is not abstract obedience to absolute laws but covenantal faithfulness in ways that are appropriate to the relationships in which they exist. Righteousness as acting in covenant faithfulness adds a further dimension. While Wesley's definitions focus on motives and intentions, the concept of righteousness adds the dimensions of consequences. The righteousness of behavior patterns, decisions, acts, or institutions is determined not only by the good intentions of the actor but also on the concrete consequences in the lives of others. Wesley's critique of slavery not only addressed the intentions of those involved in the slave trade but also focused on the concrete consequences on the bodies of the enslaved people. While some, including George Whitefield, argued that one could be involved in some forms of slavery for the benefit of others, for Wesley the clearly observed consequences of slavery countered any such argument for the legitimacy of some forms of slavery.[36] We are called to live righteously as limited and context-bound embodied creatures, and we cannot determine all the consequences of our actions, nor is the evaluation of the consequences infallible. However we are called to evaluate the potential and actual consequences of our actions. Such a conceptualization avoids the need to engage in the terminological and theological contortions of separating "sin properly so called" from "sin improperly so called" and challenges us to act in concrete love to God and our neighbors in full awareness of our limitations and failures and of the consequences of our actions. Yet it continues to affirm, with Wesley, that God does not require us to act contrary to what we genuinely believe to be God's will in a given set of circumstances, and that we are subject to error, confusion, and ignorance.

Despite its problems, the distinction between "sin properly so called" and "sin improperly so called" has an important positive contribution to make to the way we analyze and interpret both past and present human actions. When we evaluate the actions of Christians and churches, we are confronted with the reality that Christians (and other people) have engaged in activities that were carried out with good intentions but that had and have disastrously inhumane consequences. Limitations of knowledge, ideological captivity, sociological constraints, problematic theologies,

---

36   See *Thoughts upon Slavery, Works* (Jackson), 11:59–79.

and cultural blindness prevented them from seeing that what they thought was good was, as we now see with perspective of hindsight, evil. In Wesley's definition it might not have been sin properly so called, but it was still sin improperly so called—that is, a violation of the moral law—and thus can be confessed and condemned today as evil. The difficulty remains of how one determines personal responsibility and accountability. When is blindness to the evil consequences of well-intentioned action culpable? There is no easy answer to this as Wesley noted that sin cleaves to our best intentions and actions.[37] However, as I argued above, the motif of righteousness includes consequences as well as motives in the evaluation of actions. Hence the response to people who perform actions that may be well-intentioned but ultimately destructive can never be only prophetic denunciation; it must also be revealingly informative, bringing people to an awareness of the evil consequences of what they believe to be good actions or actions of no moral significance. As suggested above, Wesley's *Thoughts upon Slavery*[38] is an example of such an approach. A major part of it is a careful description of the evils of slavery designed to demonstrate its incompatibility with justice, mercy, and love. Once this incompatibility is demonstrated, Wesley calls for responsible action from those involved.

In conclusion, Wesley commented in his letter to Rev. Samuel Furley:

> I myself hear frequently unscriptural as well as irrational expressions from those whose feet I shall be joyous to be found in the day of the Lord Jesus. . . . What is wide of Scripture or reason I mildly reprove, and they usually receive it in Love. Generally they are convinced. When I cannot convince, I can bear them, yea, and rejoice at the grace of God which is in them. . . . The longer I live, the larger allowances I make for human infirmities. I exact more from myself and less from others. Go and do likewise.[39]

---

37 See Sermon 14, "The Repentance of Believers," *Works of Wesley,* 1:336–44.
38 See *Thoughts upon Slavery, Works* (Jackson), 11:59–79.
39 Letter to the Rev. Samuel Furley January 25, 1762, *Works of Wesley,* 27:284.

CHAPTER 7

THEOLOGICAL ROOTS— EPISTEMOLOGY

The word *opinions* constantly recurs in Wesley's discussion of theological diversity and disagreement. In "Catholic Spirit" he argues that a person of a catholic spirit embraces others despite their differences in opinions. In "A Caution against Bigotry" he insists that allowing differences of opinion to divide Christians is an expression of bigotry. We could summarize that a too high regard for opinions is the opposite of genuine holiness, understood as the love for our neighbors. Yet, at the same time, he maintained that Christians ought to be fixed in their opinions, and he rejected the theological vagueness of the latitudinarians; further he claimed that some theological affirmations were part of what it meant to love God. What Wesley meant by "opinions" is crucial to understanding his response to theological diversity; yet ironically, among Wesley scholars there is considerable debate and divergence of opinion (!) as to what he meant by "opinion."[1] Part of this is a consequence of Wesley's not writing with the terminological precision of contemporary systematic theologians. His writings were occasional and often directed to "plain" people; in addition, in some of his exchanges with critics, he adopts their terminology. Yet, as I will argue, there is deep consistency in Wesley's use of the concept of "opinion."

OPINIONS AND ESSENTIALS

One interpretation of Wesley proposes that his use of the language of opinions reflects an understanding that there are certain core theological affirmations that are of central and defining significance to Christian faith. These are the "essentials," and then there are a whole range of other theological affirmations of varying significance where faithful Christians disagree and

---

1   See for example David Chapman, "John Wesley on Christian 'Essentials' and 'Opinions,'" *One in Christ* 37, no. 2 (2002), 71–81; Randy L. Maddox, "Opinion, Religion, and 'Catholic Spirit': John Wesley on Theological Integrity," *Asbury Theological Journal* 47, no. 1 (1992), 63–87; John A. Newton, "The Ecumenical Wesley," *Ecumenical Review* 24 (1972), 160–75; and Colin W. Williams, *John Wesley's Theology Today: A Study of the Wesleyan Tradition in the Light of Current Theological Dialogue*, (Nashville: Abingdon, 1960), 13–22.

should be granted liberty to differ without compromising the core of the faith. These are "opinions."[2]

In numerous places in his writings, Wesley refers to fundamental or essential truths or doctrines.[3] While Wesley nowhere provided a complete list of fundamental doctrines, and he refused to do so,[4] in various places he proposed that a particular doctrine or set of doctrines is to be understood as fundamental or essential. He typically refers to these essentials as original sin, justification, new birth, and holiness— the doctrines that describe God's gracious transformation of the human person so that they love God and their fellow human beings.[5] He also referred to the Apostles' Creed[6] and to various classic Christian doctrines as essential. In a letter to John Smith, Wesley wrote: "no singularities are more or near so much *insisted* on by me as the general uncontroverted truths of Christianity."[7]

In his sermon for George Whitefield's funeral in 1770, Wesley distinguished between "the essentials of 'the faith which was once delivered to the saints'" and the "many doctrines of a less essential nature."[8] He proposed that the "fundamental doctrines" could be summed up as the new birth and justification—doctrines upon which Wesley and Whitefield agreed. Wesley's proposal was strongly opposed by one of Whitefield's followers, William Romaine, who argued that Whitefield's fundamental doctrines included predestination rooted in the covenant between God the Father and the Son. Wesley responded to this in a letter to the editor of *Lloyd's Evening Post*. Wesley rejected not only predestination but more particularly the elevation of it to an essential doctrine, which he argued effectively excluded non-Calvinists from salvation.[9] While Wesley does refer in his sermon "On the Death of George Whitefield" to opinions, the terminology he uses for both the essentials and the nonessentials is "doctrines."

---

2   See the references in n1 above and Ted A. Campbell, *Wesleyan Beliefs: Formal and Popular Expressions of the Core Beliefs of Wesleyan Communities* (Nashville: Kingsway, 2010), 17–62.

3   See for example Sermon 20, "The Lord Our Righteousness," *Works of Wesley*, 1:451; Sermon 44, "Original Sin," *Works of Wesley*, 2:183; Sermon 45, "The New Birth," *Works of Wesley*, 2:187; Sermon 97, "On Obedience to Pastors," *Works of Wesley*, 3:376.

4   See Sermon 55, "On the Trinity," *Works of Wesley*, 2:376. In Sermon 4, "Scriptural Christianity," he expressed doubt if there are fundamental doctrines. He stated: "The question moved is not concerning doubtful opinions of one kind or another, but concerning the undoubted, fundamental branches (if there be any such) of our common Christianity" (Sermon 4, "Scriptural Christianity," *Works of Wesley*, 1:175).

5   See "The Principles of a Methodist Farther Explained," *Works of Wesley*, 9:226–29 and the references in n3 above.

6   Sermon 70, "The Case of Reason Impartially Considered," *Works of Wesley*, 2:592.

7   Letter to "John Smith" September 28, 1745, *Works of Wesley*, 26:160.

8   See Sermon 53, "On the Death of George Whitefield," *Works of Wesley*, 2:341.

9   See letter to the editor of *Lloyds Evening Post*, February 26, 1771, *Letters* 5:223–26.

While Wesley drew distinctions between fundamental and less fundamental theological affirmations, and further some affirmations are rejected as errors, in some cases as fundamental errors,[10] he rarely contrasted "essentials" with "opinions." The only case where he unambiguously uses the term "opinion" as a designation of nonessential theological affirmations is in a letter to John Newton on May 14, 1765.[11] He is responding to Newton's reply to an earlier letter and adopts Newton's terminological distinction.[12] In the first letter, Wesley had referred to their different opinions; in his reply, Newton questioned the use of the term "opinions" as appropriate to refer to "any truths revealed in Scripture," because it reduces "them to matters of mere uncertainty and indifference."[13] Newton introduced three further distinctions. The first is between an opinion and the truth, and the second is between opinions and essentials. The third distinction is between an opinion and "a dangerous mistake."[14]

Wesley's response took up and affirmed the distinctions that Newton drew between essentials, opinions, and mistakes. He also affirmed the criterion that Newton proposes for determining an opinion in contrast to "a dangerous mistake"—that is, an opinion that is incompatible with "a love to Christ and a genuine work of grace."[15] He also argued that his perspective on predestination had changed from viewing it as "subversive . . . of the very foundations of Christian experience," due to his belief in the genuine Christian experience of some Calvinists, including Newton. At the end of the letter he argued that the doctrine of Christian perfection is not contrary to justification by faith or any other fundamental doctrine. He did not respond to Newton's critique of the term "opinion."

A second possible use of a distinction between essentials and opinions in relation to theological affirmations is in Wesley's second sermon on the Sermon on the Mount (1750). Here he stated that various Protestant churches "agree in essentials, and only differ in opinions, or in the circumstantials of religion."[16] It is not clear from the context that "essentials" refers to theological affirmations. I will discuss an alternative interpretation below.

---

10 See, for example, "A Word to a Protestant," *Works* (Jackson) 11:189.

11 Letter to John Newton May 14, 1765, *Works of Wesley,* 27:426–31.

12 Letter from John Newton to John Wesley April 18, 1765, Bridwell Library (Southern Methodist University), as transcribed on https://wesleyworks.files.wordpress.com/2015/09/jw-in-correspondence-1761-65.pdf, "John Wesley's In-Correspondence (1761–65)," 206–8. Wesley's earlier letter is on April 9, 1765, *Works of Wesley,* 27:420–22.

13 Letter from John Newton to John Wesley April 18, 1765, https://wesleyworks.files.wordpress.com/2015/09/jw-in-correspondence-1761-65.pdf, 420.

14 This letter is of significance to our project from another perspective in that Newton criticizes Wesley's inconsistency between his utterances about liberty in opinions and his practice in opposing predestination and promoting Christian perfection.

15 Letter to John Newton May 14, 1765, *Works of Wesley,* 27:427.

16 Sermon 22, "Upon our Lord's Sermon on the Mount, II," *Works of Wesley,* 1:508.

Wesley also referred to "opinions which do not strike at the root of Christianity"[17] as those that "do not touch the foundation."[18] He also denies that "*heresy* signifies 'error in opinion,' whether fundamental or not."[19] In "The Way of the Kingdom," he referred to the Incarnation, the doctrine of the Trinity, and the content of the Apostles', Nicene, and Athanasian Creeds as opinions.[20] Clearly Wesley's use of the word "opinions" does not necessarily relate to nonessential theological affirmations but also applies to theological affirmations, which relate either positively or negatively to the "root," "foundation," or "fundamentals" of Christianity.

Randy Maddox has proposed an alternative distinction that is between doctrine and opinion. According to Maddox, *doctrine* refers to official church teachings and *opinions* refer to an "*individual's personal* understanding, appropriation, or rejection of authoritative Christian teaching."[21] However, Wesley does not clearly make this distinction. He, for example, referred to the Reformation as churches reforming their opinions[22] and to the teaching of the Church of England, which he had received from his forefathers, as opinions.[23] As noted above, Wesley described the affirmations of the Athanasian Creed as opinions. In his funeral sermon for Whitefield, he referred to essential and less essential "doctrines," and in other places he refers to orthodoxy as a "system of right opinions."[24] His commentary on 1 Corinthians 3:10 says that a Christian must be careful that "his doctrines may be consistent with the foundation"—that is, Jesus Christ. He goes on to comment on verse 12 that judgments concerning "all doctrines, ceremonies, and forms of human invention" will be burned but "the substantial, vital truths of Christianity" will endure.[25] Further, in his sermon "Scriptural Christianity," Wesley uses "a set of opinions" and "a system of doctrines" as synonymous ways of describing the theological content of Christianity.[26] And in "Ought We to Separate from the Church of England," [27] he refers to the "*doctrine* of the Church, contained in the Articles and Homilies" as the product of "fallible men" and declares that he holds them in very high esteem or else he would not "undertake to defend every particular expression in them." Wesley clearly uses the terms *doctrine* and *opinion* interchangeably.

---

17   "The Character of a Methodist," *Works of Wesley*, 9:34.
18   *A Farther Appeal to Men of Reason and Religion*, Part III, *Works of Wesley*, 11:323.
19   Letter to Rev. James Clark July 3, 1756, *Works of Wesley*, 27:39.
20   Sermon 7, "The Way of the Kingdom," *Works of Wesley*, 1:220; see also "Ought We to Separate from the Church of England," *Works of Wesley*, 9:571.
21   Maddox, "Opinion, Religion and 'Catholic Spirit,'" 65; emphasis in the original.
22   See, for example, Sermon 61, "The Mystery of Iniquity," *Works of Wesley*, 2:465.
23   See *A Farther Appeal to Men of Reason and Religion*, Part III, *Works of Wesley*, 11:320.
24   Sermon 37, "The Nature of Enthusiasm," *Works of Wesley*, 2:46.
25   *NT Notes*, 1 Corinthians 3:10, 12.
26   Sermon 4, "Scriptural Christianity," *Works of Wesley*, 1:161.
27   "Ought We to Separate from the Church of England," *Works of Wesley*, 9:569.

OPINIONS AND REALITIES

John Newton's letter suggests a more fruitful approach to understanding Wesley's use of the word opinion. Newton on the one hand questioned the use of the term, as it indicates uncertainty; and on the other hand, he drew a distinction between opinions and the truths about which they "are conversant,"[28] *conversant* here meaning "relating to, having for its object, concerning."[29] While human opinions are to some extent uncertain, they refer to "truths revealed in scripture." This sort of distinction has its roots in the empiricist epistemology that was growing in intellectual influence in eighteenth-century Britain.[30] Wesley also argued from an empiricist epistemology, though he was probably more influenced by Aristotle than by John Locke and the British tradition.[31] Hence, for Wesley, all our knowledge of the world is derived from the senses, which perceive external realities. The data provided by the senses is processed by logic and related to other data to produce ideas.[32]

In the textbook on logic that Wesley prepared for the Kingswood School, Wesley described opinions in a way that resonates with Newton's comments about uncertainty. He states: "Opinion . . . respects a barely probable proposition and implies no certainty at all. Yet there are several degrees, whereby it approaches certainty; and the highest degree of probability is not far distant from it."[33] Wesley also used "notions" as a synonym for opinions, again pointing to a level of uncertainty.[34] If we relate Wesley's empiricism with his definition of opinions, it could be argued that in relation to the physical world, an opinion is a—to some extent an uncertain—description of reality based on data perceived through the senses and interpreted by reason. The question is then whether there is a parallel to this in Wesley's use of "opinion" to refer to theological concepts. Wesley's sermons "The Lord Our Righteousness" and "On the Trinity" suggest there is.

---

28 Letter from John Newton to John Wesley April 18, 1765, Bridwell Library (Southern Methodist University), as transcribed on wesley-works.org/john-wesleys-in-correspondence, "John Wesley's In-Correspondence (1761–65)," 206.

29 Samuel Johnson, *A Dictionary of the English Language* (London, 1785).

30 See John Locke, *An Essay Concerning Human Understanding*, Book 2, chap. 8 (Oxford: Clarendon, 1979), 134.

31 Scholars differ as to the influence of Aristotle and Locke on Wesley. Timothy J. Crutcher argues cogently for a dominant Aristotelian influence in *The Crucible of Life: The Role of Experience in John Wesley's Theological Method* (Lexington: Emeth, 2010). For arguments for a Lockean influence see Richard E. Brantley, *Locke, Wesley, and the Method of English Romanticism* (Gainesville: University of Florida Press, 1984).

32 See for example Sermon 117, "On the Discoveries of Faith," *Works of Wesley*, 3:29; and Sermon 70, "The Case of Reason Impartially Considered," *Works of Wesley*, 2:590. Crutcher explores this in detail in *The Crucible of Life*.

33 *A Compendium of Logic*, Book II, chap. 1, section 1, *Works* (Jackson), 14:176.

34 *Hymns and Spiritual Songs*, 1753: The Preface, *Works of Wesley*, 7:736.

THE LORD OUR RIGHTEOUSNESS

"The Lord Our Righteousness" was first preached in 1765 and published in 1766. In the opening paragraphs Wesley stated his aim was to contribute to bringing reconciliation between Christians who disagree with each other and devote their time and efforts to combating each other rather than carrying out God's mission in the world. He argued that the truth affirmed in the statement the "Lord our righteousness" is:

> A truth . . . which enters deep into the nature of Christianity, and in a manner supports the whole frame of it. Of this undoubtedly may be affirmed what Luther affirms of a truth closely connected with it: . . . the Christian church stands or falls with it. It is certainly the pillar and ground of that faith of which alone cometh salvation—of that *catholic* or universal faith which is found in all the children of God, and which "unless a man keep whole and undefiled, without doubt he shall perish everlastingly." (Ibid., 1:45–51)[35]

If is so, Wesley argued, then one would expect Christians to agree on this, yet on this very point they appear to have irreconcilable differences not only between Protestants and Catholics but also among Protestants. He then went on to argue that "the difference be more in *opinion* than real *experience* and more in *expression* than in *opinion*." Wesley here distinguished the "experience" of resting one's heart "only on what Christ has done and suffered for pardon, grace, and glory" (ibid., 1:461) with the "opinion" that "to all believers the righteousness of Christ is imputed" (ibid., 1:454). People who have the same experience can have different opinions, because they "may not have a *distinct apprehension*" (ibid., 1:454) of the experience, or their ideas are not clear and accurate, because there are differences in human faculties, which are intensified by differences in education. Further, even when people hold substantially the same opinion, they will use different language to describe their experience, giving rise to different expressions.

Wesley divided those who deny the imputation of Christ's righteousness into two groups. There are the Socinians and Arians who deny the deity of Christ, and thus Wesley argued they both reject the gospel. The second group is comprised of those "whose heart is right toward God," but who have "confused ideas" and use "improper language" (ibid., 1:461). Here he included many Roman Catholics, mystics, Quakers, and various members of other denominations.

In his journal entry of November 23, 1767, published in 1771, Wesley related his further reflection on the imputation of Christ's righteousness and justification by faith, and he noted that a person can be saved without being able to correctly express

---

35   Sermon 20, "The Lord Our Righteousness," *Works of Wesley,* 1:449–65.

the doctrine and without having a clear conception of it and perhaps even denying it.[36] He then asked what becomes of the thesis that this is the article by which the church stands or falls, and Wesley proposed that such bombastic assertions be put aside in favor of "the plain word, 'He that feareth God, and worketh righteousness, is accepted with him.'"[37]

Wesley regarded the imputation of Christ's righteousness as a fundamental or essential doctrine, and he regarded the evangelical Protestant interpretation as true and those of the other groups as false. However, both the Protestant view and the views of others are opinions, and what is essential for Christian faith is not the opinion, but the "experience" of faith in Christ and being accepted by God. Similarly, he wrote in *A Farther Appeal to Men of Reason and Religion*: "a true opinion concerning repentance is wholly different from the thing itself."[38] In the same work he distinguished between the way to heaven, which is "the way of faith in Christ, . . . the way of love to God and man, the 'highway of holiness,'"[39] and opinions. Of even less significance are different ways a common opinion may be expressed. What is ultimately essential is God's transforming work and not the various theological formulations that describe it.

ON THE TRINITY

Wesley wrote "On the Trinity"[40] in 1775 in Ireland. As he reflected on that context, he began by distinguishing opinions from religion and affirming that genuine Christian faith is compatible of numerous errors in opinions, referring particularly to Roman Catholicism. With regard to many opinions one can "think and let think"; however, he argued some truths are more fundamental than others because they have "a connection with vital religion."[41] He affirmed that the Trinity is such a doctrine because the Spirit witnesses to believers that they are children of God the Father, who has accepted them on the basis of the work of God the Son. While the doctrine of the Trinity is an essential doctrine, Wesley insisted that what is essential is the "*fact* . . . that God is Three and One,"[42] and this fact is derived from 1 John 5:7: "There are three that bear record in heaven, the Father, the Word and

---

36 *Journal* November 23, 1767, *Works of Wesley,* 22:114.
37 Ibid., 22:115.
38 *A Farther Appeal to Men of Reason and Religion*, Part II, *Works of Wesley,* 11:253.
39 Ibid., 11:29. We find a similar differentiation in Wesley's comments on Hebrews 6:11 in *NT Notes,* where he differentiates between assurance of faith given by the Holy Spirit and an opinion.
40 Sermon 55, "On the Trinity," *Works of Wesley,* 2:374–86.
41 Ibid., 2:376.
42 Ibid., 2:384.

the Holy Ghost: and these three are one."[43] Wesley asserted that it is not important to believe "this or that explication of the words,"[44] and terms such as *Trinity* and *Person* should not be insisted upon.

Drawing on what we have already discovered, it is possible to develop a re-construction of Wesley's approach, which goes beyond Wesley's explicit words, but I would suggest is a legitimate interpretation. The reality of God as three and one is experienced by Christians as the witness of the Spirit and as explained through di-vine revelation in scripture. For Wesley, this is the basic fact. The development of the doctrine of the Trinity is an opinion that interprets and explains this fact. The more detailed these explanations are, the more they move from the basic fact and the more uncertain they become, and hence all such explanations, including those found in the Athanasian Creed, are not to be insisted upon.

Similarly, in a letter to his brother Charles, Wesley refuses to get involved in "subtle, metaphysical controversies"[45] in relation to the person of Christ. He rejects Arianism but refuses to get into a discussion on Eutychianism or Nestorianism. He asks: "But what are they? What neither I nor anyone else understands. But they are what tore the Eastern and the Western Churches asunder."[46] Wesley consistently af-firmed the deity of Christ as a revealed fact, and hence he rejected Arianism; how-ever here, as in the doctrine of the Trinity, he refused to develop or insist on a more detailed explanation of the relationship between Christ's humanity and his deity. In both cases scripture revealed the basic facts about God; theological interpretations and explanations of these facts are fallible human opinions. In his commentary on 1 Corinthians 13:9, Wesley wrote: "The wisest of men have here short, narrow, im-perfect conceptions, even of the things around them and much more of the deep things of God."[47] Commenting on his own theology, he stated: "I cannot so prove any one point in the whole compass of philosophy or divinity as not to leave room for strong objections, probably such as I could not answer."[48] This is the case even when these opinions have been hallowed by their affirmation as criteria of orthodoxy by significant sections of the church. As I mentioned above, in "Ought We to Separate from the Church of England,"[49] he refers to the "*doctrine* of the Church, contained in the Articles and Homilies" as the product of "fallible men" and declared that while he held them in very high esteem he would not "undertake to defend every particular

---

43   Wesley was aware that the authenticity of the text is disputed but argued for its authenticity.
44   Sermon 55, "On the Trinity," *Works of Wesley*, 2:376.
45   Letter to Charles Wesley June 8, 1780, *Letters*, 7:21.
46   Ibid., 7:21–22.
47   *NT Notes*, 1 Corinthians 13:9.
48   Letter to Rev. Samuel Furley May 21, 1762, *Works of Wesley*, 27:293.
49   "Ought We to Separate from the Church of England," *Works of Wesley*, 9:569.

expression in them." He later assumed the right to revise and remove articles when preparing his own version for the Methodists in America. He also expressed reservations about the doctrine of Christ's descent into hell affirmed in the Apostles' Creed.[50] This is perhaps a reason why Wesley excluded the eighth article of the Anglican Thirty-nine Articles, which asserts that the Nicene, Athanasian, and Apostolic creeds "ought thoroughly to be received and believed," from his revised articles for the American Methodists.

OPINIONS AND RELIGION

In "A Plain Account of the People called Methodists" (1749) Wesley controversially stated, "*orthodoxy* or *right opinions*, is at best but a very slender part of religion, if it can be allowed to be any part of it at all."[51] The radicalism of this statement provoked a vigorous response from Wesley's critics and even today remains problematic for some. Rupert Davies, the editor of volume 9 of *The Works of John Wesley* added a footnote: "Wesley's definition of orthodoxy at this point should be noted. He always asserted, of course, the importance of right *doctrine*—orthodoxy in a different sense."[52] Yet as I argued above, "doctrine" and "opinion" are, in practice, synonymous for Wesley. Moreover, this is not an isolated quote but similar statements can be found in various writings from different times. Here are some examples:

In the preface to the 1746 edition of *Sermons on Several Occasions*, Wesley wrote: "For how far is love, even with many wrong opinions, to be preferred before truth itself without love?"[53] In the Sermon "The Way to the Kingdom" (published in 1746), he stated: "For neither does religion consist in *orthodoxy*, or *right opinions*; which, although they are not properly outward things, are not in the heart, but the understanding."[54] In "On the Trinity" (1775): "Whatsoever the generality of people may think, it is certain that opinion is not religion: No, not right opinion; assent to one, or to ten thousand truths. There is a wide difference between them: Even right opinion is as distant from religion as the east is from the west."[55] In "The End of Christ's Coming" (1781): "And least of all dream that orthodoxy, right opinion (vulgarly called 'faith'), is religion. Of all

---

50   *NT Notes*, Acts 2:27.
51   "A Plain Account of the People called Methodists," *Works of Wesley*, 9:254–55; emphasis in the original.
52   Ibid., 9:254, n1; emphasis in the original.
53   "Preface" to *Sermons on Several Occasions, Works of Wesley*, 1:107.
54   Sermon 7, "The Way of the Kingdom," *Works of Wesley*, 1:220; emphasis in the original.
55   Sermon 55, "On the Trinity," *Works of Wesley*, 2:374.

religious dreams this is the vainest, which takes hay and stubble for gold tried in the fire!"[56]

These statements must be understood in relation to what was described in chapter 1; that for Wesley genuine religion was God's gracious transformation of the human heart enabling people to love God and their neighbors. Hence "true Christian religion" is "not this or that opinion, or system of opinions, be they ever so true, ever so scriptural."[57] As he put it in his sermon "The Unity of the Divine Being" (1789): "True religion is right tempers towards God and man. It is, in two words, gratitude and benevolence: gratitude to our Creator and supreme Benefactor, and benevolence to our fellow-creatures. In other words, it is the loving God with all our heart, and our neighbour as ourselves."[58]

In "Of Former Times" (1787) he wrote: "By religion I mean the love of God and man, filling the heart and governing the life. The sure effect of this is the uniform practice of justice, mercy, and truth. This is the very essence of it, the height and depth of religion, detached from this or that opinion, and from all particular modes of worship."[59]

In contrast to true religion, opinions are "frothy food,"[60] and a religion of opinions is "a false religion," because it does not imply "*the giving of the heart to God.*"[61] Or as he put it in his much earlier letter to John Smith of September 28, 1745: "I love (strictly speaking) no opinion at all. I trample upon opinion, be it right or wrong. I want, I value, I preach the love of God and man. These are my 'favourite' tenets"[62] The center of religion is the transformation of the heart; when anything else is placed at the center, religion is distorted and even destroyed. This occurs when right opinions or orthodoxy are placed at the center, or when right opinions are so emphasized that it results in conflict and division in which one's opponents are despised and rejected, thus destroying love. People could be totally orthodox in their beliefs and be foreigners to true religion. In this context Wesley took up the argument that the Reformation had not gone far enough but gave it a new twist.

> Indeed many of the reformers themselves complained that the Reformation was not carried far enough. But what did they mean? Why, that they did not sufficiently reform the *rites* and *ceremonies* of the church. Ye fools and blind! To fix your whole attention on the circumstantials of religion! Your complaint

---

56 Sermon 62, "The End of Christ's Coming," *Works of Wesley,* 2:483.
57 Sermon 119, "Walking by Sight and Walking by Faith," *Works of Wesley,* 4:57.
58 Sermon 120, "The Unity of the Divine Being," *Works of Wesley,* 4:66–67.
59 Sermon 102, "Of Former Times," *Works of Wesley,* 3:448.
60 *A Farther Appeal to Men of Reason and Religion,* Part III, *Works of Wesley,* 11:321.
61 Sermon 120, "The Unity of the Divine Being," *Works of Wesley,* 4:66.
62 Letter to "John Smith" September 28, 1745, *Works of Wesley,* 26:160–61.

ought to have been, the essentials of religion were not carried far enough. You ought vehemently to have insisted on an entire change of men's *tempers* and *lives*; on their showing they had "the mind that was in Christ", by "walking as he also walked". Without this how exquisitely trifling was the reformation of opinions and rites and ceremonies![63]

Similarly, he argued in that in the eighteenth century, Protestants with different opinions had stopped fighting with each other "on account of small and unessential differences" and were uniting "on the great point wherein they all agree, the faith that worketh by love, and produces in them the mind which was in Christ Jesus."[64] The essential is not a particular doctrinal expression but God's gracious transformation of the human person. I would suggest that the reference to opinions and essentials in his second sermon on the Sermon on the Mount,[65] referred to above, is best understood in the same way, as is his statement that various Protestant churches "agree in essentials, and only differ in opinions, or in the circumstantials of religion."

Wesley further noted that there were people who were genuinely religious, whose hearts had been transformed so that they loved God and their neighbors, yet they held different and perhaps conflicting opinions on key, even essential, doctrines of the faith such as justification. Wesley believed some of these opinions were fundamentally erroneous. He wrote in his sermon "On the Trinity":

> Persons may be truly religious, who hold many wrong opinions. Can anyone possibly doubt of this, while there are Romanists in the world? For who can deny, not only that many of them formerly have been truly religious (as à Kempis, Gregory Lopez, and the Marquis de Renty) but that many of them, even at this day, are real inward Christians? And yet what a heap of erroneous opinions do they hold, delivered by tradition from their fathers! Nay, who can doubt of it while there are Calvinists in the world,—assertors of absolute predestination? For who will dare to affirm that none of these are truly religious men? Not only many of them in the last century were burning and shining lights, but many of them are now real Christians, loving God and all mankind. And yet what are all the absurd opinions of all the Romanists in the world, compared to that one, that the God of love, the wise, just, merciful Father of the spirits of all flesh, has, from all eternity, fixed an absolute, unchangeable, irresistible, decree, that part of all mankind shall be saved, do what they will; and the rest damned, do what they can![66]

---

63   Sermon 61, "The Mystery of Iniquity," *Works of Wesley*, 2:465.

64   *Hymns and Spiritual Songs*, 1753: The Preface, *Works of Wesley*, 7:736.

65   Sermon 22, "Upon our Lord's Sermon on the Mount, II," *Works of Wesley*, 1:508.

66   Sermon 55, "On the Trinity," *Works of Wesley*, 2:374–76. See also Sermon 130, "On Living without God," *Works of Wesley*, 4:175.

In his journal of February 26, 1768, Wesley commented: "How little does God regard men's opinions! What a multitude of wrong opinions are embraced by all the members of the Church of Rome? Yet how highly favoured have many of them been!"[67] And again, in his "A Letter to a Roman Catholic," he identifies true religion, not with the list of common beliefs but with a genuine love for God and neighbors, which manifests itself in a transformed lifestyle.[68]

Wesley's exclusion of the Article on the creeds from his revised Articles of Religion coheres with this, in that explicitly in the Athanasian Creed and implicitly in the creedal formulation "I/we believe" in the Apostolic and Nicene Creeds, there is an identification of true faith with assent to theological propositions. In contrast the Articles of Religion in both their Anglican and Methodist form are theological propositions without creedal formulation.[69]

Yet this does not mean that the opinions have no part in religion, or that it makes no difference what opinions one has. In a letter to Conyers Middleton (1749), Wesley set out the relationship of doctrine to genuine religion.[70] After critiquing Middleton's work, Wesley switched to a positive mode, beginning by describing in detail the character of a genuine Christian as one who truly loves God and neighbor. Having done this, he argued Christianity understood as a system of doctrine has three components: First, it "describes this character in all its parts"; second, it "promises that this character shall be mine, if I will not rest till I attain it"; and third, it describes "how I may attain the promise; namely, by faith." When Wesley developed each of these points he touched on a variety of Christian doctrines. Christianity as a system of doctrines or opinions is directed toward the transformation of people.

This emphasis that the core of genuine religion is the transformation of the human person also explains why, when Wesley offers lists of fundamental or essential doctrines, he refers to original sin, justification by faith, new birth, and sanctification. These are the doctrines that describe the core of genuine religion. His reference to these doctrines is not primarily because these are the doctrines of the evangelical revival. Nor does he emphasize these because he assumes that Christians from all traditions would accept the traditional orthodoxy of the Apostles' and Nicene Creeds. These are central doctrine because they describe the core of religion. The relationship between these theological affirmations and traditional orthodoxy is best

---

67   *Journal* February 26, 1768, *Works of Wesley,* 22:120. See also Sermon 130, "On Living without God," *Works of Wesley,* 4.175.

68   Outler, ed., *John Wesley,* "A Letter to a Roman Catholic," 498.

69   Wesley does, however, adopt a personal creedal form in "A Letter to a Roman Catholic," 493–99.

70   "A Letter to the Reverend Dr. Conyers Middleton occasioned by his late 'Free Inquiry,'" VI, Section II, *Works* (Jackson), 10:72–75.

explained by carefully interpreting his statement in "The Principles of a Methodist Farther Explained": "Our main doctrines, which include all the rest, are three, that of repentance, of faith, and of holiness. The first of these we account, as it were, the porch of religion; the next, the door; the third, religion itself."[71]

The doctrines describing God's gracious transformation of the human person *include* the other doctrines. What Wesley means here is illustrated by a quotation from Jonathan Swift to which Samuel Johnson refers in his dictionary definition of the word *include*. The quotation from Swift reads: "Instead of inquiring whether he be a man of virtue the question is only, whether he be a Whig or a Tory, under which terms all good and ill qualities are included."[72] Swift is proposing that there are certain qualities that are generally associated with a Whig and others that are associated with a Tory; so that a description of a Whig or Tory contains or presupposes a list of qualities. In a similar way the doctrines of repentance, faith, and holiness contain or presuppose other doctrines. They can only be understood in relation to a broader doctrinal framework and thus imply this framework even when it is not directly asserted. So Wesley's emphasis on the theological affirmations that describe God's gracious transformation of the human person is not to exclude other doctrines, such as Trinity, person of Christ, and atonement, that are traditionally held to be of fundamental importance. Rather it is to see these as contained within and presupposed by the doctrinal description of God's transforming work. An example of this is in his sermon "On the Trinity." The core of the doctrine that God is one and three is, in Wesley's understanding, the key to explaining the witness of the Spirit to the transformation brought about by God.

This affirmation that the core of religion is the transformation of the human person and that the fundamental doctrines are those that describe this transformation in the context of the broader framework of Christian doctrine has an important corollary; namely, that theological propositions that deal with issues closer to the core message of God's transformation of the human person are of greater significance than those that are further away. As Wesley wrote in *A Farther Appeal to Men of Reason and Religion*: "No stress has been laid on anything as though it were necessary to salvation but what is undeniably contained in the Word of God. And of the things contained therein the stress laid on each has been in proportion to the nearness of its relation to what is laid down as the sum of all—the love of God and our neighbor."[73]

When Wesley addressed key theological issues in debate, he sought to show their relationship with this central core of genuine religion. As we noted above,

---

71 "The Principles of a Methodist Farther Explained," *Works of Wesley*, 9:227.
72 Samuel Johnson, *Dictionary of the English Language*, 6th ed. (London, 1785)
73 *A Farther Appeal to Men of Reason and Religion*, Part III, *Works of Wesley*, 11:277.

Wesley argued that the affirmation that God is one and three has fundamental significance as the theological framework for understanding God's transformative work. However, more detailed attempts to work out how God can be three and one or details of the divine persons are of lesser significance, because they do not relate as directly to God's transformative work and are therefore open to debate and disagreement. Similarly, in "Catholic Spirit" Wesley argued that some opinions about basic rights with regard to God and Christ are necessary for the existence of true religion; yet as noted in the discussion of this sermon, he is not totally consistent in identifying these.[74]

Negatively, Wesley grappled with the issue of the impact of erroneous opinions on the life of Christians. As I stated in chapter 3, a key element of Wesley's early argument against Calvinism was that it undermined the pursuit of holiness of heart and life and hence was a dangerous error. In his response to critics of his statement that "right opinions are only a slender part of religion," he added a number of qualifications.[75] These qualifications continued to emphasize that genuine religion is not constituted by right opinions, but added that wrong opinions are detrimental to genuine religion as they lead to wrong practices and tempers. Thus while criticizing the overemphasis on orthodoxy and its equation with true religion, he argued that Methodists were thoroughly orthodox in their theology.[76] In the genuinely religious person, right tempers are dependent on at least some right opinions, and right opinions promote growth in right tempers. He thus states in his letter to Rev. James Clark in 1756: "I rejoice to please all men for their good to edification, if happily I may gain more proselytes for genuine scriptural Christianity, if I may prevail on more to love God and their neighbor and to walk as Christ walked. So far as I find them obstructive of these, I oppose opinions with all my might."[77]

---

74   See chapter 3 above, and note also his discussion in Some Remarks on "A Defence of the Preface to the Edinburgh Edition of 'Aspasio Vindicated,'" *Works of Wesley*, 13:396.

75   See A Second Letter to the Author of the Enthusiasm of Methodists, *Works of Wesley*, 11:425; Letter to Rev. James Clark September 18, 1756, *Works of Wesley*, 27:62; A Letter to the Right Reverend The Lord Bishop of Gloucester, *Works of Wesley*, 11:479; Some Remarks on "A Defence of the Preface of the Edinburgh Edition of '"Aspasio Vindicated,'" *Works of Wesley*, 13:395; and Sermon 127, "On the Wedding Garment," *Works of Wesley*, 4:146. Maddox argues that there is a progression of qualification as Wesley responds to different critics, while there is some explicit progression. Most of the qualifications are implicit in Wesley's earlier critiques of Calvinism and Catholicism, his rejection of latitudinarianism, and his description of a genuinely catholic spirit included theological affirmations in "Catholic Spirit" and his discussions of error in relation to Christian perfection. More explicitly he commented on 1 Corinthians 3:17 in *NT Notes* published in 1754. He referred to "doctrines fundamentally wrong" that had the potential to "destroy a real Christian."

76   See for example A Farther Appeal to Men of Reason and Religion, Part III, *Works of Wesley*, 11:276.

77   Letter to Rev. James Clark September 18, 1756, *Works of Wesley*, 27:61.

Wesley combines both the positive and negative dimensions in his critique of the German mystic Jacob Böhme. (Wesley used the spelling Behmen, which was common in English at the time). Wesley defended the necessity of holding to a doctrine of God's wrath by first arguing that if God was not angry with sinners, then his wrath could not have been turned away from them, and thus God was not reconciled to sinners. This logic undermines the foundations of the doctrine of justification, which is the root of holiness. He then went on to argue that a denial of God's wrath undermines various dimensions of holiness.[78]

These points are well illustrated in a letter Wesley wrote to his nephew Charles, when his nephew Samuel converted to Roman Catholicism. He states:

> I doubt not but both Sarah and you are in trouble because Samuel has "changed his religion." Nay, he has changed his *opinions* and *mode of worship*. But that is not religion; it is quite another thing. "Has he, then," you may ask, "sustained no loss by the change." Yes, unspeakable loss; because his new opinion and mode of worship are so unfavorable to religion that they make it, if not impossible to one that once knew better, yet extremely difficult.

> "What, then, is religion?" It is happiness in God, or in the knowledge and love of God. It is "faith working by love, producing righteousness and peace and joy in the Holy Ghost." In other words, it is a heart and life devoted to God; or communion with God the Father and the Son; or the mind which was in Christ Jesus, enabling us to walk as He walked. Now, either he has this religion or he has not. If he has, he will not finally perish, notwithstanding the absurd, unscriptural opinions he has embraced and the superstitious and idolatrous modes of worship. But these are so many shackles which will greatly retard him in running the race that is set before him. If he has not this religion, if he has not given God his heart, the case is unspeakably worse: I doubt if he ever will; for his new friends will continually endeavor to hinder him by putting something else in its place, by encouraging him to rest in the form, notions, or externals, without being born again, without having Christ in him, the hope of glory, without being renewed in the image of Him that created him. This is the deadly evil.[79]

To summarize, genuine religion is God's gracious transformation of the human heart so that people love God and their neighbors. This is the essential or fundamental core of Christianity.[80] Theological opinions are secondary as descriptions of God's

---

78 See "Thoughts upon Jacob Behmen," *Works* (Jackson), 9:513.
79 Letter to his nephew Charles Wesley May 2, 1784, *Letters*, 7:216. See also letters to his nephew Samuel Wesley on August 19, 1784, *Letters*, 7:230–31, and on March 18, 1788, *Letters*, 8:47.
80 See for example Sermon 4, "Scriptural Christianity," *Works of Wesley,* 1:160.

transforming action and the consequent transformation. However, the theological description of this transforming action can only be understood within the context of a broader system or network of theological affirmations. The significance of a particular theological opinion depends on its relationship with the central core, that is, God's transformation of the human heart. All theological opinions are human constructs and hence subject to error, and the significance of the theological error depends on its relationship to the core. While it is possible for a person to experience God's transforming work and hold to false opinions that are directly related to the core, such opinions undermine the spiritual well-being of the person.

OPINIONS, ESSENTIALS, AND ETHICS

If the core of true religion is that God transforms the human heart so that persons love God with all their being and their neighbors as themselves, then ethics is integral to the core of Christianity. Nevertheless, true religion cannot be reduced to morality; it is possible to be moral without experiencing the inner renewal and transformation of the heart.[81] Wesley can thus describe the essential doctrines of Christianity theologically as those that describe this process of transformation (original sin, justification, the new birth, and inner and outer holiness) or ethically as the commandment to love God and our neighbors.[82] Hence Wesley argued "zeal for all good works is . . . an essential ingredient of true religion."[83] In another context he stated: "this religion has no mixture of vice or unholiness. It gives no man . . . the license to sin."[84] However, the inevitable diversity of opinions that are a consequence of human finitude and fallenness does not only relate to issues of doctrinal theology but also to ethics, as we noted in the previous chapter.

Wesley noted in his sermon "A Caution against Bigotry" that one area of divergence in opinions among genuine Christians related to "the nature and use of the moral law."[85] He recognized that diversity of opinions will lead to diversity of practices. Developing Wesley's proposal, we can argue that, in relation to ethics, the issue of diversity has a triple reference. First, human finitude will necessarily lead to diversity in interpretation of the biblical, ethical, and material. Second, human finitude will lead

---

81   See for example Sermon 7, "The Way of the Kingdom," *Works of Wesley,* 1:219–20; and
      Sermon 62, "The End of Christ's Coming," *Works of Wesley,* 2:483.
82   See "An Answer to Roland Hill's Tract," *Works of Wesley,* 9:405; *A Farther Appeal to Men
      of Reason and Religion,* Part I, *Works of Wesley,* 11:129; and Letter to Mr. 'G.R.', alias R.A.,
      alias 'M.H.', alias 'R.W.' February 17, 1761, *Works of Wesley,* 27:243.
83   A Letter to the Right Reverend the Lord Bishop of Gloucester, *Works of Wesley,* 11:459.
84   *A Farther Appeal to Men of Reason and Religion,* Part III, *Works of Wesley,* 11:278.
85   Sermon 38, "A Caution against Bigotry," *Works of Wesley,* 2:70.

to diversity in the understanding of human beings, creation, and societies. And third, human finitude will lead to diverse ways of correlating the interpretation of the biblical material with the understanding of human beings, creation, and societies.

Wesley defined sin as "a voluntary transgression of a known law,"[86] yet faithful Christians disagree on what the law requires in particular contexts. In Wesley's context there was little debate around key issues of Christian ethics, with traditional positions being accepted without much debate. There were, however, three issues of contention that Wesley did address.

- The first was that of money, which became a constant theme in his ethical instructions to Methodists.[87] Wesley's radical rejection of the pursuit of wealth was rooted in his understanding of the commands to love God and one's neighbor. While this was controversial, Wesley argued views on money could not be compromised, as they were deeply rooted in what he understood to be the core of Christianity.

- The second issue was slavery. Wesley's uncompromising rejection of slavery was similarly rooted in his view that it was incompatible with justice and mercy and hence violated the command to love one's neighbor as one's self.[88] Wesley's position is particularly interesting given that there was a growing debate on slavery with people arguing for slavery on the basis of the Bible.[89] There was an exchange of letters between Wesley and Whitefield on slavery in which Whitefield argued for slavery on biblical grounds. But this does not appear to have become an issue that divided them the way that predestination did; possibly because at that time it was not a major issue on Wesley's agenda.[90]

---

86 Sermon 76, "On Perfection," *Works of Wesley,* 3:79.

87 See all the following in *Works of Wesley*: "Upon our Lord's Sermon on the Mount, VIII," 1:612–31; Sermon 50, "The Use of Money"; Sermon 51, "The Good Steward," 2:266–80 and 282–98; Sermon 87, "The Dangers of Riches"; Sermon 107, "On God's Vineyard"; and Sermon 108, "On Riches," 3:228–46, 503–17, 519–28.

88 See *Thoughts upon Slavery, Works* (Jackson), 11:59–79.

89 See David N. Field, "John Wesley as a Public Theologian: The Case of *Thoughts upon Slavery,*" *Scriptura* 114 (2015), 1–13, http://scriptura.journals.ac.za/pub/article/view/1136/1081.

90 Whitefield argued in a letter to Wesley that slavery was permitted in the Bible, citing the case of Abraham and the references to "servants" in the New Testament, arguing that some of them were slaves. He proposed that if one treated one's slaves humanely then it was legitimate to own and use slave labor in situations where slave labor was required. He further proposed that by buying slaves he would make their lives comfortable (in contrast

• A third issue revolved around Wesley's strong opposition to the American struggle for independence. At the core of Wesley's theological argument was that loving and honoring the king was inseparable from loving and fearing God.[91] Here Wesley goes as far as to state: "Do any of you blaspheme God and the King? None of you I trust who are in connexion with me. I could no more continue in fellowship with those who continued in such a practice, than with whoremongers, or Sabbath-breakers, or thieves, or drunkards, or common swearers."[92] As we noted in chapter 3, when Wesley argued that belonging to a different party should not divide Christians, he was probably referring to political parties; yet here in the heat of this controversy, his catholic spirit seems to have been forgotten.

In addressing all three of these contentious issues, Wesley justified his radical stand on the basis that these issues were fundamentally related to the commands to love God and one's neighbor. Here, in Wesley's view, there was no room for diversity of opinion. While one might disagree with Wesley's view on the American War of Independence, his statements suggest that there are ethical issues where there is no place for compromise. The early American Methodists originally took this approach to slavery—including a rejection of slavery in the General Rules and the first *Discipline of the Methodist Episcopal Church*, even though they were later to compromise on that. For us, the contemporary challenge is to develop criteria by which churches can discern whether a particular issue is one that invites people to "think and let think" or one that accommodates no deviation.

SOURCES FOR THEOLOGICAL OPINIONS

The discussion on the sources of theological propositions in Wesley's theology has since the 1970s centered on Albert Outler's argument that Wesley drew on four elements: scripture, experience, tradition, and reason in constructing his theology,

---

to other slave owners) and that his slaves would be brought up to hear the gospel. It appears that Whitefield is replying to a letter from Wesley but this letter has not survived. See Iva A. Brendlinger, *Social Justice through the Eyes of Wesley: John Wesley's Theological Challenge to Slavery* (Ontario: Joshua, 2006), 56–58.

91 See "A Calm Address to the Inhabitants of England," in *Works* (Jackson), 11:129–40. He states his principle most simply in his broader political pamphlet "A Word to the Free-holder" in *Works*, 11:97.

92 "A Calm Address," *Works* (Jackson), 11:139.

with scripture carrying the most weight. Outler dubbed his construct the "Wesleyan quadrilateral."[93] While it is generally acknowledged that Wesley did make use of these four sources, how they should be weighted; how they relate to each other; what is exactly meant by each of them; and whether the geometrical image is useful, has been a subject of considerable debate. The inclusion of the quadrilateral in the 1972 United Methodist *Book of Discipline* resulted in entangling this debate with the complexities of theological politics in The United Methodist Church. A detailed discussion of all these issues would take us beyond the scope of this book.[94] The purpose of this section is to provide a brief description of a viable alternative model to the quadrilateral but one that acknowledges its contribution.

A few preliminary points need to be made. First is that while Wesley refers to the four elements, he never refers to all four together; at the most he refers to three. Second, Wesley's writings are occasional and sometimes polemical, and he adopts those elements that best suit his purposes. Third, Wesley never developed his theology from a theological *tabula rasa*. He was from his childhood rooted in the Anglican tradition, which he developed and adapted, and hence he never really argues from the ground up.

The starting point for our discussion must be what I have argued throughout; that is, for Wesley all theology is in the service of the Christian life. His goal was that people grow in grace and holiness. He did not intend to develop a systematic conceptual theory of the Christian faith. Theological reflection is thus primarily to be understood as a means of grace—a means the Spirit of God can use to transform people. The crux of the issue is not the development of a perfectly coherent theological methodology. It is rather to discern how the Spirit uses scripture, tradition, experience, and reason, and anything else needed to transform human lives. The priority is thus the gracious work of the Spirit—or to use Wesleyan terminology—prevenient, justifying, and sanctifying grace.[95]

---

93   See Albert Outler, "The Wesleyan Quadrilateral in John Wesley," in Thomas C. Oden and Leicester R. Longden, *The Wesleyan Theological Heritage: Essays by Albert C. Outler* (Grand Rapids, MI: Zondervan, 1991), 21–38.

94   For details of this debate see David B. McEwan, *Wesley as a Pastoral Theologian: Theological Methodology in John Wesley's Doctrine of Christian Perfection*, (Milton Keynes, UK: Paternoster, 2011), 5–36; Ted A. Campbell, "The 'Wesleyan Quadrilateral': The Story of a Modern Methodist Myth," in Thomas A. Langford, *Doctrine and Theology in the United Methodist Church* (Nashville: Kingswood, 1991), 154–61; Randy L. Maddox, "Honoring Conference: Wesleyan Reflections on the Dynamics of Theological Reflection," in *The Renewal of United Methodism: Mission, Ministry, and Connectionalism*, ed. Rex D. Matthews (Nashville: General Board of Higher Education and Ministry, 2012), 55–97; and W. Stephen Gunter, Scott J. Jones, Ted A. Campbell, Rebekah L. Miles, and Randy L. Maddox, *Wesley and the Quadrilateral: Renewing the Conversation* (Nashville: Abingdon, 1997).

95   This is a major theme of David B. McEwan, *Wesley as a Pastoral Theologian*.

As argued above, Wesley held to an empiricist epistemology.[96] Knowledge is obtained through the sensory perception of reality; it is then processed by reason. Experience is central to knowledge but not in the sense of an inner psychological or religious event but as the encounter with a reality. Hence experience is verifiable; if other persons are in a similar context, they will experience this reality in a similar but never exactly same way. As we cannot individually experience many aspects of reality, we are dependent upon the testimony of others who have experienced dimensions of reality that we have not experienced. In this sense, knowledge is dependent upon reliable testimony. Human reason is not a source of knowledge but the tool that the mind uses to process the data obtained by the senses in order to construct ideas. This empiricist epistemology encounters a major difficulty when applied to theology, in that spiritual realities are not perceived by the bodily sense organs, although Wesley believed that they did impact the physical world. In order to cope with this difficulty, Wesley made two modifications to his empirical epistemology. First, he added a second source of knowledge, God's revelation in scripture, which provides information of theological realities that cannot be perceived by the physical senses. Second, he argued that at the new birth, the human soul acquires spiritual senses, which enables it to perceive spiritual realities in a manner analogous to the physical senses.

In a number of his writings, Wesley laid out principles for interpreting scripture.[97] He argued that the literal interpretation of scripture is to be preferred. However, Wesley understood that one of the consequences of inspiration was that the biblical texts cohered with each other. Hence the emphasis on the literal sense was qualified in four ways.

- First, individual texts should not be interpreted in a way that contradicts other texts. Wesley insisted in numerous places that scripture is the only authoritative source for determining Christian teaching. However, while scripture reveals God, God's purposes and God's work must be interpreted by fallible and fallen human beings using the gift of reason; hence these interpretations are subject to the limitations, mistakes, and errors of human thinking.

---

96 For much of what follows I am dependent on the argument of Crutcher, *The Crucible of Life,* and refer the reader to this work for detailed argument and references to Wesley's work.

97 For a fuller discussion see Scott J. Jones, *John Wesley's Conception and Use of Scripture* (Nashville: Kingswood, 1995); Randy Maddox, "The Rule of Christian Faith, Practice and Hope: John Wesley on the Bible," *Methodist Review* 3 (2011), 1–35; Robert W. Wall, "Wesley as a Biblical Interpreter," in *The Cambridge Companion to John Wesley,* ed. Randy L. Maddox and Jason E. Vickers (Cambridge: Cambridge University Press, 2010), 113–28; and Crutcher, *The Crucible of Life,* 141–83.

- Second, the individual passages should be interpreted in terms of the overarching message of the Bible, which he described as the "whole scope and tenor of scripture"[98] or the "analogy of faith."[99] He provided a number of descriptions of this overarching message, and in some cases he referred to inward and outward holiness, which is constituted by love for God and our neighbors. In other cases, the entire tenor of scripture provides key steps in the process by which people are restored in the image of God, so that they love God and their neighbors. This begins with original sin, then repentance, faith, and justification, leading to sanctification. We can summarize Wesley's understanding of the "whole tenor and scope of scripture" to be that God is love and loves humanity; and that out of love God has acted to forgive and transform sinful human beings, so that they are empowered to love God and their neighbors.[100]

- The third qualification is that the interpretation of scripture must not be absurd, hence the use of reason is an integral component of interpretation.

- Fourth, once the literal meaning in its original context had been discerned, then it must be "applied to ordinary Christians" in a manner that allows "for different times and circumstances."[101]

Because interpretation is fallible and subject to error, it is always open to correction. Hence in a number of places Wesley not only acknowledges this but also asks others to critique his interpretation when they believe he is in error.[102] It is thus also important to consult the work of others as points of comparison and correction as well as a way of developing deeper insights into the meaning of scripture. This process is often identified as tradition in the quadrilateral.

---

98   Sermon 110, "Free Grace," *Works*, 3:552.

99   See *NT Notes* on Romans 12:6.

100 Wesley's discussion of predestination provides the most developed example of this hermeneutic at work. In the sermon "Free Grace" he argues that the Calvinistic interpretation of specific biblical texts is illegitimate because it contradicts the "whole scope and tenor of scripture." The biblical passages cannot mean what the Calvinists say they mean as this would be a denial of God's love revealed in the whole of scripture (Sermon 110, "Free Grace," *Works of Wesley*, 3:552).

101 "An Answer to the Rev. Mr. Church's Remarks," *Works of Wesley*, 9:116.

102 See for example Preface, *NT Notes*.

Experience functions in five important ways in relation to the interpretation of scripture.

1. A transforming experience of God's grace is the goal of the interpretation and hence of the theological affirmations that emerge.

2. As a result of the Spirit's action, experience prepares the way for the interpretation of scripture. One can see this, for example, in the development of Wesley's own understanding of salvation by faith. His journey to a new understanding began with a deepening dissatisfaction with his spiritual life that was emphasized by his encounter with possible death during his stormy passage to America. Here he could not help but compare his fear and anxiety with the calmness and faith of his Moravian fellow travelers. This experience opened the way for him to listen to their understanding of salvation by faith, leading him back to the study of the Bible to evaluate their message. In a different way in his *Original Sin,* Wesley describes the experience of evil in human society, both historically and in his context, providing the basis for showing how a doctrine of original sin developed from the Bible.[103]

3. Experience functions as a test of interpretation—if an interpretation is valid it will be manifested in the lives of people. After Wesley came to the conclusion that the Bible did teach instantaneous conversion through faith in Christ, he then asked his Moravian dialogue partners for testimonies of people who had experienced it to confirm this interpretation. In the case of ethics, experience is a vital test of the adequacy of an ethical decision by evaluating its consequences on the well-being of the people involved. In the eighteenth century and earlier, philosophers and theologians de-

---

103 See *The Doctrine of Original Sin: According to Scripture, Reason and Experience,* Part I, *Works of Wesley,* 12:160–211.

veloped ethical propositions and biblical arguments that defended some forms of slavery. Wesley's rejection of slavery in *Thoughts upon Slavery*[104] arose in part through a concrete evaluation of what slavery was like based on his own experience (observation) of slavery in America and the testimony of others to its cruelty.

4. Experience provides data that must be interpreted and responded to by the interpretation of scripture. Hence when he discussed the possibility of contemporary miracles, Wesley referred to this testimony to provide information as to what had occurred, and then he turned to the Bible to interpret these phenomena.[105] In dealing with ethical issues such as slavery or poverty, experience—either Wesley's own or that of those he considered trustworthy witnesses—provided the description of the ethical issue, which was then responded to on the basis of scripture.

5. Experience will at times influence the interpretation of scripture. Wesley noted in his sermon "The Means of Grace" that people in exceptional circumstances experienced God's grace in isolation from the world, and hence God can be experienced by abstaining from the means of grace.[106] This interpretation, however, he rejected. Experience is not infallible, because human beings are open to deception—what some think is an experience of God at work might be of human or demonic origin. The testimony of others, and hence of tradition, provides an important test of the validity of the experience. The application of scripture to the experience of Christians raises new questions and hence directs us back to scripture again.

---

104 See *Thoughts upon Slavery, Works* (Jackson), 11:59–79.
105 *A Farther Appeal to Men of Reason and Religion*, Part III, *Works of Wesley*, 11:310.
106 Sermon 16, "The Means of Grace," *Works of Wesley*, 1:380.

OPINIONS AND DIVERSITY—WITH WESLEY AND BEYOND WESLEY

We can summarize the key elements of Wesley's thought as follows.

- The essence of true religion is the gracious transformation of the human heart, so that a person loves God and neighbor. This transformation is manifested in outward behavior.

- Orthodoxy as a system of correct opinions/doctrines is not to be identified with true religion.

- Theological reflection is a means of grace directed toward the transformation of human hearts.

- Theological opinions are human theoretical constructions that describe theological/spiritual realities.

- The realities described are revealed in scripture and may be experienced by humans.

- Human beings will describe the theological realities differently as a result of personal and social factors, giving rise to different opinions.

- As a consequence of human fallenness and finitude, all opinions are subject to error.

- People who agree on an opinion might also express that opinion in different terminology.

- Opinions vary in their significance relative to their connection to the core of true religion.

- Not all opinions are equally valid; some opinions provide better descriptions of the theological reality than others. Some opinions are mistaken and erroneous. Hence there is a need to ascertain as comprehensibly as possible that one's own opinions are correct.

- There is considerable room for accepting people with divergent opinions whose lives manifest a genuine faith that expresses itself in love, even when the differences relate to core issues such as justification.

- Certain opinions are incompatible with a genuine acceptance and experience of the theological reality.

- While correct opinions are not to be identified with true religion, erroneous and mistaken opinions have detrimental effects on the spiritual well-being of people. Further, correct opinions promote growth in holiness. Hence Christians have a duty to seek and promote true opinions.

- Ethical opinions are also human constructions with the same fallibility as other opinions.

- Ethical opinions that are most directly related to the central core of loving God and neighbor have precedence over issues that are less directly related to this core.

- The primary source for theological opinions is scripture rightly interpreted. Tradition provides an important check on the interpretation of scripture, and reason functions positively as an interpretative and theory-constructing tool and negatively to ensure that our interpretation is not absurd.

- Experience prepares the way for right interpretation of scripture, confirms the right interpretation, and provides the necessary information for ethical decision making.

The above points provide the theological background for understanding Wesley's sermons on "Catholic Spirit" and "Caution against Bigotry" and form a bridge to our consideration of his understanding of the church and schism, which we examine in the next chapter.

In contemporary terms, Wesley's approach might be described as a form of critical realism that affirms spiritual and theological realities and that our opinions are human constructs that we (as flawed, finite, and fallen creatures) build to describe these realities, thereby making our descriptions and interpretations of them fallible and open to revision.[107] And the development of a contemporary Wesleyan perspective requires that we move critically and constructively beyond Wesley in at least four significant ways.

---

107 For a contemporary example see N. T. Wright, *The New Testament and the People of God* (London: SPCK, 1992), 31–44. Interestingly, in his preface, Wright echoes Wesley when he states that some of his ideas are wrong but that he does not know which parts are wrong; see page xvii and Sermon 39, "Catholic Spirit," *Works of Wesley*, 2:84.

• Wesley generally has a negative perspective on theological diversity, seeing it as a product of the Fall and giving rise to false opinions, which will be overcome eschatologically.[108] An affirmation of the inherent embodied character of human life suggests that such diversity is not necessarily the product of mistake and error but is an intrinsic aspect of our humanity. As embodied creatures we experience reality from diverse contexts and conditions. Our differing perspectives can be mutually enriching and provide the opportunity to learn from each other, rather than one perspective being wholly right and the other completely wrong. Hence it is only together that we get a fuller understanding of the multidimensional character of God, God's purposes and actions, and faithful Christian living. Wesley comes close to such a view, though still in a negative fashion, in his proposal that different Christian denominations have retained aspects of Christian truth and practice and that those who "desire to follow the whole word of God" should "gather up" all these "fragments" and join them "together in one scheme of truth and practice."[109] Emphasizing the positive character of diversity does not eliminate the need to discern which perspectives are true and which are false and which build up people in the love of God and humanity and which will destroy this. Not all perspectives are valid. Nor does it mean that we should not hold our own perspectives with deep conviction.

• Wesley's understanding of the Bible is best described as precritical. The development of historical criticism in the nineteenth century and other critical interpretative tools in the twentieth and twenty-first centuries have raised major questions for our understanding of the Bible and how it can function authoritatively for Christian theology and practice. This further raises two important issues. The first is that these tools have, at best, provided us with rich new insights into the Bible; but they have also made us much more aware of the complexity and diversity of the biblical material as

---

108 See *NT Notes*, Ephesians 4:13; and Sermon 109, "The Trouble and Rest of Good Men," *Works of Wesley*, 3:538–39.

109 "Advice to the People called Methodists with Regard to Dress," *Works* (Jackson), 11:467.

well as its historical situatedness. Current methodologies of interpretation do not rule out a theological reading of the Bible, but all critique any simple movement from a biblical text to a contemporary theological and ethical opinion. Second, the rise of historical criticism occurred within the context of increasing debate about how to relate the human and the divine dimensions of scripture, and hence how the Bible functions as an authoritative source within the church. There is extensive diversity of opinion even within the Methodist and Wesleyan tradition. This creates considerable complexity in seeking to overcome theological disagreement or in seeking unity where there is unresolved disagreement. However, all disagreement should not be reduced to differences in understanding the Bible and its authority, nor should the complexity and nuance of diverse positions be simplified into two or more contradictory positions.

• With regard to ethical opinions, the triple complexity in interpretation, that is, the diversity of interpretation and potential error in interpreting the Bible, diversity of interpretation and potential error in interpreting the reality to be addressed, and diversity of interpretation and potential error in correlating the Bible with this reality, must be noted. A further complicating element must also be noted, and that is the relationship between contemporary contexts and biblical contexts. We face many issues that require ethical response but which did not exist at all or did not exist in their contemporary form in the biblical context. There are some issues that seem, at a surface level, to be parallel to the biblical context but on a deeper investigation prove to be different. This complexity I suggest should lead to greater humility in making ethical pronouncements, recognizing that even when people have similar interpretations of the biblical ethical imperatives, they may have diverse interpretations of the contemporary reality and how the Bible does and should address it. This, however, does not have to reduce us to ethical passivity but rather to critical engagement and mutual discernment with other Christians. Nor does it exclude the possibility that certain ethical issues are related in a very direct and intrinsic way to the core of the gospel message. In such cases there is a need to speak with clarity and boldness as Wesley did in relation to slavery, or to take a more contemporary issue, the rejection of racism and apartheid as contrary to the gospel. And we must remember that the context in which the church engages in mission also changes the understanding of the meaning and significance of the theological core. It is important to discern the points of contact and conflict between the message of God's accepting and transforming grace and the realities of a particular context.

- With Wesley it is important to affirm that what is ultimately important is the reality of what God is doing and God's transformative impact rather than our limited human description of it. However, as a consequence of the reality of human participation in God's transforming process, the way that we describe what God is doing impacts the process. Hence our theological opinions have significance, and this significance is in proportion to their relationship to the core reality of God's acceptance and transformation. The less a theological opinion has to do with this core or the more abstract it becomes, the less significance it has and the greater acceptance of difference is possible. The more that the opinion has to do with the core, the greater the significance of the difference and the less room there is for acceptance of diversity. In some cases, a theological or ethical perspective can be judged to be in fundamental conflict with the core and therefore must be rejected.

Paul Chilcote and others have proposed that Wesley's theology is to be understood as being a conjunctive theology that creatively relates opinions that are held to be contradictory or in tension in other traditions.[110] A similar proposal argues that theology in the Wesleyan tradition is a *via media* or an "extreme center," and hence the theological task in a context of theological conflict is to find a way to do justice to the "truths" in both positions.[111] While at times Wesley's theology clearly displays correlative and/or *via media* features, an understanding of his interpretation of theo-

---

110 See Paul Chilcote, *Recapturing the Wesleys' Vision: An Introduction to the Faith of John and Charles Wesley* (Downers Grove, IL: InterVarsity, 2004), 12–13.
111 See, for example, Scott J. Jones, *United Methodist Doctrine: The Extreme Center* (Nashville: Abingdon, 2002).

logical opinions and essentials suggests an alternative. Wesley did draw on different and at times contesting theological positions; the goal was not to find a middle way or even hold things in tension, but to best describe the gracious action of God and its transformative effect in order to promote people's growth in love for God and their fellow human beings. Hence the criterion for evaluating theological and ethical views is their adequate description of and promotion of holiness. Theological opinions that clearly undermine holiness of heart and life are to be rejected, as are ethical opinions that run counter to a genuine love for God and our fellow human beings. In these cases there is no place for a *via media*.

I conclude this chapter with Wesley's own summary of the importance of opinions. Writing in "Advice to the People called Methodists" he states:

> And perhaps there is no such people . . . who lay *so much*, and yet *no more* stress than you do on the rectitude of *opinions* . . . *so much* stress on right *opinions* as to earnestly desire to have a right judgment in all things, and are glad to use every means which you know or believe may be conducive thereto; and yet *not so much* as to condemn any man upon earth merely for thinking otherwise than you do, much less to think that God condemns him for this, if he be upright and sincere of heart.[112]

> Lay so much stress on opinions that all your own (if it be possible) may agree with truth and reason, but have a care of anger, dislike or contempt towards those whose opinions differ from yours. . . . Condemn no man for not thinking as you think. Let everyone enjoy the full free liberty of thinking for himself. Let everyman use his own judgment, since everyman must give an account of himself to God.[113]

---

112 "Advice to the People called Methodists," *Works of Wesley*, 9:125–26; emphasis in the original.
113 Ibid., 9:130.

CHAPTER 8

THE IDENTITY OF THE CHURCH AND THE THREAT OF SCHISM

As discussed in the preceding chapters, Wesley's interpretation of and response to theological diversity arose out of his understanding of holiness and the mission of the Methodist movement to promote scriptural holiness. The pressing problem in the contemporary context is how theological diversity should be dealt with in a church or between churches. Hence there is a necessity to locate the discussion within the context of ecclesiology.

Such concerns were not foreign to Wesley; the often problematic relationship between early Methodism and the Church of England resulted in Wesley addressing aspects of the ecclesiological dimension. Aspects of this relationship have been sketched in chapter 3. As Methodism developed, there was increasing pressure from within the Methodist movement to separate from what many Methodists regarded as a corrupt and dead church. Some Methodist preachers wished to administer Communion, and a few went ahead and did so, despite not being ordained clergy. Some of the Methodist societies registered their meeting houses as Nonconformist chapels to avoid opposition from the authorities. This tension gained a new intensity when after the American War of Independence, Wesley ordained preachers to serve in America and appointed Thomas Coke as superintendent of the work there—establishing Methodism as a separate church in America. In addition, he provided the church with a liturgy, The *Sunday Service of the Methodists in North America*,[1] which included a revised version of the Church of England's Thirty-nine Articles of Religion reduced to twenty-four articles. It was in the aftermath of these developments that Wesley wrote the two sermons "On the Church" (1785) and "On Schism" (1786). These are complemented by a number of brief comments on the identity and mission of the church in his other writings. It is important to note that the context is the issue of diverse and even contradictory opinions and practices within an institutional church. It is not the relationships among people within the revival movement or Wesley's connection. As Wesley viewed

---

1   *John Wesley's Sunday Service of the Methodists in North America* (Nashville: United Methodist Publishing House and United Methodist General Board of Higher Education and Ministry, 1984).

Methodism as an embodiment of the church,[2] Wesley's explicit ecclesiological statements can be enriched by an examination of the implicit ecclesiology embodied in the organization of early Methodism. In this chapter we will examine Wesley's understanding of identity of the church, of schism and heresy, and related to this, the issues of church discipline.

THE IDENTITY OF THE CHURCH

Wesley proposed that reforming the church was a significant component of the mission of Methodism;[3] however, this reformation was directed toward the inner transformation of its members and not to church structures, ceremonies, or opinions.[4] The theological identity of the church was not a major focus of his attention. He gives even less attention to issues of church polity and structure and how they relate to its theological identity. What Wesley does say about the church is rooted in the center of this theology—that is, God's gracious transformation of the human person—but is developed within the context of early Methodism's complex and contested relationship with the Church of England. On the one hand, Wesley was defending himself against members of the Anglican establishment who argued that various Methodist practices, such as the employment of lay preachers, the establishment of societies, unpermitted preaching in the parishes of others, and field preaching, were violations of church law and constituted separation from the Church of England. On the other hand, a significant group within Methodism wanted Wesley to clearly separate from the Church of England and for Methodism to become a dissenting church—a significant issue from this perspective was pressure to permit lay preachers to celebrate Communion.

In the first paragraph of his sermon "On the Church," Wesley states that "a more ambiguous word than this, the 'church' is scarce to be found in the English language."[5] In order to clarify what he means by the church, Wesley draws on the traditional distinction between the visible and the invisible church but interpreted it in terms of his understanding of God's transformative mission in the world.

---

2   In a letter to Revd. Gilbert Boyce May 1, 1750, he wrote: "I have not found any community who (in my apprehension) come so near the scripture plan, or so nearly answer the original design of a church, as the people called Methodist," *Works of Wesley,* 26:419.

3   See "Minutes of Several Conversations between the Reverend Mr. John and Charles Wesley and Others," *Works of Wesley,* 10:845.

4   See *A Farther Appeal to Men of Reason and Religion,* Part III, *Works of Wesley,* 11:322.

5   Sermon 74, "On the Church," *Works of Wesley,* 3:46.

THE INVISIBLE CHURCH

In his sermon "On the Church" Wesley provides a description of the invisible or universal church through an exposition of Ephesians 4:1-6, arguing that this passage provides a list of the distinguishing characteristics of those who belong to the universal church. He explains the characteristics as follows: there is one Spirit "who animates all members of the church of God." Wesley notes two possible interpretations. It could refer to the Holy Spirit who is "the fountain of all Spiritual life," or it could refer to "spiritual gifts and dispositions."[6] In his *Explanatory Notes upon the New Testament,* he argues that the presence of the Holy Spirit is a distinguishing characteristic of Christians, and he ascribes the development of spiritual gifts to the presence and work of the Spirit,[7] so one could argue that there is no substantial difference between the two options. The Spirit inspires within these people a common hope of immortality and the Resurrection. Through the Spirit they are enabled to receive Christ as the one Lord.[8] To affirm one Lord is not a mere theological affirmation, but rather the subjection of one's self to God's reign over one's life that gives rise to eager obedience to God's commandments. The one hope arises out of one faith, which is deep confidence that Christ "loved me and gave himself for me." The outward sign of God's grace to the church is the one baptism given by the one Lord. This is a means by which many receive the one faith and one hope. The Spirit assures these people that the Creator and Ruler of the universe is their Father.

All people who experience these things are constituted as the one body of Christ. In this one body "all believers" are "closely connected together in Christ";[9] it unites people "who are at the greatest distance from each other by nature" (Jews and Gentiles) and "at the greatest distance by law and custom" (slaves and free persons).[10] Hence the unity of the church is constituted by the common relationship of all believers to Christ as members of his one body. The unity of the church is a gift from God and not the achievement of human effort.

The attribute of catholicity describes this one body as present throughout the earth and not a particular confession. In a letter to the editor of the *London Chronicle* in 1761 defending the ecclesial integrity not only of Methodism but also of Protestantism,[11] Wesley describes the church catholic as "the *whole body* of men endued

---

6   Ibid., 3:49–50.
7   See *NT Notes,* 1 Corinthians 12:3-4 and Galatians 5:18-25.
8   See *NT Notes,* 1 Corinthians 12:3.
9   *NT Notes,* Romans 12:5.
10   *NT Notes,* 1 Corinthians 12:13.
11   Letter "To the Editor of the *London Chronicle*" February 19, 1761, *Letters* 4:135–4. He included a copy in his journal entry of February 19, 1761, *Works of Wesley,* 21:303–8.

with faith, working by love dispersed over the whole earth."[12] The various institutional churches are particular branches of this one catholic church. As only genuine believers transformed by the presence of the one Spirit can be members of this catholic or universal church, then by definition the church is holy in its members for "every member thereof is holy though in different degrees."[13] As he emphasizes in his letter to the *London Chronicle*, "no unholy man can possibly be a member of it."[14] Further this church is orthodox because all genuinely holy people are "secured from error," not in every aspect of their theology nor even in every important or fundamental doctrine (as we discussed in chapters 6 and 7) but "in all things necessary to salvation" and are directed by the Spirit "in the truth that is after godliness."[15] Significantly Wesley leaves open what the doctrines are whose affirmation is necessary for salvation.

Wesley's exposition of the Ephesians passage and his interpretation of the traditional marks of the church are shaped by his understanding of the core of genuine Christianity as being the experiential reality of God's gracious action within the human person and the human response to this action. This reshapes the description of the identity of the church from being a series of doctrinal affirmations to being a portrayal of the transforming presence of the one Spirit within the community of those who genuinely believe in Christ.

THE VISIBLE CHURCH

The visible church is the ecclesial communities in which the invisible church becomes visible in particular concrete locations.[16] One of Wesley's favorite descriptions of the visible church is taken from Article 19 of the Thirty-nine Articles of the Church of England, which said:

> The visible Church of Christ is a congregation of faithful men, in which the pure Word of God is preached, and the sacraments be duly ministered according to Christ's ordinance, in all those things that of necessity are requisite to the same.[17]

---

12   *Journal* February 19, 1761, *Works of Wesley*, 21:304. See also *Popery Calmly Considered*, *Works* (Jackson), 10:142.

13   Sermon 74, "On the Church," *Works of Wesley*, 3:55–56.

14   *Journal* February 19, 1761, *Works of Wesley*, 21:305.

15   Ibid.

16   See Sermon 92, "On Zeal," *Works of Wesley*, 3:313–14.

17   See Sermon 74, "On the Church," *Works of Wesley*, 3:51; "A Letter to the Rev. Mr. Fleury," *Works of Wesley*, 9:391; *An Earnest Appeal to Men of Reason and Religion*, *Works of Wesley*, 11:77; *Journal* February 4, 1740, *Works of Wesley*, 19:138; "The Minutes of the London Conference of June 25–29, 1744," *Works of Wesley*, 10:131–32; and his letter to Charles Wesley August 19, 1785, in *Letters*, 7:284–85.

Wesley both quotes and paraphrases this definition in numerous places in his writings, interestingly on occasions changing "men" to "people." The crux of the definition for Wesley lies in the word *faithful*. In his journal entry of February 4, 1740, he explains this as "holy believers." He goes on to explicitly exclude all whom he regarded as outwardly unholy; in *An Earnest Appeal to Men of Reason and Religion* he defines the faithful as "true believers." In his 1771 letter to Mr. Fleury, he describes them as "true believers who have 'the mind that was in Christ' and 'walk as Christ walked,'" and in his sermon "On the Church," he proposes "men endued with a living faith." In another reference in the *Explanatory Notes upon the New Testament,* he describes the church as "the believing, loving, holy children of God,"[18] and commenting on the description in Acts of the communal sharing of possessions and the deceit of Ananias and Sapphira, he describes the church as "a company of men, called by the gospel, grafted into Christ by baptism, animated by love, united by all kind of fellowship, and disciplined by the death of Ananias and Sapphira."[19] According to Wesley, genuine love for each other naturally gave rise to community of property, and hence the sin of Ananias and Sapphira was the expression of their failure to be genuinely transformed by God's love.

While there is some variation of expression for Wesley, the main idea is that the visible church is a community of people who have experienced the grace of God. And through the church, the community of faith, people are led to their personal transformation, which is manifested in lives characterized by love for God and their fellow human beings. The visibility of the church does not consist of its institutional structures but in its embodiment of love.[20] The church is the gathering of the scattered members of the invisible church in a particular location. This location can range from a relatively small community to a nation. Such a visible church is "a branch of the one, true, Church of Christ."[21] So the Church of England is the visible gathering of the members of the invisible church in England, which is not to be confused with or understood as being completely identifiable with the institutional Church of England.

Wesley argued in his journal entry for February 6, 1740 (published in 1744), on the basis of Article 19, that those whose lives were not characterized by holiness were the real dissenters regardless of their professions and outward church membership.[22] Nevertheless, Wesley recognized that the visible church in its institutional forms was a mixed body; it included not only genuine believers but also others who only profess

---

18 *NT Notes*, Acts 20:28.
19 *NT Notes*, Acts 5:11.
20 See Sermon 24, "Upon our Lord's Sermon on the Mount, IV," *Works of Wesley,* 1:539–41.
21 Letter to the Revd. Gilbert Boyce May 22, 1750, *Works of Wesley,* 26:426.
22 See *Journal* February 6, 1740, *Works of Wesley,* 19:138.

to believe,[23] and those who "have the form of godliness without the power."[24] In his comments on the parable of the wheat and the tares (or darnel), Wesley contrasts darnel with thistles and brambles. The darnel depicts those who have the "form of godliness." They must be left to grow because they cannot be gathered up without damaging the wheat; but the brambles and thistles are open "sinners, such as have neither the form nor the power"[25] of godliness; these must be rooted up. This distinction between wheat and darnel and tares can be compared to the membership requirements of early Methodism, which was open to all who were "fleeing the wrath to come," even if they had not yet come to personal faith; but it was expected that they would express their seeking after God through keeping the General Rules (the form of godliness). Those who did not were excluded from the societies.

In *An Earnest Appeal to Men of Reason and Religion* (1743), Wesley proposed that the first part of the definition of the church, that is, as a "congregation of faithful men," described the "essence" of the church and the second part, "in which the pure Word of God is preached, and the sacraments be duly ministered," the "properties" of the church.[26] Forty-two years later he declared with regard to the second part that he would "not undertake to defend the accuracy of this definition."[27] This is despite his inclusion of it in the Articles of Religion he had prepared for the American Methodists in 1784, but it accords with his earlier affirmation in "Catholic Spirit" that churches that celebrated the sacraments in a radically different fashion or even not at all were still genuine congregations of believers.[28] The major reason for his reservation was because it excluded "the Church of Rome," yet like similar statements in other Reformation documents, this exclusion was the intention of the writers. Even in his staunchly anti-Catholic work *Popery Calmly Considered* (1779), Wesley described the "Church of Rome" as a "branch of the catholic or universal Church of Christ."[29] The Catholic Church included genuine believers despite its "wrong opinions" and "superstitious modes of worship." He then went further and argued that he would have no objection to receiving them as "members of the Church of England."[30]

---

23 See "Minutes of the London Conference of June 25–29, 1744," Wednesday June 27, *Works of Wesley*, 10:133.

24 *NT Notes*, Matthew 13:28.

25 Ibid.

26 *An Earnest Appeal to Men of Reason and Religion*, *Works of Wesley*, 11:77; see also the statement in "Minutes of the London Conference of June 25–29, 1744," Wednesday June 27, *Works of Wesley*, 10:134.

27 Sermon 74, "On the Church," *Works of Wesley*, 3:52.

28 See Sermon 39, "Catholic Spirit," *Works of Wesley*, 2:86–87.

29 "Popery Calmly Considered," *Works* (Jackson), 10:142.

30 Sermon 74, "On the Church," *Works of Wesley*, 3:52.

Hence in Wesley's interpretation of the second part of the definition ("in which the pure Word of God is preached, and the sacraments be duly ministered") there is a considerable development. This can be seen by comparing his journal entry of February 4, 1740. Here Wesley had interpreted the preaching of the pure Word of God to exclude those who deny the various doctrinal affirmations, including the justification by faith and present salvation (holiness). Accordingly, the sacraments are not duly administered when Communion is given to those who "have neither the power nor the form of godliness."

For Wesley, the visible church as a manifestation of the universal church ought to manifest a catholic spirit. Commenting on Acts 11:17, he said:

> And who are we that we should withstand God particularly by laying down rules of Christian communion which exclude any whom he has admitted into the Church of the first born, from worshipping God together. O that all Church governors would consider how bold an usurpation this is on the authority of the supreme Lord of the Church! O that the sin of thus withstanding God may not be laid to the charge of those, who perhaps with a good intention, but in an over fondness for their own forms, have done it, and are continually doing it.[31]

THE CHURCH AS PARTICIPANT IN THE *MISSIO DEI*

In our analysis of "A Caution against Bigotry" in chapter 5, we saw how Wesley located the mission of Christians within the mission of God. God is "the great ocean of love" who created human beings "to love."[32] As creatures created in the image of God, their hearts were filled with love for God and neighbor. This love was lost in the fall, resulting in societies characterized by injustice, cruelty, and falsehood. God's mission in the world is to overcome sin and evil and its consequences so that love reigns throughout creation. Through the death and resurrection of Christ and the outpouring of the Spirit at Pentecost, God's kingdom of love has entered into history. The kingdom comes when God reigns in the heart of the believers, resulting in them loving God and their fellow human beings. The result of God's kingdom coming is that God's will is done on earth. God's love fills and transforms human societies as increasingly people submit to God's reign in their life. But until the time comes when the vast majority of the world's population has been transformed by God's love and united in a global society, the world will not have peace, justice, or equity.[33]

---

31 *NT Notes*, Acts 11:17.

32 Sermon 26, "The Law Established through Faith, II," *Works of Wesley*, 2:39.

33 See Sermon 4, "Scriptural Christianity," *Works of Wesley*, 1:159–80; Sermon 63, "The General Spread of the Gospel," *Works of Wesley*, 2:485–99; and Sermon 26, "Upon our Lord's Sermon on the Mount, VI," *Works of Wesley*, 2:581–82.

The invisible church is made up of those who have experienced God's transforming reign in their lives, so that the visible church is the community of these people
in a particular location; however, as we described above, it also includes others who
have only the outward form of Christianity. When Christ established the kingdom of
God he did not only transform individuals, he also established a society, the body of
Christ.[34] The church is an "appointment . . . of God. He saw it was 'not good for men
to be alone,' even in this sense, but that the whole body of his children should be 'knit
together, and strengthened, by that which every joint supplieth.'"[35] Hence the unity of
the visible church, like that of the invisible church, is a gift from God.

The church is now the firstfruits of the coming transformation of human society.[36] As such, the church is both a present manifestation of that kingdom and a
means through which God's kingdom of grace comes. As a present manifestation of
God's reign, the visible church is a community that embodies the radical love of God
and neighbor—a holy community. It is the presence of such love that authenticates
a community as a visible manifestation of the invisible church. As Wesley described
it in stanzas 9 and 10 of his poem "Primitive Christianity," which was published as a
conclusion to some editions of his *An Earnest Appeal to Men of Reason and Religion*:

> Ye different sects, who all declare,
> 'Lo! Here is Christ!' or 'Christ is there;'
> Your stronger proofs divinely give,
> And show me where the Christians live.
>
> Your claim, alas! Ye cannot prove,
> Ye want the genuine mark of love:
> Thou only, Lord, thine own canst show,
> For sure thou hast a church below.[37]

As the means of grace through which the kingdom comes, it is to be a place
where the people of God grow in holiness and reach out into the world bringing
about transformation through their acts of mercy. As Wesley expressed it in "The
Reformation of Manners":

> Men who did fear God, and desire the happiness of their fellow-creatures,
> have, in every age, found it needful to join together, in order to oppose the
> works of darkness, to spread the knowledge of God their Saviour, and to pro-
> mote his kingdom upon earth. Indeed He himself has instructed them so to

---

34 See *NT Notes*, Matthew 3:2, 4:17.
35 Sermon 92, "On Zeal," *Works of Wesley*, 3:318.
36 Sermon 22, "Upon our Lord's Sermon on the Mount, II," *Works of Wesley*, 1:509.
37 "Primitive Christianity," *Works of Wesley*, 11:91.

do. From the time that men were upon the earth, he hath taught them to join together in his service, and has united them in one body by one Spirit. And for this very end he has joined them together, "that he might destroy the works of the devil;" first in them that are already united, and by them in all that care round about them. This is the original design of the Church of Christ. It is a body of men compacted together, in order, first, to save each his own soul; then to assist each other in working out their salvation; and, afterwards, as far as in them lies, to save all men from present and future misery, to overturn the kingdom of Satan, and set up the kingdom of Christ.[38]

These two dimensions, the church as a manifestation of God's kingdom and as a means through which the kingdom comes, are integrally related, for it is only as the church embodies the love of God in its own life that it can become a means of spreading the love of God to others. There is however an unresolved tension in Wesley's ecclesiology that arises out of his strong emphasis on individual salvation. In the quotation immediately above, the first goal of joining the church is to save one's "own soul." Similarly in the sermon "On Zeal," the role of church is understood as the promotion of individual holiness.[39] Even when holiness is understood as being transformed by and for love, the focus is on the individual, which remains Wesley's major emphasis. This emphasis on the individual stands in unresolved tension with the communal dimensions of Wesley's thought, which, while underemphasized in his theology, was integral to the life of early Methodism. The consequence of this is a tendency to focus on the church as an instrument of holiness understood in a narrow individualistic manner.

In Wesley's understanding, the essence of the kingdom of Satan is its opposition to and destruction of the love of God and our fellows, hence of all good deeds and words. In his sermon "Of Evil Angels" (1783), he described Satan's agenda:

Next to the love of God, there is nothing which Satan so cordially abhors as the love of our neighbour. He uses, therefore, every possible means to prevent or destroy this; to excite either private or public suspicions, animosities, resentment, quarrels; to destroy the peace of families or of nations; and to banish unity and concord from the earth. And this, indeed, is the triumph of his art; to embitter the poor, miserable children of men against each other, and at length urge them to do his own work, to plunge one another into the pit of destruction.[40]

---

38   Sermon 52, "The Reformation of Manners," *Works of Wesley*, 2:302. See also his description of the church in Sermon 92, "On Zeal," *Works of Wesley*, 3:313.

39   See Sermon 92, "On Zeal," *Works of Wesley*, 3:313–14.

40   Sermon 72, "Of Evil Angels," *Works of Wesley*, 3:22–23.

Wesley regularly emphasized that the great hindrance to mission was the Christian who, instead of embodying the love of God and neighbor, expressed the opposite—the ethos of the kingdom of Satan. A particular expression of this is the constant strife over theological opinions. Wesley said:

> How dreadful and how innumerable are the contests which have arisen about religion! . . . even among the children of God; those who had experienced "the kingdom of God within them;" who had tasted of "righteousness, and peace, and joy in the Holy Ghost." How many of these, in all ages, instead of joining together against the common enemy, have turned their weapons against each other, and so not only wasted their precious time, but hurt one another's spirits, weakened each other's hands, and so hindered the great work of their common Master! How many of the weak have hereby been offended!—How many of the lame turned out of the way! How many sinners confirmed in their disregard of all religion, and their contempt of those that profess it! And how many of "the excellent ones upon earth" have been constrained to "weep in secret places!"[41]

In his journal of May 6, 1742, he describes how he was opposed by someone defending the Church of England and comments that "his speech bewrayed him to be of no church at all, zealous and orthodox as he was."[42] The word *bewrayed* was used in the eighteenth century as a synonym for betrayed, meaning to make something visible or reveal. Wesley is asserting that the way this person attacked him showed that he was not a genuine member of the (invisible) church. His behavior contradicted the central attribute of the church: love.

CONNECTIONALISM AND THE STRUCTURES
OF EMBODIED LOVE

As the revival spread and his followers increased, Wesley developed institutional structures to provide for the needs of his connection or "connexion," to use the eighteenth-century spelling. Over the years a complex institutional network was put in place, giving rise to a structure that has come to be described as connectionalism. While these structures were largely developed pragmatically and contextually, they can be understood to give expression to an implied ecclesiology that provided a structure for the community of embodied love.[43]

---

41 Sermon 20, "The Lord Our Righteousness," *Works of Wesley,* 1:449.
42 *Journal* May 6, 1742, *Works of Wesley,* 19:261.
43 On the significance of connectionalism for ecclesiology, see Brian E. Beck, "Connexion and Koinonia: Wesley's Legacy and the Ecumenical Ideal," in *Rethinking Wesley's Theology for Contemporary Methodism,* ed. Randy L. Maddox (Nashville: Kingswood, 1998), 129–41; and Michael Nausner, "Kulturalle Grenzerfahrung und die Methodistische Konnexio,"

At the local level, Methodists were members of small groups (classes, bands, and select societies). These groups provided mutual accountability and responsibility directed toward spiritual development, which nurtured and encouraged growth in love. Moreover, it was within the context of the classes, and not in open-air or indoor preaching events, that most early Methodists experienced the new birth. Class and band leaders had responsibility for the group and in turn were responsible for the leadership of the society. The society was on the one hand led by society stewards and on the other by traveling preachers. Both the stewards and the preachers were appointed by Wesley. The societies held regular meetings, conducted love feasts and covenant renewal services, provided for needy members, and engaged in mission to the communities in which they lived. The societies were then linked together in circuits. The preachers were appointed by Wesley to particular circuits and were responsible for the spiritual well-being of members of the societies as well as proclaiming the gospel to nonmembers. The societies in Wesley's connection were expected to submit to his authority. Wesley invited many, but not all, traveling preachers to attend the yearly Conference. Wesley envisaged that after his death the responsibility for ordering the societies would go the members of Conference, who entered into a mutual agreement with each other. Wesley engaged on extensive travels visiting the societies as well as preaching to others.

In addition to the institutional structures, Wesley published and circulated sermons, tracts, books, hymnbooks, and magazines. Methodists across England, Scotland, Wales, and Ireland, and to some extent in America, read the same literature, sang the same hymns, participated in the same covenant renewal services, and read accounts of Methodists in other areas. Wesley's journals and his various accounts of the rise of Methodism gave them a common history and a common sense of mission.

The combination of the connectional structures and the common literature created a sense of being part of a community that encountered, included, and bridged social, theological, cultural, linguistic, and national boundaries. They were the one, but diverse, people called Methodist. Importantly, the connectional structures ensured that this community was real, not only imagined, as members of Methodist societies participated regularly in their community of faith. At a local level, they were brought into personal relationship with people from the same locality but from various social classes. Traveling preachers and visits from Wesley brought them into personal contact with Methodists from beyond their locality. The traveling preachers related to and ministered to people in different locations and contexts and through the yearly Conferences engaged in intensive dialogue with preachers from other con-

in *Kirchlichers Leben in Methodistischer Tradition: Perspektiven aus Drei Kontinenten,* ed. Michael Nausner (Göttingen: Edition Ruprecht, 2010), 273–95.

texts. It is not insignificant that Wesley wished to be succeeded by John William Fletcher (Jean Guillaume de la Fléchère), a French-speaking, Swiss immigrant.[44]

The ecclesiology implied in connectionalism was an important corrective to the individualistic tendencies within Wesley's theology in general and his ecclesiology in particular. In its small-group expression, connectionalism showed the church to be a midwife of faith and the enabler of spiritual growth. In its diverse local and trans-local expressions, it provided the structural framework for people to be for each other, with each other, and before each other in relationships of love and responsibility. Such mutual responsibility was also an important corrective to the dangers posed by an emphasis on the liberty of individual conscience. Liberty of conscience was to be exercised by being in loving, responsible relationship with those whom one disagreed with. In its inclusion and transcending of boundaries, the connection was seen as an expression of the kingdom of God's grace and a foretaste of the kingdom of glory. Its use of a common hymnbook and the celebration of a common order of worship for covenant renewal services expressed the identity of the invisible church as a diverse body whose unity arose out of its worship of and obedience to God— Father, Son, and Holy Spirit. Thus to be part of the people called Methodist was to be part of a transnational, countercultural, and interconnected network of communities with a mission to embody holiness; that is, the love of God and our fellows in the face of an often hostile world.

CHURCH STRUCTURES AND THE IDENTITY OF THE CHURCH

As I described above, Wesley regarded the visible Church of England as composed of all faithful people in England. The relationship between this understanding of the visible Church of England and an institutionally structured body of believers became deeply ambiguous in Wesley's writings. His understanding of the institutional structure of the church changed and developed. During his time in America, he understood the episcopal structure to reflect the divinely authorized structure of the church as set out in the New Testament and the early church. His views went through a fundamental change, the details of which are not significant for our purposes.[45] In later years, he regarded the office of ordained ministry (presbyters or priests) as a divinely established order; he came to reject the idea of the episcopacy

---

44   For a more detailed exploration of this in a contemporary context see Nausner, "Kulturalle Grenzerfahrung."

45   Full details can be found in Baker, *John Wesley and the Church of England*; and Gwang Seok Oh, *John Wesley's Ecclesiology: A Study of Its Development and Sources* (Lanham, MD: Scarecrow Press, 2008).

as a separate divinely established order, which alone had the authority to ordain.[46] Rather, every presbyter had the authority to ordain; but in particular churches this authority had been given to a select group of presbyters who were consecrated as bishops. This episcopal ordering of the church was compatible with scripture but not required by it. In 1755 he strongly defended the right of the government to order the affairs of the church,[47] but in his 1785 sermon "On Obedience to Pastors" he refused to discuss the issue.[48]

Wesley adopted a pragmatic understanding of the development of the various forms of church government as responses to mission in particular contexts. Even those forms of government described in the New Testament are not necessarily binding in a different context.[49] For Wesley, any church order included both divinely established elements and pragmatic human solutions.[50] In developing the institutional structure of the church, the goal was to wisely arrange and relate the divinely ordered elements with the human pragmatic aspects in such a way as to best promote the mission of the church in the world. He thus proposed: "What is the end of all ecclesiastical order? Is it not to bring souls from the power of Satan to God? And to build them up in his fear and love. Order then is valuable as far as it answers these ends; and if it answers them not it is nothing worth."[51]

The order of the church, however, was always to remain subservient to its mission, thus "wherever the knowledge and love of God are, true order is not wanting. But the most apostolic order where there are not is less than nothing and vanity."[52] Hence a Wesleyan approach to church order is characterized by flexibility, pragmatism, and the willingness to change in line with its mission. While Wesley did not promote the structural reformation of the Church of England, his theology provided the basis for such a reformation when the structures no longer serve their missiological goal. It is in the light of this approach to ecclesiastical order that we can understand, on one hand, his selective noncompliance with aspects of the Anglican church order when he viewed it as hindering his mission, which we will discuss below. On the other hand, his approach to ecclesiastical order provided the basis for the various structures he developed for the emerging Methodist movement.

---

46   See *Journal* January 20, 1746, *Works of Wesley,* 10:112, and *Letters,* 7:238ff.
47   See "Ought We to Separate from the Church of England?" *Works of Wesley,* 9:570.
48   See Sermon 97, "On Obedience to Pastors," *Works of Wesley,* 3:375–76.
49   See his comments in his Letter to James Clark September 18, 1756, *Works of Wesley,* 27:60.
50   See The Disciplinary *Minutes* 1749, *Works of Wesley,* 10:812–14, and "A Plain Account of the People called Methodists," *Works of Wesley,* 9:258.
51   Letter to "John Smith" June 25, 1746, *Works of Wesley,* 26:206.
52   Ibid.

SCHISM, HERESY, AND THE UNITY OF THE CHURCH

Prominent figures within the Church of England accused Methodism of being a schismatic and heretical movement that was contrary to the order and doctrine of the Church. Wesley rejected this and argued strongly that Methodist doctrine was the recovery of the doctrine of the Church of England as set out in its Thirty-nine Articles and the Homilies. However, his defense of Methodism went further, in that he raised significant questions about the standard definition of heresy and schism.

Schism and Heresy in the Explanatory Notes upon the New Testament (1754)

Wesley provides a summary of his views in his comments on 1 Corinthians 11:18:

> It is plain that by schisms is not meant any separation from the church, but uncharitable divisions in it; for the Corinthians continued to be one church; and, notwithstanding all their strife and contention, there was no separation of any one party from the rest, with regard to external communion.... Therefore, the indulging any temper contrary to this tender care of each other is the true scriptural schism. This is, therefore, a quite different thing from that orderly separation from corrupt churches.... Both heresies and schisms are here mentioned in very near the same sense; unless by schisms be meant, rather, those inward animosities which occasion heresies; that is, outward divisions or parties: so that whilst one said, "I am of Paul," another, "I am of Apollos," this implied both schism and heresy. So wonderfully have later ages distorted the words heresy and schism from their scriptural meaning. Heresy is not, in all the Bible, taken for "an error in fundamentals," or in anything else; nor schism, for any separation made from the outward communion of others. Therefore, both heresy and schism, in the modern sense of the words, are sins that the scripture knows nothing of; but were invented merely to deprive mankind of the benefit of private judgment, and liberty of conscience.[53]

This summary reveals key aspects of Wesley's views:

- First, in his understanding schism is not the separation from the church in the sense of separating from a particular institutional church; rather it is division within the church that has its root in a lack of genuine love for our fellow Christians.[54]

---

53   *NT Notes*, 1 Corinthians 11:18.
54   This contrasts to some extent with his earlier statement in the 1745 *A Farther Appeal to Men of Reason and Religion*, where he defined schism as a "*causeless* separation from the church of Christ" but questioned whether this could be applied to separation from a "*particular national* church" (emphasis in the original, *A Farther Appeal to Men of Reason and Religion*, Part III, *Works of Wesley*, 11:312).

Schism is "alienation of affection from each other"[55] or indulging a "temper contrary to tender care" (ibid., 1 Cor 11:18). Unity in the church is constituted by having the same "affections and desires." The core issue for Wesley is inner holiness—a deep love for each other despite differences in theology or practice. Schism is a failure to love expressed in the tempers, which he describes elsewhere in relation to church conflict such as bitterness, pride, anger, distrust, intolerance, and the despising of others.

- Second, heresies are not errors in doctrinal fundamentals but the creation of opposing parties or divisions within the church. Hence a heretic is one who causes "strife and animosities, schisms, and parties in the church" (ibid., Titus 3:10).

- Third, the traditional definition of heresy as false doctrine, which he elsewhere describes as "Popish" (ibid.) deprives people of their right to "private judgment" and "liberty of conscience." Hence, even in relation to fundamental doctrines, people must have liberty to disagree and not be pressured to conform to official doctrine. Wesley does, however, recognize that the presence of those who deny Christ in their "doctrine and their works" can result in "heresies," that is, divisions; but, on the other hand, he argues that division can also lead people to deny Christ in their doctrine and lives (ibid., 2 Pet 2:1).

- Fourth, he asserted that schism is "not orderly separation from corrupt churches." Here Wesley is defending the legitimacy of the Reformation against the Roman Catholic charge of schism. He is acknowledging that there are situations where an institutional church is so corrupt that separation from it is legitimate. In his comments on Jude 19, he states that separation from the church is a "very heinous" sin, but then qualifies this to say "by the church is meant a body of living Christians," and by separating he means "renouncing all religious intercourse with them; no longer joining with them in solemn prayer, or the other public offices of religion" (ibid., Jude 19). Schism and heresy are thus not issues of theology or of church discipline but are failures to live in love with other believers.

---

55 *NT Notes,* 1 Corinthians 1:10.

"Farther Thoughts upon Christian Perfection (1763)"

Wesley wrote "Farther Thoughts upon Christian Perfection"[56] in the context of intense debates over Christian perfection, which had as their consequence the withdrawal of Thomas Mansfield, a Church of England priest and prominent preacher, and his followers from the Methodist society in London. Here Wesley described schism "making a rent in the Church of Christ"[57] and instructed Methodists to beware of it and anything leading to it. The root of schism was the lack of "reciprocal love" that in turn gave rise to "contention" resulting in "outward separation." Contradictory opinions and opposition from those who disagreed with one will not lead to separation when there is reciprocal love between those who disagree.

Having diagnosed the root of schism as a lack of "reciprocal love," Wesley sought to correct the problem by describing in practical terms what it entails. He noted the following:

- Particular leaders or preachers must not be exalted or denigrated.

- Excessive and unnecessary criticism is to be avoided.

- Relationships should be strengthened by active participation in the small groups.

- All thought of separating must be avoided.

- One must not overevaluate the significance of one's own opinions.

- People must not be rejected because they hold contrary opinions nor must their opinions be condemned as sinful merely because they are contrary to one's own.

- Contradiction and opposition are part of normal Christian life and should be approached with patience, humility, and gratefulness as opportunities to grow in grace and holiness.

- One should beware giving others reason to separate from one and thus seek to avoid giving offence to others.

---

56   "Farther Thoughts upon Christian Perfection," *Works of Wesley*, 13:95–135.
57   Ibid., 13:121.

"On Schism" (1786)

Wesley develops his understanding of schism and separation from the church in more detail in his sermon "On Schism."[58] He introduces the sermon by setting it in the context of debates about Protestant separation from the Roman Catholic Church and Nonconformist separation from the Church of England. The first main section is a repeat of the basic argument found in the *Explanatory Notes upon the New Testament* with some expansions. Schism is internal division within the church, which it is sometimes characterized by "anger and resentment."[59] Wesley further notes that one of the causes of "schism" in Corinth was not doctrinal disagreement but the misuse of the Lord's Supper, which resulted in the poor going hungry and the rich overindulging. Biblically speaking: "The word 'schism' . . . means the want of this tender care for each other. It undoubtedly means an alienation of affection in any of them toward their brethren, a division of heart, and parties springing therefrom, though they were still outwardly united together; though they still continued members of the same external society" (ibid., 3:63).

In a similar way Wesley rejects the understanding that heresy refers to "erroneous opinions" (ibid., 3:62) and argues that the reference in 2 Peter 2:1 "does not appear to have any reference to opinions, good or bad" (ibid., 3:63). It is worth noting in the light of our discussion in the previous chapter that he substitutes terminology of opinions for doctrines.

Having cleared the ground from what Wesley sees as the terminological confusion, he addresses the issue of "separation from a body of living Christians," which he describes as "both evil in itself, and productive of evil consequences" (ibid., 3:64). It is evil because it is "a grievous breach of the law of love" (ibid.). Love unites people together, and the growth in love leads to growth in unity, so that where love is strong nothing can break the unity. It is only where love has grown cold that people could think of separating themselves from their fellow Christians. Lack of love is the root cause of all separation even when other reasons, such as theological disagreement, are provided as the cause for it. Separation is a violation of all God's commands that we love our fellow Christians.

Separation has evil consequences, because it "leads directly to a whole train of evil surmisings, to severe and uncharitable judging of each other" (ibid., 3:65). This in turn can lead to prejudice, anger, resentment, bitterness, malice, and hatred. These evil tempers produce evil words as when one denigrates one's opponents, giving rise to "if not lying and slandering (which yet will hardly be avoided), bitter words, tale

---

58 Sermon 75, "On Schism," *Works of Wesley*, 3:59–69. Wesley presents the same argument in two letters written to James Clark in 1756. See letters of July 5, 1756 and September 18, 1756, *Works of Wesley*, 27:36–40, 59–63.

59 Sermon 75, "On Schism," *Works of Wesley*, 3:61.

bearing, and evil speaking of every kind" (ibid.). This in turn leads to further evil works. Wesley goes on to warn that these evil consequences bring with them the threat of eternal judgment.

These evil consequences herald the decline of genuine religion as the parties engage in blaming and attacking each other and ceasing their pursuit of true righteousness—that is, the love of God and their fellows. It destroys both the power and the form of godliness. This in turn alienates non-Christians from the church and the gospel. Thus separation has a negative impact on the persons involved, on the particular church, and on the world in which the church is charged to minister.

This process of decline is described in Wesley's journal entry of May 26, 1767:

> But misunderstandings crept in between the leaders, and between some of them and the preachers. And these increased sevenfold when one of the leaders was expelled from the society—some believing him faulty, some not, and neither side having patience with each other. Hence a flame of anger succeeded the flame of love, and many were destroyed by it. At the same time, some of our brethren learned a new opinion and warmly propagated it. This heat was almost as destructive as the former, and the effect of both was, the Spirit of God was grieved, his blessing was withheld, and of course the flock was scattered. When they are convinced of their sin and humbled before him, then and not before, he will return.[60]

Finally, Wesley turns to the question of whether there are situations in which separation is justifiable because a person could not continue in the church without violating his or her conscience. He agrees that this is possible in two cases. The first is when remaining as members of that particular institutional church requires people to do something that they are convinced that the Word of God forbids. The second is when it prevents people from doing something that they are convinced the Word of God requires them to do.

Wesley gives three examples of what he means.

- First, he argues, in a traditional Protestant manner, that one should not remain in the Roman Catholic Church if one was forced to engage in idolatrous worship. In his 1787 sermon "On Attending the Church Service," he proposed that the Reformers did not separate from the Church of Rome but were not allowed to continue within it unless they subscribed to its teaching and practices.[61]

---

60   *Journal* May 26, 1767, *Works of Wesley*, 22:83.
61   Sermon 104, "On Attending the Church Service," *Works of Wesley*, 3:475.

- Second, he states that he personally could not remain in the Church of England if he was forbidden to preach the gospel.

- Third, he notes that separation would be legitimate if one could not remain without committing sin or if one was forced into preaching doctrines that one did not believe. In these cases, the fault for the separation lies with the church, which requires "terms of communion as I could not in conscience comply with."[62] A church that is genuinely characterized by love will seek to structure itself so that its members are not forced to act against their consciences. He goes on to affirm that if the church of which one is now a member "does not require me to do anything which the scripture forbids, or to omit anything which the Scripture enjoins, it is my indispensable duty to continue therein."[63]

The deciding point is being forced to act contrary to one's conscience or being prevented from acting in accordance with it. If this point is not reached, then separation is wrong. Any separation can only be entered into after deep and serious consideration, and Christians have an obligation to prevent the formation of divisions and work for peace and reconciliation. Wesley said: "If I were in the Church of Rome I would conform to all her doctrines and practices. So far as they are not contrary to plain scripture. And (according to the best of my judgment) I conform so far only to those of the Church of England."[64] Separation is not required or permitted when a church is corrupt, has corrupt ministers and bishops, and has unscriptural practices as long as the individual is not required to directly participate in this corruption.

In Wesley's view the root of division in the church is not theological or practical disagreement but a lack of love. Difference of doctrine does not necessarily cause division, but it is the way in which the doctrines are affirmed and promoted that will advance either unity or division.[65] A church with a genuinely catholic spirit provides room for theological and practical diversity. Such love, as we will argue below, does not require complete ecclesial conformity, especially when a person is convinced that obedience to God requires disobedience to the church order. The implication is that if there is true love then it would be possible to deal with the theological and practical disagreements as well as a measure of disciplinary nonconformity.

---

62 Sermon 75, "On Schism," *Works of Wesley,* 3:67.
63 Ibid., 3:67. See also his letter to Revd. Samuel Walker September 24, 1755, *Works of Wesley,* 26:593.
64 Letter to the Revd. Gilbert Boyce May 22, 1750, *Works of Wesley,* 26:426.
65 See "A Letter to Rev. Mr. Thomas Maxfield," *Works of Wesley,* 9:423.

CHURCH DISCIPLINE AND CONSCIENCE OBJECTION

Wesley's argument that the church authorities should respect the freedom of conscience of its members raises an issue that was a central point of contention both within early Methodism and between Wesley and the Church of England. As we noted in our discussion of the catholic spirit in chapter 4, Wesley viewed Methodism as an embodiment of the catholic spirit where people holding diverse theological and liturgical beliefs could become members if they accepted the discipline of the movement. However, the majority of Methodists were members of the Church of England, Wesley and several other key leaders were Anglican priests, and Wesley viewed his movement as being bound to the Church of England. Each of these relationships reveals aspects of Wesley's understanding of the church.

Discipline within Early Methodism

Wesley's understanding of the ecclesial character of Methodism is complex. On one hand he clearly saw it as being in some sense a form of the visible church. On the other hand, he adopted the structures of the religious societies that were common in the eighteenth century. As a network of religious societies, Methodism existed alongside the structures of the Church of England, from where it drew most of its members. As the movement developed, Methodism began to draw members from Nonconformist churches with the stated policy that they were welcome to be part of a Methodist society and at the same time remain members of their own denomination. Wesley rejected transforming his societies into a church, arguing that the goal was the renewal of the Church of England and spreading "scriptural religion . . . among people of every denomination."[66] He encouraged Church of England members to participate in their local parish churches, refused to ordain preachers in England, and refused to allow his unordained preachers to celebrate the sacraments.

Perhaps equally significant, Methodism's organizational structure was a network centered on Wesley himself. It was Mr. Wesley's connection, and he understood himself as the leader raised up by the providence of God to lead the movement. When people joined Wesleyan Methodism either through becoming a member of a society or as a preacher, they were voluntarily submitting to Wesley's authority and committing themselves to following the General Rules of the societies.[67] And Wesley strongly resisted challenges to his authority, arguing that if people were not prepared to accept it, they could

---

66 Sermon 107, "On God's Vineyard," *Works of Wesley,* 3:511.
67 See "The Nature, Design and General Rules of the United Societies," *Works of Wesley,* 9:69–75. In the *Journal* November 23, 1779, Wesley records that a Mr. McNab did not want to submit to Wesley's system of appointments and was informed by Wesley that he could only become a preacher if he agreed to submit, *Works of Wesley,* 23:155.

leave the movement.[68] One of the distinctive features that Wesley developed was the regular Conference of preachers, which became the policy-making body in early Methodism. The results of these discussions were published in the minutes. Unfortunately, these only record the decisions and not the discussion. While this added a corporate decision-making dimension to early Methodism, it was clear that Wesley remained the dominant leader. He invited selected preachers to the Conferences and the role of the preachers in Conference was to advise Wesley and not to make decisions.

However, the minutes of Conference enshrined the principle of freedom of conscience. In the "Disciplinary *Minutes* of 1749" it was affirmed that members of the Conference were only required to submit to the judgment of the majority in "as far as his judgment shall be convinced" in relation to "speculative things" and on practical issues "so far as we can without wounding consciences."[69] This "right to private judgment" was to be applied to all human religious authorities as: "Every man must think for himself, since every man must give an account of himself to God."[70] No Christian could be required to go beyond this, for it denies the right of private judgment and personal responsibility before God. The Methodist movement was open to all regardless of their "opinion," because Methodists "think and let think." Hence there was only one requirement for membership: "a real desire to save their soul."[71] Yet how this worked out in practice was more complicated, as Wesley balanced this right of private judgment with his sense of responsibility before God as the leader of Methodism. Hence he argued that as such he could not permit certain practices and on occasions expelled people from the movement when they taught or acted contrary to his views.

An example of this was his response to lay preachers who administered the sacraments. Wesley made a clear theological distinction between those called only to preach and those called to administer the sacraments; the latter required legitimate ecclesiastical ordination in Wesley's opinion.[72] However, some of Wesley's actions in this regard ran counter to the spirit of toleration of difference that was integral to Methodism.[73] In a letter to Nicholas Norton in 1756, he strongly defended himself against the charge of inconsistency in this regard. He affirmed that he did not tolerate lay preachers administering Communion, but that this was compatible with his fundamental principle of freedom of

---

68 Wesley provided a detailed justification of his authority in the "Annual Minutes of Some Late Conversations, 1766," Q. 29, *Works of Wesley*, 10:326–31. See the extended discussion in Henry D. Rack, *Reasonable Enthusiast: John Wesley and the Rise of Methodism* (London: Epworth, 2002), 237–50. Compare the letter to John Mason, January 13, 1790, in *Letters*, 8:196.

69 Disciplinary *Minutes*, 1749, Q. 5, *Works of Wesley*, 10:823.

70 Ibid., Q. 6, 10:823–24.

71 "Thoughts upon a Late Phenomenon," *Works of Wesley*, 9:537.

72 See Sermon 121, "Prophets and Priests," *Works of Wesley*, 4:75–84.

73 See the discussion in Henry D. Rack, "Introduction: The Conference History" and *Minutes*, *Works of Wesley*, 10:62–73.

conscience, as he did not force people holding this view to change their mind. He merely refused to allow them to implement this practice in his movement. He regarded it as contrary to the Word of God, and his conscience required him to forbid it. Wesley argued this was not persecution, as people were free to follow their own consciences outside of his movement. Further, by administering Communion, people were separating themselves from the Methodist movement that he led.

Given the qualifications referred to above, the preachers in Wesley's connection were expected to hold to and teach the agreed doctrine of the connection. In the Model Deed of 1763, Wesley set out that Methodist societies were only to accept preachers who preached "no other doctrine than is contained in" the *Explanatory Notes upon the New Testament* and the first four volumes of his sermons (the "Standard Sermons").[74] This formulation left room for some disagreement in belief but not in proclamation. But it also leaves open what is meant by "doctrine . . . contained in." The sermons and the *Notes* are not clearly delineated doctrinal statements.

Wesley acknowledged in his introductions to both his sermons and the *Explanatory Notes upon the New Testament* that they were open to correction, and he asked people to correct him.[75] Clearly they could not be binding in every detail. For example, there is the issue of eating blood referred to in chapter 1. In his *Notes* on Acts 15, Wesley argued that the eating of blood was clearly forbidden, yet in his journal he argued that, while he believed it was forbidden, this was a matter where legitimate disagreement was possible.[76] While the journal entry is dated October 29, 1745, it was published in 1753 and the *Notes* were published in 1754, indicating that the two references reflect Wesley's thought at the same period. Hence just because something is taught in the sermons and *Notes* does not mean that it belongs to authoritative doctrine. I would suggest that the doctrines referred to here are the broad contours of Wesley's theology, particularly his understanding of sin, justification, the new birth, and holiness. Given the discussion of schism and heresy in the *Notes* and the sermons "Catholic Spirit" and "A Caution against Bigotry," space for diversity of theological opinion is an integral part of the doctrine contained in the Standard Sermons and the *Explanatory Notes upon the New Testament*.

The sermons are occasional documents. Some deal with key themes in Wesley's theology, others relate these themes to pressing contextual issues, and some are focused on specific issues with little overt reference to central theological themes. This does not prevent them from being used as doctrinal standards but suggests an

---

74   "The 'Large' *Minutes*, 1753, 1763," *Works of Wesley,* 10:869–70.

75   See the preface and the introduction to Revelation in *NT Notes* and the "Preface" to *Sermons on Several Occasions, Works of Wesley,* 1:107.

76   See *Journal* October 29, 1745, *Works of Wesley,* 20:97–98, and compare his comment on Acts 15:29, *NT Notes.*

alternative understanding. The sermons do indicate the contours of the central doctrinal distinctives of the Methodist movement, but more than that they provide exemplars of how to relate these to particular contextual issues. Part of their authority lies in challenging us to do the same.

Wesley did go a step further in providing his revised list of Articles of Religion for the American Methodists, but he did not describe the exact function of the articles and stated that the American Methodists were at liberty to follow the Bible and the "primitive church." This suggests a freedom in interpretation and application of the articles. As we noted above, Wesley expressed disagreement with the part of the definition of the church included in the articles, a disagreement that reflects the theology of the "Catholic Spirit" and "A Caution against Bigotry." His understanding of private property as set out in his *Explanatory Notes* on the early church's practice of a community of property and his sermon "Scriptural Christianity" also stands in considerable tension with that set out in the Articles of Religion.[77]

While Wesley was alive he was the final determiner of what was and what was not part of authoritative doctrine for the Methodist movement and how it should be related to contextual issues. After his death, this function passed to the Conference, a transfer of leadership that had already taken place in the American wing of the movement. Wesley himself recorded in minutes of the 1747 Conference:

> Q. 4. In our first Conference it was agreed to examine every point from the foundation. Have we not been some way fearful of doing this? What were we afraid of? Of overturning our first principles?

> A. Whoever was afraid of this, it was a vain fear. For if they are true, they will bear the strictest examination. If they are false, the sooner they are overturned the better. Let us all pray for a willingness to receive light; an invariable desire to know of every doctrine whether it be of God.[78]

A further important aspect of the discipline within the Methodist societies was the requirement that members demonstrate their commitment to saving their souls by living in conformity to the General Rules. Failure to conform would result in a person being excluded from the Methodist society. In his journals, Wesley

---

77 Compare *NT Notes*, Acts 2:45, 4:32-34, and 5:1-12; and Sermon 4, "Scriptural Christianity," *Works of Wesley*, 1:165, in which the holding of property in common is regarded as the natural expression of love and the insistence on the right of private property within the church as a detrimental aberration, with the article that states: "The riches and goods of Christians are not common as touching the right, title, and possession of the same, as some do falsely boast" (Article 23 in Wesley's original version and 24 in the present United Methodist Articles of Religion).

78 "MS Minutes: London Conference, June 15–18, 1747," *Works of Wesley*, 10:189.

reports on his occasional visits to particular Methodist societies, during which he examined the members and warned or expelled those whose lives did not match their profession.[79] The goal of the disciplinary procedure was to ensure that the Methodist societies maintained their character as communities that embodied the love of God. Where personal or communal behavior threatened that character, then disciplinary action was taken. This was not, however, simplistic conformity to rules; Wesley expressed relative flexibility in issues he regarded as disputable. Hence discipline was compatible with ethical diversity as long as it was demonstrably compatible with a commitment to the dual love command. Among the grounds for being excluded was causing strife over differences of opinion. Theological uniformity was not expected of Methodists, but what was expected was a disciplined lifestyle demonstrating a love for God and one's fellow human beings.

METHODISM AND THE CHURCH OF ENGLAND

Throughout his life Wesley maintained that he was a loyal member of the Church of England and that he carried out his ministry as one commissioned through ordination to the Anglican priesthood. However, in practice he often disregarded the canons of the Church of England and the instructions of bishops. Key issues included his preaching in the parishes without the permission of the incumbent clergyperson, commissioning lay preachers, open-air preaching, and founding of societies.[80] The latter two were also of questionable legality in terms of the Conventicle Act and the Act of Toleration. While Wesley incurred the opposition of individual priests and bishops, the laxity of discipline and the lack of centralized authority within eighteenth-century Anglicanism meant that no action was taken to discipline him.

Wesley vigorously defended the legitimacy of his actions and attempted to defend their legality. However, he argued that, while he affirmed the authority of the church and its bishops, if his actions were contrary to ecclesiastical or civil law, God had commissioned him to preach the gospel and no human authority had the right to stop him.[81] His famous statement that "I look upon the whole world as my

---

79   See for example *Journal* February 24 and 28; March 6, 1741; and March 12, 1743, *Works of Wesley*, 19:183–86, 317–18.

80   See Baker, *John Wesley and the Church of England*, 58–87; Ryan Nicholas Danker, *Wesley and the Anglicans: Political Division in Early Evangelicalism* (Downers Grove, IL: InterVarsity, 2016), 71–127; W. Stephen Gunter, *The Limits of "Love Divine": John Wesley's Response to Antinomianism and Enthusiasm* (Kingswood: Nashville, 1989), 27–34; and Rack, *The Reasonable Enthusiast: John Wesley and the Rise of Methodism*, 275–81.

81   See the Letters to [recipient uncertain: Rev. John Clayton?] of [March 28, 1739?], *Works of Wesley*, 25:614–17; to Revd. Samuel Walker September 24, 1755, *Works of Wesley*, 26:592–96; and to William Legge, 2nd Earl of Dartmouth April 10, 1761, *Works of Wesley*,

parish"[82] was not primarily a statement of missionary vision. It was a statement of ecclesiastical defiance, rejecting the authority of canons of the Church of England, which restricted priests from preaching in other parishes without the permission of the responsible priest. The use of lay preachers, he argued, was a necessity so people could hear the gospel.

In things that Wesley considered indifferent or where he disagreed with an aspect of the church order but saw no necessity to act contrary to it in pursuit of his commission to preach the gospel, he submitted to it. Hence, while he came to believe that as a presbyter he had the right to ordain, he did not do so as there were sufficient Anglican parish churches with ordained priests who could administer the sacraments. He decision to ordain people for service in America was based on a two-fold argument. First, most Anglican priests had left in the wake of the Revolution, thus denying Methodists of the sacraments. Second, he argued that in the light of the Revolution, America lay outside of the jurisdiction of the Church of England.

Hence for Wesley neither membership of a particular church nor ordination in it required absolute obedience to its order. While he affirmed his agreement with the doctrine of the Church of England set out in the Thirty-nine Articles, he regarded these as human opinions and felt free to critique them, as we saw in his understanding of the identity of the church. Wesley's critical commitment to the church is boldly expressed in his preparation of *The Sunday Service of the Methodists in North America*, where he assumed the right to edit not only the liturgy but also the doctrine contained in the Articles of Religion, while maintaining his loyalty to the church. Wesley was convinced that it would be a sin for him to leave the Church of England and a sin not to act contrary to its order when he was convinced this was necessary to do so.[83] He consistently insisted on the right to private judgment based on his responsibility before God.[84]

Wesley also had to defend Methodism's Anglican credentials against the critique from within the Church of England as the revival progressed and Methodism expanded. And challenge came from within Methodism as increasing numbers of Methodists wished to separate from the Church of England and saw no benefit in participating in its services.[85] The argument for separation was that the church was

---

27:251–56; *An Earnest Appeal to Men of Reason and Religion, Works of Wesley,* 11:45–101; *A Farther Appeal to Men of Reason and Religion,* Part I, *Works of Wesley,* 11:176–86; and "The Principles of a Methodist Farther Explained," *Works of Wesley,* 9:185–96.

82 Letter to [recipient uncertain: Rev. John Clayton?] of [March 28, 1739?], *Works of Wesley,* 25:616.

83 See Sermon 121, "Prophets and Priests," *Works of Wesley,* 4:121.

84 See *Journal* June 7, 1746, *Works of Wesley,* 20:122.

85 The accusations and Wesley's response can be found in "Reasons against a Separation from the Church of England," "Farther Thoughts on Separation from the Church," and

corrupt; its ministers were unholy; the evangelical understanding of the gospel was not preached; and preachers railed against Methodism and evangelical religion.

But was the corruption of the Church of England so thorough that separation was legitimate? Wesley's response was threefold:

- First, he denied that the Church of England was as corrupt as was claimed by those who wanted to separate. There were holy ministers who preached the gospel, and the articles, homilies, and liturgy in most parts gave expression to the truth of the gospel.

- Second, he argued that even if the church was corrupt, its ministers unholy, and preaching did not express the gospel, this was not grounds for separation. This was true even when some of the leadership of the Church of England were "heathenish priests and mitred infidels."[86] To bolster this argument, he surveyed the Bible to show that in both Testaments faithful people of God were not called to separate from corrupt religious institutions. On the contrary, Wesley held that Methodism as a movement was called to promote true religion; that is, God's loving transformation of human persons within the Church of England, and they could only do this by their being part of the Church of England. Rather than becoming entangled in controversies leading to all sorts of unholiness in attitudes, words, and behavior, Christians should work in love and peace for the renewal of the church.

- Third, Wesley argued that the consequences of separation would be increasing alienation between those who left and those who remained, resulting in acrimony, conflict, and bitterness—unholiness of heart and life. Such unholiness would blemish the image of the church in the minds of nonbelievers. Wesley toward the end of his life did grant that in specific

---

"Ought We to Separate from the Church of England," *Works of Wesley,* 9:334–49, 538–40, and 567–80; and Sermon 104, "On Attending the Church Service," *Works of Wesley,* 3:465–78.

86   Letter to his brother Charles August 19, 1785, *Letters,* 7:284; John Wesley is quoting from a poem by Charles Wesley published as *Elegy on the Death of Robert Jones, Esq. of Fonmon Castle in Glamorganshire,* South Wales (Bristol, UK: Farley, 1742)

local cases it might be right for Methodists to separate from
a particularly corrupt parish and minister, but this was the
exception and not a precedent for a general separation.

Love required that Wesley should seek to keep Methodism within the Church
of England even though he regarded it as corrupt. Love required that Methodism
should seek to bring renewal to a corrupt church and thus promote the spiritual
well-being of its corrupt members and office bearers. Hence it can be argued that
love motivated Wesley to keep Methodism within the Church of England not despite
its corruption but rather because it was corrupt. To leave the Church of England was
contrary to love, for it was the abandonment of its members to their spiritual disaster.

A WESLEYAN VISION FOR
THE CONTEMPORARY METHODIST CHURCHES

Wesley never provided a detailed depiction of how the diverse aspects of his ecclesiology could be fitted together into a vision of the church, and how it could
be institutionally manifested. The guidelines he provided for the Methodists in
North America consisted of a reaffirmation of the Methodist doctrine and discipline as set out in the Standard Sermons, the *Explanatory Notes upon the New
Testament*, and "The 'Large' *Minutes*";[87] a liturgy based on the Church of England's
Book of Common Prayer (which included services for the ordination of elders
and superintendents), and a doctrinal statement based on the Church of England's
Thirty-nine Articles. Beyond that, he encouraged the American Methodists to follow the "Scriptures and the Primitive Church."[88] While Wesley anticipated that he
would continue to play a role in American Methodism, he emphasized that they
were freed from the Church of England's hierarchy and said that the American
Methodist Conference could plan its own future. The Episcopal Methodist Church
in America not only separated itself from Anglicanism but also rejected Wesley's
attempts to assert control as they sought to develop their own way.

As Methodism has spread, so Wesley's legacy has given rise to many different
denominations, which seek to embody at least some aspects of his thought. These denominations are neither broad-based national churches, like the Church of England
was in Wesley's time, nor parachurch renewal movements, like Wesley's Methodist
connection. Some are limited to a single nation while others have developed international structures such as the Methodist Church of Southern Africa and The United
Methodist Church, which is the largest.

---

87   See his letter to the Preachers in America October 3, 1783, *Letters*, 8:191.
88   Letter to Our Brethren in America September 10, 1784, *Letters*, 8:239.

EMBODIED LOVE AT THE CENTER

The center of a Wesleyan vision for the visible church is a community that embodies God's love, both in its internal life and in its engagement with society. Hence the authenticity of a particular institutional form of the church claiming to be a manifestation of the invisible catholic church is determined by the extent to which it embodies love for God and human beings. An institutional church is part of the church universal only when characterized by a deep concern for and practical commitment to the holistic well-being of its members and the society in which it lives. An institutional church that is consumed by strife, giving rise to bitterness, denigration, backbiting, anger, distrust, arrogance, and pride is no longer embodying love; and to the extent that this permeates the church, it ceases to be a manifestation of the body of Christ. This is why *schism* and *heresy*, as defined by Wesley, are so serious. They strike at the heart of what it means to be the church. Equally important is a practical and deep commitment to meeting the spiritual, bodily, and psychological needs of those outside the church. This was at the heart of Wesley's nonconformity to the institutional rules of the Church of England, as these rules prevented him from carrying out his calling to bring the gospel to people. A community is only a manifestation of the body of Christ when it is engaged in an active, concrete, and holistic ministry of love to those outside the church—particularly to those who suffer; those who are excluded, exploited, and victimized; and those who are vulnerable, voiceless, and powerless.[89] A church that embodies love is inherently a missional church participating in God's mission of love in the world.

A CHURCH WITH A CATHOLIC SPIRIT

One important aspect of what it means to be a community that embodies love is to be a community that is characterized by a catholic spirit. As we have discussed earlier this means, positively, the recognition of the transforming love of God in the lives of fellow Christians, even when they hold to radically different theological opinions. Negatively, it is the rejection of bigotry that refuses to recognize the work of God in groups other than one's own.

The challenge that every church faces is how to give institutional form to a catholic spirit. In Wesley's Methodism it meant that membership was open to all

---

89   Wesley in a number of places emphasized that Methodism had a special calling to reach the poor and others whom he described as the "outcasts of men." See David N. Field. "Holiness, Social Justice and the Mission of the Church: John Wesley's Insights in Contemporary Context," *Holiness: The Journal of Wesley House Cambridge* 1, no. 2 (2015), 186–87, http://www.wesley.cam.ac.uk/wp-content/uploads/2015/10/03-field.pdf.

genuinely seeking salvation in its fullness regardless of denominational membership. Members were expected to respect the theological convictions of others. However, preachers were required to preach the doctrine contained in the Standard Sermons and the *Explanatory Notes upon the New Testament*, and those who taught contrary to this could expect to be excluded. Nevertheless, as we noted above, neither this provision nor the addition of the Articles of Religion for the American Methodists provide absolute clarity as to what this authoritative doctrine is. Further, Wesley strongly argued that certain theological positions were detrimental to growth in holiness. Yet he insisted on individuals' responsibility before God and hence their right to private judgment.

With regard to the Church of England, it appears that he envisaged a greater institutional diversity. He sought in various ways to work with others who held to core doctrines of justification by faith and the new birth, even when they were not Arminians or they rejected his understanding of Christian perfection. In the sermon "Catholic Spirit," Wesley argued for the legitimacy of separate denominations to cater to people with contradictory opinions.[90] Yet in "On Attending the Church Service," he criticized some nonconformists for leaving the Church of England when they were not constrained to act against their conscience.[91]

In "On Zeal" he was very critical of disputes over what he saw as minor issues that had led to separation from the Church of England, taking as his example the wearing of liturgical vestments.[92] In "Thoughts upon Liberty," he was very critical of the Act of Uniformity, which resulted in the expulsion of numerous clergy who could not in good conscience conform to its provisions.[93] In "On Schism," he argued that a church needs to make provision for those who have diverse opinions; no one must be forced to act against his or her conscience, and no one must be prevented from acting in accordance with his or her conscience. Rather than the creation of new denominations to give expression to diverse opinions and practices, Wesley seems, at least here, to be arguing that a church that is genuinely characterized by love should be structured in such a way as to enable its members to act with a good conscience before God. What remains unclear is the extent that this is institutionally possible and how this relates not only to members but also to leaders and clergy. In Wesley's context, he determined the boundaries; in a post-Wesleyan context it would be the Methodist Conferences that decide. But acting in accordance with a catholic spirit entails a bias to be as inclusive as possible, yet at the same time to guard the core

---

90   See Sermon 39, "Catholic Spirit," *Works of Wesley*, 2:93–94.

91   Sermon 104, "On Attending the Church Service," *Works of Wesley*, 3:475; see also Sermon 75, "On Schism," *Works of Wesley*, 3:68.

92   Sermon 92, "On Zeal," *Works of Wesley*, 3:317.

93   See "Thoughts upon Liberty," *Works* (Jackson), 11:39.

identity of the church as the community of people accepted and transformed by God through Christ by the power of the Spirit so that they love God and their fellows. As I argued in chapter 2, participation in a diverse church has the potential to become a means of grace through which its members grow in love for God and each other.

The international Methodist churches provide another significant embodiment of the catholic spirit by virtue of their including churches from different countries with diverse cultures. But this complexity gives them particular challenges. Even so, reaching across national borders helps provide a particular manifestation of the body of Christ, which transcends national and cultural boundaries and creates the opportunity for the church to express catholic love in a world divided by culture, ideology, language, national identity, and economic structures.[94] This is particularly significant given what I argued in chapter 7. The realities of our bodily existence both limit and enhance our understanding of God's revelation as we seek to relate it to our context. The contextual particularity of specific branches of international churches provides opportunities for them to discover what it means to embody holiness in their location. Hence participating in the life of an international church provides for both the correction of some human limitation and the enhancement of our understanding of God's revelation and hence of what it means to be holy. Yet this requires the humility, the willingness to listen to the experience of others and to appreciate and learn from their embodiments of holiness, even when we might have substantial disagreements with them. For such a community of mutual learning to flourish requires the development of structures that overcome the dangers of domination and allowing the voices of those with fewer resources and less power to be genuinely heard.

DIVERSITY AND BOUNDARIES

Does the emphasis on a catholic spirit mean that there are no theological and ethical boundaries? Clearly Wesley did not think that all theological opinions were to be included or that all behavior patterns were acceptable. He clearly rejected the classic christological heresy of Arianism and the more recent one of Socinianism,[95] and his practice of examination and discipline resulted in people being excluded from the movement. Discerning where to draw the lines is a complex procedure. For Wesley, it was not merely enough to argue that a particular belief or practice was contrary to scripture. Rather the core issue was to demonstrate the relationship between this issue and the core of Christian faith and life; that is, God's gracious transformation of human persons so that they love God and their

---

94   See Nausner, "Kulturalle Grenzerfahrung."
95   See for example Letter to Rev. James Clark July 3, 1756, *Works of Wesley,* 27:38.

fellow human beings. The closer the perceived error was to this, the more direct the action that needed to be taken against it. Hence for Wesley the christological heresies were particularly significant, because they threatened the understanding of God's gracious salvific action in Christ.

A similar pattern can be observed in his dealing with ethical issues. As we noted, Wesley argued on biblical grounds that the command not to eat blood was still binding on Christians, but it was an issue where he argued that Christians should be free to disagree. Even with regard to the General Rules, he was on occasion prepared to accept variations in compliance.[96] This contrasts with the radical stance he took against slavery toward the end of his life. He argued that slavery was totally irreconcilable with the Golden Rule and hence with the command to love one's neighbor as oneself. In the General Rules and elsewhere in his writings, he argued that consuming alcoholic spirits or participating in the manufacture of and trade in such spirits was incompatible with Christian faith, even though there is no direct reference to this in the Bible. For Wesley the destructive consequences of the abuse of such alcohol made any involvement with it incompatible with the command to love one's neighbor as one's self. In a similar way during the twentieth century, churches in response to Nazism, apartheid, and the denial of civil rights in the United States have come to show clearly that racism is incompatible with the command of love for one's neighbor, and the theological legitimation of it is heresy (in the traditional sense of the term).

The catholic spirit does not mean unconditional acceptance of all theological and ethical opinions. Churches can and must draw boundaries that reflect their fundamental affirmation of God's transforming love. The theological task lies in showing the relationship between a particular opinion or pattern of behavior and this fundamental core and hence what is excluded by the commitment to this core. But instituting boundaries entails a process of discernment, which needs to take place in the context of a genuine catholic spirit and a communal listening to determine what the Spirit is saying to the church today. Boundaries cannot really be determined *before* but only *as* the church is confronted with a context of decision. Such a situation should lead not to a mere reiteration of a past decision but to a renewed and bold reexamination of issues.

A SELF-DISCIPLINED MISSIONAL COMMUNITY

A Wesleyan vision for the church includes a disciplined missional community. While Wesley emphasized the need to reach people with the gospel, his focus was not on the numbers of people who professed faith but on the number of people

---

96   See the letter to Wesley from Thomas Willis and Wesley's comments on it in *Works of Wesley*, 26:116–18.

who experienced the transforming grace of God and who manifested it in lives of love for God and their neighbors. He was convinced that the most effective way for Methodism to grow was when the lives of its members and the communal life of its societies embodied the love of God. The whole structure of early Methodism with its small groups, love feasts, and covenant renewal services was directed toward this goal. It was this emphasis on the quality of the personal and communal life of Methodism that led to the disciplinary procedures and exclusion of those who were not pursuing this goal. In this sense discipline and even exclusion were methods to ensure the long-term growth of the movement.

In the contemporary European and North American context, many of Wesley's methods appear to be an unwanted intrusion into people's personal lives. Yet in increasingly secular societies, the credibility of the gospel of God's transforming grace is the existence of communities that embody God's love. Hence there is a need to recover the identity of the church as a self-disciplined, missional community characterized by voluntary mutual accountability without succumbing to authoritarianism or sectarianism. The goal of being a mutually accountable self-disciplined community is missional—that is, it is shaped by its participation in God's mission in the world and is directed toward the concrete and comprehensive good of others. The church denies its own reason for existence when it focuses on self or institutional preservation.

A CHURCH WITH AN ECUMENICAL PRAXIS

The Wesleyan vision for the church extends beyond the confines of denominational structures and impels Wesleyan and Methodist churches to engage in seeking deeper communion with other churches. This drive toward greater ecumenism is integral to our identity as churches in the Wesleyan tradition. The understanding of holiness as love embodied in praxis also opens a new approach to ecumenical (and intra-Methodist) relationships. As I argued in chapter 2, holiness is only possible in the context of interpersonal interaction; as embodied love, it only exists as it is concretely expressed in the diversity, conflicts, and complexity of human relationship. It is through this expression that inner attitudes are transformed. Analogously, Methodist churches only embody holiness in dynamic relationships with other churches and hence on their denominational boundaries, not because we agree with each other or we share common practices, but because we disagree with each other and have contradictory practices. It is only as we live with each other and engage in mission together in our diversity and disagreements seeking to break down the barriers that divide us that we embody love for each other. In this way holiness becomes Methodism's gift to ecumenical relationships, not primarily in terms of theological affirmation but rather in terms of the embodied praxis of love. It is precisely here on the boundaries engaged with the other in love that we manifest our particular identity.

CONCLUSION

In a Wesleyan perspective the church is a community of people who have been transformed by the grace of God so that personally and communally they embody the love of God. Negatively this means that division and separation within churches arise out of a lack of love. Positively it means that institutional churches need to be structured to express the catholic spirit by allowing for considerable diversity. This diversity is not to be confused with an absolute inclusiveness. There are boundaries, but these lie at the center of the church's existence—the gospel message of the transforming love of God that must be concretely embodied in the encounter with others, particularly the excluded others. The responsibility for the development of both the structures of the church and the articulation of the boundaries lies with the Conference. This raises significant issues as to what is meant by Conference and how it should function.

CHAPTER 9

SANCTIFIED AND SANCTIFYING CONFERENCING

In early Methodism, John Wesley had decisive authority over the theological and disciplinary boundaries of the movement; yet while he retained this right for himself believing that he had been called by God to this position, he also emphasized the importance of consultation with others. Since Wesley's time, Methodism in its various forms has not given any one person Wesley's decisive role but rather developed structures within the regular Conference of the church to take on this function. This development was not merely a pragmatic solution but was deeply rooted in aspects of Wesley's theology and praxis.

The deep differences in theological and ethical positions within Methodist churches and the calling to engage in seeking the unity of the broader church that arises out of a catholic spirit challenge Methodist churches to rediscover the meaning of "conferencing." This is not merely an aspect of church polity but is an expression of Methodist identity as a community called to express and promote holiness—that is, the dynamic love for God and our fellow human beings. This resonates with the call for holy conferencing that one often hears in some Methodist circles. While the terminology of holy conferencing does not go back to Wesley, there are elements in Wesley's theology and practice that can be used to develop a model for what I have called "sanctified and sanctifying conferencing." By this I mean an engagement with each other in relation to the controversial themes that divide us in a way that manifests holiness and as a means by which we can grow in holiness. Given that the core of Wesley's understanding of holiness is love, the question becomes how can we engage each other in a way that expresses love and helps us to become more loving.

CONFERENCE AND CONFERENCING

The Wesleyan roots of the concept of sanctified and sanctifying conferencing are twofold. The first is the development of regular Conferences as an essential aspect of the growing organizational structure of early Methodism, which continues to be a characteristic feature of Methodist churches. The second is Wesley's understanding of Christian conferencing or conversing as a means of grace.

THE HISTORICAL ORIGINS OF THE METHODIST CONFERENCE

Soon after its emergence, the eighteenth-century Evangelical revival split into three main streams: Moravian, Calvinist, and Wesleyan. Given Wesley's commitment to a catholic spirit, it is not surprising to discover that he tried to bring the three streams together to foster relationships between the leaders and to work together in common mission. From 1739 to 1743 he made a number of attempts to call the leaders of the different streams to Conferences in order to promote greater unity. Since representatives of the other streams did not attend, Wesley resolved to organize a Conference for his own connection.

The first Conference of Wesley's connection took place in 1744, when John Wesley met with nine other Methodist preachers. The agenda was to discuss what to teach, how to teach it, and what to do—that is "doctrine, discipline, and practice."[1] Wesley understood the function of the Conference to be to advise him in his role as leader of the Methodist movement, and participation was based on invitation from Wesley. While discussions about relationships with the other streams within the revival occurred from time to time, the focus was on the development of Wesleyan Methodism. It is not surprising Hugh Harris, the leader of Welsh Calvinistic Methodism, attended a number of the early Conferences.[2] The details of the development of the Conference within early Methodism are not relevant to our discussion, but two issues are significant. The first is that the early Conferences had the particular aim of dealing with theological and practical differences between the various streams of the revival. The second is that an important aspect of the Conferences was the determination of core doctrine and practices. While the early Conferences also dealt with administrative issues, their primary function was to provide leadership to the movement by discerning together what it meant to be a holy people and how the life of the movement should be best structured in order to express that holiness. A key element of this was how to deal with theological diversity and disagreement. At the end of the 1766 Conference, which included intense debate on Wesley's own position and the role of the preachers, Wesley stated: "An happier Conference we never had, nor a more profitable one. It was both begun and ended in love, and with a solemn sense of the presence of God."[3] It is therefore not enough that Conference decides on how best the church can embody the love of God in its context; the processes of decision making itself ought to be an embodiment of that love.

---

1   The minutes of the London Conference of June 25–29, 1744, "The Agenda," *Works of Wesley,* 10:120.

2   On the history and the development of Wesley's Conferences, see Rack, "Introduction: The Conference History, and the *Minutes,*" *Works of Wesley,* 10:1–109.

3   *Journal* August 12, 1766, *Works of Wesley,* 22:57.

SANCTIFIED AND SANCTIFYING CONFERENCING IN THE CONTEXT OF THEOLOGICAL DIVERSITY

Wesley published a summary of the Conference minutes as guidelines for Methodist belief and practice; these have become known as "The 'Large' *Minutes*." In the 1763 edition "Christian Conference" is listed as means of grace.[4] This a reference not to the regular Conferences but rather to conversation, as I described in chapter 2, as times of intense fellowship and conversation about spiritual things aimed at fostering spiritual growth: promoting "faith, or love, or holiness" and ministering grace to the participants.[5] Wesley expected the early Methodists to regularly engage in conversation about spiritual topics to encourage each other in their Christian life. This was further fostered by the various small groups within early Methodism, which provided a structured context for such conversation. Conversation was not only a means of grace; it could also be an expression of grace (or of sin). Wesley took people's speech very seriously as the expression of their tempers and affections, so that it became a window through which people might see into each other's hearts. Speech that is destructive, deceitful, cruel, scornful, derogatory, intolerant, rude, or haughty gives expression to unholy tempers and sinful affections. Such unholy conversation is destructive and to be avoided by Christians. Speech that is honest, kind, edifying, caring, trusting, respectful, and tolerant gives expression to holy tempers; as such it is the fruit of the Spirit's work within a believer.

The significance of this is seen when located within the broader context of Wesley's theology. God's purpose in sending Jesus Christ was to overcome the power of evil in the world by creating a community of people who had been transformed and empowered to love God and their neighbors. Relating to each other and communicating with each other in love is both God's goal for the church and a means by which the goal is achieved. Thus for Methodism, conferencing is an integral part of what it means to be the church.

Theological disagreement provides a unique context for and a danger to the church as an embodiment of love. I argued in chapter 1 that for Wesley, theological disagreement has a unique potential to destroy relationships that embody love. These differences can easily descend into intense arguments in which opponents believe they are representing God and the truth and those that disagree with them are

---

4   See "The 'Large' *Minutes*, 1753, 1763," *Works of Wesley*, 10:856–57; see the detailed discussion in Richard P. Heitzenrater, "The Exercise of the Presence of God: Holy Conferencing as a Means of Grace," in *Perfecting Perfection: Essays in Honor of Henry D. Rack*, ed. Robert Webster (Eugene, OR: Pickwick Publications, 2015), 61–80.

5   Sermon 89, "The More Excellent Way," *Works of Wesley*, 3:272. See also Sermon 8, "The First Fruits of the Spirit," *Works of Wesley*, 1:236–37; Sermon 51, "The Good Steward," *Works of Wesley*, 2:294.

unfaithful and disobedient, representing, at best, their own ideas and, at worst, those of the devil. In chapter 2, I argued that participation in a theologically diverse community can be a unique opportunity to develop loving affections as people exercise love to those with whom they strongly disagree, recognizing each other as siblings in Christ, with a common mission of participating in God's reign. Even when the differences seem insurmountable, and opponents on different extremes find it difficult to recognize the others as siblings in Christ, participation can be a means of grace when the commitment to deeply loving each other is present.[6]

Scattered throughout Wesley's writings we find advice and examples of how Christian conferencing can be both sanctified (embodying love for each other) and sanctifying (promoting the embodiment of love in the church and society). In developing these insights, I will in places go beyond Wesley and against some of his practices.

THE GOAL—PROMOTING THE EMBODIMENT OF HOLINESS

The goal of conferencing in a community characterized by theological diversity and disagreement is the embodiment of God's transforming love in the life of the community. The same is true for dialogue between Christian communities. In this case discussions of theological differences that impede greater levels of unity are directed at developing relationships that more fully manifest their common love for God and each other. In both cases, it is the communal seeking to discern in the presence of God that holiness is to be expressed in this particular context in response to God's revelation in and through the scripture by the Spirit. This focus on holiness recognizes the importance of theological opinions, for, as Wesley argued, right opinions promote growth in holiness and wrong opinions are destructive to holiness.

Truth matters in our understanding of God's revelation, the realities of the world, the people to whom we proclaim the gospel, and the way in which we understand the relationships between God's revelation, the world, and people. However, recognition of human fallibility means that we can never unequivocally associate our theological opinions, no matter how well grounded they are, with God's truth. So the aim of conferencing is not to win the theological argument or to provoke disagreement, nor is it to use political means to impose the opinions on others, but rather to seek together to discern the voice of the Spirit. The goal is the embodiment of love through loving means. Wesley aptly describes this goal in the preface to his *Explanatory Notes upon the New Testament*: "Would to God that all party names and unscriptural phrases and forms which have divided the Christian world were forgot,

---

6   See Sermon 80, "On Friendship with the World," *Works of Wesley*, 3:130–31.

and that we might be able to sit down together, as humble loving disciples, at the feet of our common Master, to hear his word, to imbibe his Spirit and to transcribe his life in our own!"[7]

THE FUNDAMENTAL TEMPER—HUMILITY

For Wesley one of the central characteristics of a heart transformed by God is humility. Humility is the recognition of our own limitations and failings and the recognition of the work of God in the life of others. This has important consequences for the way in which we approach theological disagreements. Wesley argued that ignorance, errors, mistakes, wrong opinions, and thus wrong interpretations of scripture are fundamental characteristics of fallen humanity. This is not changed by the new birth and sanctification. As we noted he argued that sanctification might lead to greater errors, because a sanctified person will, out of love, be inclined to believe what someone says even when it is false. The temptation that we face is to assume the ideas of those with whom we disagree as errors but our own beliefs as true. While Wesley assumed the truth of his core beliefs and rigorously critiqued the views of others, he notes in "Catholic Spirit":

> Although every man necessarily believes that every particular opinion which he holds is true (for to believe any opinion is not true, is the same thing as not to hold it); yet can no man be assured that all his own opinions, taken together, are true. Nay, every thinking man is assured they are not, seeing . . . "To be ignorant of many things, and to mistake in some, is the necessary condition of humanity." This, therefore, he is sensible, is his own case. He knows, in the general, that he himself is mistaken; although in what particulars he mistakes, he does not, perhaps he cannot, know.[8]

This means that on the very point we are arguing about, it might be possible that those with whom we disagree are right and we are wrong. Hence in the preface to his *Sermons on Several Occasions*, 1–33, Wesley states: "But some may think I have mistaken the way myself, although I take it upon myself to teach others. It is probable that many will think this; and it is very possible that I have. But I trust, whereinsoever I have mistaken, my mind is open to correction. I sincerely desire to be better informed. I say to God and man, 'What I know not, teach thou me.'"[9]

In a number of other places in his writings, Wesley asked those who thought he was wrong to graciously show him his error by reason and scripture, by what

---

7   Preface, *NT Notes*.
8   Sermon 39, "Catholic Spirit," *Works of Wesley,* 2:83–84; see also 2:93.
9   "Preface" to *Sermons on Several Occasions*, 1–33, *Works of Wesley,* 1:107.

we might call today a carefully argued interpretation of the Bible.[10] An interesting contrast to this can be found in Wesley's journal entry of September 12, 1751, where he comments on the writings of William Dell: "From his manner one may learn that he was not very patient of reproof and contradiction, so that it is no wonder there is generally so much error mixed with the truth he delivers."[11] The pursuit of truth in the service of the love of God and our neighbors requires a mutual willingness to listen to the critique of others who hold different and even contrary opinions. This does not mean an indifference to issues of truth or a lack of conviction about what one believes. One ought to be firmly convinced of the truth of one's opinions and argue for them but at the same time recognize one's own fallibility and be open to correction and to learning from others.

Humility also opens a person to listening and learning from those with whom they disagree in relation to other issues. Given the embodied character of all human knowledge and manifestations of holiness, people in different contexts will, through their own particular experience, have opportunities to develop particular insights into God, God's work in the world, and what it means concretely to be a holy people. It is by engaging with people from diverse social, cultural, geographical, national, economic, and political contexts that one can discover new theological, ethical, and practical insights, and so engage in new ways of embodying God's love in the world. It is in difference that they can provide an important critique and challenge to assumptions one takes for granted. However, conversing with others requires humility to hear and learn from this challenge, particularly when one is convinced that the views of these people are deeply defective in other areas. It is by such deep listening that we discover together what it means to manifest God's love and grow together to greater maturity as the one body of Christ.

THE CONNECTIONAL CONDITION

Christian conferencing is a particular expression of connectionalism and must be characterized by the central features of connectionalism. Three features are particularly important.

- The first is representation; I argued above that the embodied character of the human person leads to diverse expressions of holiness as God's love unfolds in particular people in relation to who they are and the context in which they live.

---

10 See for example his letters to Richard Tompson ('P. V.') of June 28, 1755; to Rev William Dodd of March 12, 1756; to Henry Venn June 22, 1763; and to the *London Magazine/Philosophaster*, January 4, 1765, *Works of Wesley*, 26:567; 27:19, 337, 407.

11 *Journal* September 12, 1751, *Works of Wesley*, 20:401.

The strength of connectionalism is that it brings people with diverse expressions of holiness and diverse and even contradictory interpretations of God's transforming work into relationship with each other. Hence authentic conferencing in this context requires the genuine and equal participation of all members of the connection, particularly those who have been disempowered and silenced. The voices of all need to be heard and their participation in decision making assured.

• The second characteristic is being responsible for and with each other. Decisions are to be made in such a way that the Conference takes collective responsibility for the decisions made or by authorizing actions for the whole. Conference decisions ought not to be the expression of a simplistic majority vote. Decisions have to be made in a way that genuinely respects the opinions of all, even when some opinions are rejected. Discussion at a Conference thus need to be structured in such a way as to promote as much participation as possible in the decision making with the goal of seeking consensus without silencing prophetic voices. The difficulty is that such discussion is difficult in any large gathering. Hence there is a need for rigorous discussion in smaller groups, the results of which can be fed into a larger discussion that seeks to be as inclusive as possible. Such restructuring of decision making is particularly problematic in the context of large and international denominations. Here the possibility of devolving decision making on many issues to lower regional levels needs to be explored. The building of voting blocks and voting slates needs to be strongly discouraged—in some cases such groups function as the promoters of what Wesley understood as schism. In the end, complete consensus might not be possible, and some form of majority voting system might be inevitable, but this should only take place within the context of the striving for consensus.

• Finally, it entails accountability. Decision making in Conference is done in the context of a deep awareness of the impact of particular decisions on the lives of those participating, of the church they represent, and of the broader societies in which the church lives. Love requires that decisions must seek the comprehensive well-being of all, and hence there is a need for a deep awareness of the potential negative impact of decisions. The participants in conferencing are accountable not only to each other for their decisions but also ultimately of greater significance to God, who is love.

THE DETERMINING ORIENTATION—LOVING ONE'S OPPONENTS

Conferencing that is sanctified and sanctifying will be determined by love for those one disagrees with. In various writings Wesley describes what such love practically entails.[12]

The first major point is to focus on the issues and not on the person. The great temptation when engaging in theological debate is to attempt to win the debate by discrediting people who hold contrary opinions by displaying them in a bad light, by highlighting their failures, and by denigrating their person. In a digital age this temptation is intensified by the possibilities for engaging in such denigration without ever physically meeting the other person. The denigration of the other and thus the harm done is multiplied as it spreads uncontrollably over the Internet. For Wesley, a true love for one's neighbor should result in the opposite. One should refuse to denigrate one's opponents or treat them contemptuously.

When describing an opponent's opinions, one must be careful to do it in a way that does not lead to the person being denigrated or subjected to contempt. One should refuse to spread bad rumors about one's adversaries and refuse to listen to accounts of their failures and sin. One should rejoice not in their faults but rather in the good they do. One should weep over their failings and sins, and despite disagreeing, one should affirm and rejoice in all positives seen in one's opponents. One should defend these opponents and their reputation in the face of attacks from others and seek to cover up their failures where this does not contribute to evil.

Second, bitterness, anger, hatred, harshness, unfriendliness, and any attitude of unkindness toward one's opponents are to be rejected as evil tempers, which are an "abomination to the Lord."[13] On the contrary we should treat our opponents with tenderness, kindness, and affection.

---

12 See for example from *Works of Wesley*: Sermon 22, "Upon our Lord's Sermon on the Mount, II," 1:500–506; Sermon 38, "A Caution against Bigotry," 2:71–72; Sermon 39, "Catholic Spirit," 2:77–78, 94–95; and preface to "The Principles of a Methodist," 9:48–49. Also, Outler, ed., *John Wesley*, "A Letter to a Roman Catholic," 493–94, 498–99.

13 Outler, ed., *John Wesley*, "A Letter to a Roman Catholic," 493.

Third, one's arguments should be characterized by truth, justice, and mercy.[14] Truth requires integrity in describing and evaluating the evidence and the arguments for a particular position. Justice requires that we treat the arguments of others fairly and not misrepresent them or impute to them ideas or attitudes that they do not hold. Mercy requires that we understand the circumstances and context from which a person argues.

Fourth, love requires that we refuse to be suspicious of our opponent's motives, but always attribute to them the best motives and put the best construction on their words and behavior.

Fifth, one should pray for the spiritual well-being and growth of one's opponents and ask them to pray for oneself in return. Love leads one to encourage and support others in their spiritual life and the work they do in the service of God's reign. One should also join with them where appropriate.

Sixth, one should speak the truth to one's opponents and where necessary be prepared to warn and correct them when their behavior is contrary to the fundamentals of loving God and one's neighbors. Yet, one needs to do so in a loving, gentle, and mild manner and not seek to denigrate one's opponents or open them to public shame.[15]

This acting in love toward those one disagrees with is not dependent upon the attitudes and behavior of the opponents. Even if they do not act in love, one should patiently and in self-denial bear with them and continue to act in love. However, a mutual love will provide the basis for finding a way forward. Without it there is little hope of success. Wesley commented in his journal that reconciliation between Arminians and Calvinists would require a change of "their hearts."[16]

THE TRANSFORMATIVE FOUNDATION—HAVING THE SAME HEART

In a Wesleyan perspective the transformative foundation for all such engagement is the mutual recognition that despite strong disagreement, the conversing parties have the same heart. That is, while they might describe it in radically different language and manifest it in very dissimilar and possibly even contradictory ways, they have experienced the forgiving, accepting, and transforming grace of God that empowers them to love God and their fellows. It is the recognition and affirmation of having the same heart that provides the foundation for genuine community

---

14 Wesley complained that some of his opponents did not treat him with justice, mercy, and truth. See for example his "*A Second Letter to the Author of* The Enthusiasm of Methodists and Papists Compared (1751)," *Works of Wesley,* 11:429.

15 See Sermon 65, "The Duty of Reproving our Neighbour," *Works of Wesley,* 2:511–20.

16 *Journal* February 25, 1777, *Works of Wesley,* 23:43.

and transforms intense disagreements into conversations among siblings, God's children, who deeply love each other. Hence such conversations start with hearing each other's faith stories. While it is obviously possible to engage in such a process through media, it is the face-to-face encounters in which one engages in "Christian conferencing" that provide the best possibility for the mutual recognition of possessing the same heart.[17] The promotion of the unity of the church would therefore be encouraged through the praxis of Wesleyan small groups made up of people with radically diverse opinions.

There are, however, situations where the contradiction is so great that a mutual recognition of having the same heart is not possible. When that is the case an approach suggested by a Wesleyan theology is to find a foundation through a recognition that one's opponents are created in the image of God, that Christ died for them, and that God is at work in them in prevenient grace.

THE SEARCH FOR A WAY FORWARD—FINDING COMMON GROUND

A common attitude of love and humility will facilitate a dialogue between people of differing opinions; it will not itself hold a diverse community together. Love should become the basis for seeking a way forward for a diverse group. A common feature of Wesley's approach to engaging people with whom he disagreed was to find common ground—to seek to set out what the opposing groups had in common. One interesting example of this is his "A Letter to a Roman Catholic."[18] This is in many ways a remarkable document given that Wesley was a fierce critic of Roman Catholicism. As I described in earlier chapters, he regarded Catholic theology as fundamentally denying the core gospel message of justification by faith. He viewed Catholic worship as idolatry and an abomination, accused the Catholic Church of making one of the Ten Commandments disappear, and believed that many of its traditions, doctrines, and practices were not scriptural. Further he claimed that persecution of Protestants and the political subversion of Protestant countries were the normal outcome of Catholic theology and ethics.

"A Letter to a Roman Catholic" sets out the areas of doctrinal agreement between Catholics and Protestants. It covers most of what one could call the common

---

17 An interesting example of this in the ecumenical context is the Global Christian Forum (GCF). Earlier attempts to promote the ecumenical unity of the church have focused on finding unity in doctrine (faith and order), ethical action (life and work), or mission. The GCF has focused on a mutual hearing of each other's faith stories. See www.globalchristianforum.org.

18 Outler, ed., *John Wesley*, "A Letter to a Roman Catholic," 493–99. Note the discussion on sanctification and holy living in various sections on pages 495–97.

doctrines of historic Christianity and has a substantial section on sanctification, which Wesley proposed was a strength of Catholic teaching in contrast to some forms of Protestantism (particularly Lutheranism).[19] Perhaps strange for modern Methodists, it included a statement affirming the perpetual virginity of Jesus' mother, Mary. Apart from a brief reference at the end to Romans 5:1-2, it does not deal with justification. Yet Wesley wrote in his pamphlet "A Word to a Protestant" that the Catholic understanding of justification was one of the three "fundamental errors of Popery," saying, It "strikes at the root of Christian faith, the only foundation of true religion."[20]

The letter also expresses Wesley's characteristic appreciation of the experience of God's transforming love in the lives of some Roman Catholics, despite their substantial and even fundamental differences. The letter is an attempt to explore what Protestants and Catholics have in common theologically despite their substantial disagreements. It points to a way of seeking unity by focusing on the commonalities flowing out of the recognition of a common experience of God's transforming grace. It suggests that this is one way of responding to diversity, which recognizes but is not defeated by real differences of opinion.

This approach is not unique in Wesley's writings. In a volume of his journal that contains substantial criticism of the Moravians, he begins with an introduction setting out what they agreed upon and what he appreciated about them.[21] This initial focus on common ground expresses love and forms the basis for future discussion on issues where there is disagreement. Ted Campbell has argued that within Wesley's writings and within the doctrinal statements of the Methodist churches, it is possible to discover central theological issues. Some pertain to the common Christian tradition, others reflect the heritage of the Protestant Reformation, and a few express the heritage of the Wesleyan revival.[22] While Campbell's identification of these as theological essentials in contrast to opinions is problematic for the reasons set out in chapter 7, they are a helpful identification of different levels of theological commonality that can form the basis for various forms of unity.

Methodist churches have historically engaged in ecumenical dialogue with people who share the first level of commonality, seeking to develop relationships and sacramental Communion. In relation to the second level, Methodist churches are in full communion with various Protestant churches, with full recognition of sacraments and ordination. In some cases, Methodist churches have entered into union with

---

19   See Sermon 107, "In God's Vineyard," *Works of Wesley*, 3:505–6.

20   "A Word to a Protestant," *Works* (Jackson), 11:188.

21   "To the Moravian Church" June 24, 1744, *Introduction to An Extract of the Rev. Mr. John Wesley's Journal of November 1, 1739 to September 3, 1741, Works of Wesley*, 19:116–18.

22   Ted A. Campbell, *Wesleyan Beliefs: Formal and Popular Expressions of the Core Beliefs of Wesleyan Communities* (Nashville: Kingswood, 2010), 17–62.

such churches and have brought to that union their Wesleyan distinctives. While the common affirmation of the Methodist unity for Methodist churches, Campbell's list of common doctrines has significant potential for finding a way forward together, not only in ecumenical but also in inter-church relationships. However, in the contemporary context, significant differences exist as to how these theological commonalities are to be interpreted; hence there is a need to reexamine both the content and the interpretation of these doctrines in the way Wesley did with the doctrines of the Trinity and justification, which we examined in chapter 7.

Disagreements exist not only in doctrine but also, from a Wesleyan perspective, in more significant areas of life and ethics. In the twentieth century most churches came to a common agreement that racism was incompatible with the central values of love for one's neighbor. Some traditions argued that participation in war is similarly incompatible; and, in the contemporary context, debate rages over globalization, economic systems, environmental concerns, abortion, homosexuality, and other issues. Methodists have historically been prepared to affirm concrete statements on ethical issues, making them binding not only on the leadership but also on the membership. The classic example is Wesley's General Rules. These statements do not cover all areas of ethics but attempt to set forth what Methodists mean by loving God and one's fellows, while leaving room for disagreement in other areas. Such attempts to make concrete ethical statements, expressing the mind of the church and requiring compliance, are fraught with difficulties.

Then there are situations where despite the controversy and disagreement, even within the church, the fundamental dual love command requires a clear, bold statement. Compromise is impossible, and there can be no attempt to find common ground. In other situations, the church may discern that Christians, equally committed to the love commands, may legitimately come to different conclusions. Different analyses of an ethical problem can lead to different responses that genuinely express a desire for the comprehensive well-being of the other. Love for each other and the humble recognition of one's own fallibility must lead to a careful listening and a desire to find common ground, recognizing that a divisive decision might still need to be made. Such issues should be approached by first identifying areas of agreement in general principles, in biblical interpretation, and in the analysis of the situation. Then areas of disagreement must be identified. It is on this basis that decisions need to be made about how far it is possible to find a way forward together.

THE NECESSARY HONESTY—RECOGNIZING THE DEPTH OF DIVISION

I have emphasized in a number of places in this book that Wesley's openness to the genuine faith of those he disagreed with and his commitment to working with them as participants in God's mission in the world was not incompatible with his strong critique of opinions that he held to be wrong and even spiritually dangerous. Some of Wesley's critiques of other positions express stereotypical critiques and a tendency to emphasize the most problematic expressions of opposition rather than seeking genuine deep dialogue. Yet Wesley remains a very important reminder that important differences must not be covered up, obscured, or downplayed as having little significance. The depth of difference needs to be acknowledged before a way toward genuine unity can be uncovered.

There is, of course, a danger that in the polemics of a conflict situation the degree of difference is overestimated or genuinely mediating positions are overlooked and excluded. Love requires honesty in identifying and explicating genuine significant difference as well as recognizing that not all difference carries the same significance and the possibility of mediating positions. Particularly problematic is the attempt to clearly define and stereotype different positions in opposition to each other when greater nuance is possible. This becomes even more problematic when people are classified according to these stereotypes even when they reject them.

THE DANGER TO BE AVOIDED—REJECTING THE SPIRIT OF PERSECUTION

One of the fundamental principles of Wesley's theology is that every person is accountable to God. This means that every person must be given the freedom to think, speak, and act in accordance with his or her conscience. Given that we are all fallible, we do not have the right to encourage, coerce, or force others to act or speak contrary to what they sincerely believe to be true. Wesley insists: "They must not act contrary to their conscience, though it be an erroneous one."[23] It is always possible that they are right and we are wrong. We are responsible to God and therefore must always act before God in accordance with what we believe to be right and true. Wesley insisted that Christians must reject a persecuting spirit as having its roots in not knowing Christ.[24] By this he did not mean merely the use of force or violence to force people to change their minds, but he included the use of all forms of pressure to make someone act contrary to his or her conscience to what he or she sincerely believes to be true.[25]

The goal in engaging with each other is to discover the truth, and if we sincerely believe that our opinions are true then we must seek to convince the other person

---

23 *Journal* June 3, 1776, *Works of Wesley*, 23:18.
24 See *NT Notes*, John 16:3.
25 See Sermon 37, "The Nature of Enthusiasm," *Works of Wesley*, 2:59; "Advice to the People called Methodists," *Works of Wesley*, 9:130; and *A Farther Appeal to Men of Reason and Religion*, Part III, *Works of Wesley*, 11:279.

through the means of reason, patience, gentleness, long-suffering, and love. Yet for Wesley this did not mean that every belief and practice was tolerated within Methodism, but rather that enough space must be created for legitimate diversity.

CENTERS AND BOUNDARIES

As we have seen in earlier chapters, Wesley's commitment to a catholic spirit and the rejection of a persecuting spirit did not mean there were no boundaries. While membership in early Methodism was open to all seeking the salvation of their souls, evidenced in their behavior and commitment to participation in the life of a local Methodist society, preachers were expected to submit to stricter disciplinary boundaries imposed by Wesley. The content of their preaching was to conform to the doctrine contained in the *Explanatory Notes upon the New Testament* and the Standard Sermons. They were also expected to submit to the authority of John Wesley. While some of the preachers had input into the interpretation of the doctrinal commitments and establishment of the discipline through their participation in the Annual Conferences, Wesley still made the final decisions. Wesley regarded himself as responsible before God for the doctrine and discipline of the Methodist movement and argued that, for example, forbidding the lay administration of the sacraments was not an expression of a persecuting spirit but the exercising of his responsibility. In the post-Wesley context, the communal responsibility for doctrine and discipline now lies with Methodist Conferences in their various forms and polities. The process of sanctified and sanctifying conferencing includes determining disciplinary procedures and theological boundaries. Both arise out of the goal of embodying holiness.

In Wesley's understanding, while theological opinions were always fallible and were not a determinative dimension of religion, they nevertheless were important, as false opinions could undermine the experience of God's transformative grace and lead to wrong practices. The closer an opinion was related to the center of genuine religion, that is, God's gracious transformation of the human person enabling them to love God and their neighbors, the more serious was the consequence of potential error. The boundaries are determined by the center. The task of Conference in the context of intense theological and ethical disagreement is to determine the relationship between the diverse and contradictory theological opinions and the central core of the faith. How much diversity is compatible without compromising the core? In the case of ethical issues, the test lies in the relationship and compatibility of a particular ethical position and the double love commandment.

The amount of diversity permitted lies in the dynamic relationship between affirming personal responsibility before God and exercising communal responsibility before God. There is no definitive solution to this tension. As the church encounters new theological and ethical challenges, so it must engage again in the process of communal discernment as to the relationship of the new challenge to the center of the Christian faith. If the church follows Wesley's example, different levels of conformity can help create space for genuine personal responsibility before God and maintain the integrity of the teaching and praxis of the church as an embodiment of God's transforming love.

CONCLUSION

The invitation to sanctified and sanctifying conferencing is not an easy way out of conflicts. It is not a broad way or a middle way. It is a call to costly self-denial, humility, love, and vulnerability in the service of a greater goal—a church that embodies the love of God. It is such a church that will stand in stark contrast to the divisiveness and conflicts that dominate so much of our contemporary society and thus will bear witness to the transforming and reconciling grace of God, who empowers us to be new people in Christ.

AFTERWORD

I have argued throughout this book that the core of Wesley's theology of holiness is love. God—Father, Son and, Spirit—is love. Out of love, God brought creation into existence. God loves all human beings; they were created to manifest God's moral character by loving God and loving their fellow human beings. Humans have rejected God's love for them and have turned in on themselves, so that they can no longer truly love God or their fellows. In fact, without knowing God as revealed in Christ Jesus, humans cannot know the depth of what unselfish love looks like in practice. Despite our turning away, God refused to stop loving human beings and maintained a desire to transform us by love, renewing the divine image within us so that we could have characters dominated by love for God and our fellow human beings.

In order to achieve God's purpose, God became a human being in Christ Jesus, who took upon himself human sin and its consequences in order to reconcile human beings with God. With prevenient grace, God draws all human beings into a relationship with Godself, revealing to all, in rudimentary form, what it means to love God and their fellows. God had called the people of Israel into being and gave them a more detailed exposition of love in the moral law. God's relationship with humanity and Israel took a dramatic new turn when the Divine Word became human in Jesus of Nazareth, who not only taught God's way of love, but was himself the Incarnation of divine love. The imperative of love led Jesus to the cross. God raised him from the dead as the firstfruits of the transformation of creation. The life, death, and resurrection of Jesus the Christ reveal the true character of love. This lies at the heart of the Christian understanding of the confession that God is love and prevents the simplistic reversal of the statement into the deeply problematic affirmation that love is God, which opens the way to defining the character of God through diverse cultural understandings of love. In the aftermath of the Resurrection, God sent the Holy Spirit upon the followers of Jesus, filling them with the divine love, uniting them into a new community, the church, and equipping them to be witnesses to God's love through their words, the example of their communal life, and their acts of loving service toward humanity. The Holy Spirit is active in the world to overcome sin and evil and their consequences and to so transform human beings and human societies that love reigns throughout the earth, anticipating the eschatological transformation of creation.

At the center of the Spirit's work is the transformation of human persons, who then transform the societies in which they live. God unites these transformed persons into God's church, which has its origins in God's love for humanity. God's purpose is to enable and sustain a community whose love for God gives rise to a radical commitment to enable and sustain the well-being of others. It is this participation in the divine love that distinguishes the church from the broader society, constituting it as a countercultural community. Hence, it is as an embodiment and reflection of this love that the church is holy and thus distinct from the surrounding cultures. The universal church manifests itself as concrete communities of love in the real world. Ecclesial communities are the visible manifestation of the church to the extent that they embody God's love. Institutional churches that fail to embody love deny their own identity and are obstacles to God's mission in the world.

The church, as the community of those transformed by God's love, is located in a multitude of social, cultural, ethnic, national, and other contexts. A consequence of this multiplicity is diversity in the expressions of holiness, because different contexts provide multiple opportunities for love to be embodied in relation to concrete particular realities. Thus, holiness and diversity are not contradictory. Theological disagreement, even the holding of deeply contradictory theological propositions resulting in diverse ethical practices, is not necessarily contradictory to love and hence holiness. Wesley described this particular expression of holiness as a catholic spirit. However, opportunities to give expression to holiness are often accompanied by threats to holiness. The danger of theological diversity is that it can be responded to in a manner that is contradictory to holiness. This happens when theological disagreement leads to strife and division. Wesley noted that in theological disagreement we quickly associate our particular viewpoint with God's viewpoint and our cause with God's cause, and hence opponents are viewed as opposing God's truth and purposes and in some cases as the enemies of God. Disagreement is often associated with deep emotions, resulting in alienation from each other as well as bitterness, anger, misrepresentation, mutual recriminations, personal attacks, degrading comments, and a host of other unloving attitudes and actions. These are the manifestation of a lack of love and a contradiction to the holiness that God desires for the church. Acting in ways that do not lead to holiness strikes at the heart of what it means for a given community to be a visible expression of God in the world—the church.

As churches and Christians face theological and ethical diversity, either within their own church structures or in relation to other churches and communities of faith, the challenge before them is how to respond to such diversity and even contradiction in a manner that manifests holiness by embodying love and thus becoming a countercultural witness to the power of God's love. Wesley's theology provides a theological framework for responding to theological differences so that participation in a diverse community can become both a means of grace and a manifestation of that grace. This can be summarized as follows:

- Human beings are finite and fallen creatures, and as such their knowledge is limited and subject to error and confusion. This includes their knowledge of theological realities. All theological propositions, even those hallowed by tradition, are human opinions and hence are limited and subject to error.

- Theological opinions have consequences for people's spiritual well-being and growth in holiness. Truth is important, and people have a duty to ensure that their opinions are correct.

- Human beings are responsible before God for their opinions, and hence their opinions must be held with a clear conscience. No one should be forced to accept or practice opinions against his or her conscience.

- Acting in accordance with ultimately wrong opinions is not sinful (properly so-called) when we act out of genuine love and in accordance with what we authentically believe to be God's will. This must be qualified in two ways. First, by the recognition that well-meant actions might be sinful (improperly so-called); that is, violations of the moral law, objectively viewed, and as such they may be deeply destructive of the well-being of others. This might not be the intention of the actor and might not be seen to be so by the actor. It might only be recognized in hindsight or from a different contemporary context; hence there is a need to hear the voices of others. Second, in Wesley's understanding, as demonstrated in his discussions of slavery, consequences as well as motives matter in ethical decision making. Ethical decision making is an act of responsibility that needs to look not only at motives but also at norms and consequences. Actions that have destructive consequences are unethical even when they are justified by appeals to norms and motives.

- Truth and the pursuit of truth are subordinate to love. Truth is to be pursued out of love for God and others, and hence the methods and modes of seeking truth must conform to love.

- Love requires that churches be structured in such a way as to allow for as much liberty of opinion as compatible with and required in order to protect their identity as the embodiment of God's transformative love.

- Institutional churches are not simply "big tents," nor are they uncritically inclusive communities. At the center of the life and message of the church is the reality of God's gracious action in Christ by the Spirit to forgive and transform human beings so that they love God and their neighbor. Theological affirmations and ethical propositions that contradict this central reality must be rejected.

- However, given the recognition of human fallibility, there is diversity of theological and ethical viewpoints that are compatible with this central core.

- Within a given institutional church, the challenge is to determine in the light of scripture and the voices of tradition, both in relation to the particular tradition of the church and the witness of other Christians, what is acceptable diversity within this particular institutional church. Different standards ought to be applied to those with teaching and leadership responsibilities given that an institutional church can come to the conclusion that certain ideas and practices have the potential to seriously endanger growth in love for God and neighbor, even though it is possible for a person to genuinely love God and their neighbors and hold to such opinions and practices.

- The historic wisdom of the Methodist tradition is that the best way of determining the limits of diversity is through sanctified and sanctifying conversation.

- Institutional churches may and will come to the conclusion that certain theological and ethical positions are not compatible with their understanding of the core of Christian faith and the doctrinal and ethical positions that interpret it. It is thus not possible to grant people who hold to such positions the liberty to teach or practice them. People who are members of a particular institutional church may come to the conclusion that they cannot in good conscience conform to the teaching and structures of a church, because they are forced to do or teach that which contradicts their personal theological convictions, or they are prevented from doing or teaching that which they believe God calls them to do and to teach. In such cases some form of division may be inevitable in order to preserve peoples' good conscience before God. In such situations a way forward needs to be found that manifests love in the midst of separation. However, people may decide to remain within a church they disagree with in order to reform it.

- Where separate institutional churches exist or come into being, such churches have an obligation to seek as much cooperation and communion as possible, giving expression of love for each other and supporting each, seeking communion with each other even where institutional union is not possible at a given time and context. However, the goal of visible union as the embodiment of divine love remains the goal to be achieved.

Those who stand in the Wesleyan and Methodist tradition who believe that God has called this tradition to spread scriptural holiness—that is, the embodiment of love for God and one's neighbor—have a particular calling to fulfill in this regard. This calling is a passionate commitment to the unity of the church in theory and in practice so that in this way God will be glorified. The question remains as to how this is to be worked out in the context of contemporary debates and divisions. In a wide variety of denominational and ecumenical contexts, not the least within various Methodist churches, the inclusion of LGBT people and the affirmation of homosexual relationships has become a major point of conflict and division. It thus provides an important case study for the Wesleyan approach to the unity of the church developed in this book.

WESLEYAN UNITY AND THE DIVIDE OVER HUMAN SEXUALITY

Any attempt to address this debate over human sexuality is fraught with complexity, and it is impossible to do justice to it in the context of a short afterword. Bearing this in mind, my aim is to briefly describe how the theology and praxis we have developed in the previous chapters can provide a framework for addressing the divisions caused by diverse responses to the debate around human sexuality.

For reasons of space, I will confine the discussion to homosexuality. One factor in the complexity is the considerable diversity of positions. L. R. Holben has identified six approaches. These are condemnation, a promise of healing, costly discipleship, pastoral accommodation, affirmation, and liberation.[1] For the purposes of illustrating

---

1   See for example L. R. Holben, *What Christians Think about Homosexuality: Six Representative Views* (North Richland Hills, TX: Bibal Press, 1999).

the usefulness of Wesley's ideas, I will refer to two broad and somewhat stereotypical approaches, recognizing that I am bracketing out a range of other issues and perspectives related to both heterosexual and homosexual relationships. The one maintains that sexual relationships can only be affirmed between members of the opposite sex in the context of heterosexual marriage—for want of a better term, I will refer to this as the traditional approach. The second maintains that Christians should also affirm sexual relationships between members of the same sex within the context of committed covenant relationships or marriages (where this is possible). I will refer to this as the affirming approach.

Given the centrality of love, the starting point of any discussion of this debate, and of primary importance within it, is to affirm that at the center is not an issue or a problem but people—loved by God to whom love (that is, a genuine commitment to their well-being) is owed by all. People who are, in many cases, members of the body of Christ—they are members of a fellowship that, in Wesley's theology, ought to be characterized by reciprocal love expressed in benevolence and delight. Their presence within the church is not a problem to be solved but an opportunity to discover in new ways what it means to be a community of love.

The process of finding a way of unity for the church begins with the discovery of having the same heart—that is, the mutual recognition of the work of God's transforming grace in the lives of those with whom we disagree. It starts with developing relationships with each other, hearing each other's faith stories, and a deep listening to how and why people came to their particular viewpoints on this issue. There is a need to put away all prejudgments on the motives or reasons why people hold particular viewpoints. Given what was stated in the first point above, there is a particular need for the diverse voices, experiences, and faith stories of lesbian and gay Christians to be heard.

However, this raises the major issue of what happens when some people in the dialogue are not able to recognize a common heart—the divisions appear to be of such a nature that they cannot recognize others as siblings in Christ. In this case the dialogue, from a Wesleyan perspective, can continue on the basis of three affirmations. The first is the duty to love one's neighbors, even if one regards them as the enemies of God. Such loving involves rejecting prejudices, respectful listening, a commitment to seeking understanding, a commitment to fairness, and the trust of the other. The second is that loving one's neighbors includes the duty of seeking their spiritual welfare and thus in a loving and respectful manner explaining one's own position and why one believes the other's position is wrong. Third, while the center of Wesleyan theology is God's transformation of the human heart, it also affirms that God is at work in prevenient grace in all human beings.[2] Prevenient grace

---

2   For discussion of Wesley's understanding of prevenient grace see Charles Allen Rogers, "The Concept of Prevenient Grace in Theology of John Wesley" (PhD Diss., Duke University, 1967); Randy L. Maddox, *Responsible Grace: John Wesley's Practical Theology*, 83–93; J. Gregory Crofford, *Streams of Mercy: Prevenient Grace in the Theology of John and Charles*

begins the process of transformation in all human beings, bringing them to an awareness of God's moral law, convincing them of sin, and drawing them to Christ. Hence even when one cannot recognize another as a sibling in Christ, one can affirm them as a neighbor in whom God is at work.

Recognizing each other as siblings in Christ or at least neighbors should transform the spirit in which the issue is discussed. In a context where people's faith, motives, sincerity, and intentions are often called into question by their opponents, an approach shaped by sanctified and sanctifying conferencing in the spirit of love, requires us to accept the genuine character of people's affirmations and not denigrate their motivations and intentions, unless substantial public evidence to that contradicts their stated intention.

While love should shape the character of the conversation, it does not on its own provide the solution. Contradictory opinions still need to be addressed. The first step in doing so is to seek common ground, both in terms of understanding of the central core of the Christian faith and of the ethics of human sexuality as the particular issue at stake. One way of doing this would be to draw up a statement, similar to Wesley's "A Letter to a Roman Catholic," that sets out the common agreements in relation to central theological themes and to sexual ethics. It might be necessary to draw up more than one such statement. Having observed the debate within a number of churches, I would propose that you would probably come up with the following:

- There are people who substantially agree both on theology and sexual ethics whether holding affirming or traditional views.

- There are people who substantially agree on major theological issues and on most aspects of sexual ethics but only disagree with regard to homosexual relationships, with some being committed to a traditional view and others to an affirming view.

- There are people who agree on core theological issues but have different views on a broader range of sexual ethical issues.

- There are people who agree on an affirming or traditional view on homosexual relationships but have significant disagreements in other areas of theology.

In seeking to identify common ground, the complexity of the differing viewpoints will become clearer. If groups are to work toward unity, then the realities of difference need to be recognized. Obviously the issue of unity is not a problem among

---

Wesley (Lexington: Emeth, 2010); and W. Brian Shelton, *Prevenient Grace: God's Provision for Fallen Humanity* (Anderson: Francis Asbury Press, 2014), 120–74.

those who hold position 1; unity among themselves is no problem. The question is how they relate to those who are part of the same church or to other churches that disagree with them on issues of theology or sexual ethics or both. The challenge for people in groups 2 and 3 is how to evaluate the differences in sexual ethics. Are these of such a nature as to override the unity in other issues? In many denominations it is not uncommon for members to disagree on ethical issues around the economy or war and still remain united because of commonalities in other areas. However, a disagreement around issues of racism would not be tolerated. Is the debate about sexuality like that about economics and war, or is it like that around racism?[3] In debates within churches over sexuality, one solution that has been proposed is that churches split into two new denominations—one traditional and one affirming. The question then is, can one's position on homosexuality become the focus of unity above other significant theological issues? The following will not attempt to address all these complexities but rather focus on the issue of the affirmation or rejection of homosexual sexual relationships but recognizing the greater complexity.

From the perspective of Wesleyan theology, the theological question at stake in the debate is one of moral law. As such, it cannot be addressed by drawing dichotomies between grace and law, or holiness and love, or inclusion and exclusion. While these categories might function in other theological traditions, in Wesleyan theology these dichotomies are transcended. So the question is: Does the moral law forbid all sexual relationships between members of the same sex or does it affirm them in the context of covenanted monogamous relationships (or marriages)? For Wesley, debates about the meaning and implications of the moral law were a context where Christians often held to different opinions. He regarded Roman Catholic worship as idolatrous and thus a violation of the moral law—he could go as far as to designate it superstitious. Yet this did not mean that a Roman Catholic could not be a person transformed by God's grace and even a model of Christian holiness. He regarded the commandment not to eat blood as part of the moral law and binding on Christians but held equally strongly that it should not be a point of division. People who did not agree with him on this were welcome in his societies. The challenge is to determine when differences in the interpretation of the moral law become a question like slavery—a question where difference is unacceptable.

A difference of the interpretation of the moral law arises out of differences in the interpretation of the Bible, both in relation to individual texts and as to how human sexuality is to be interpreted in relation to the overarching message of scripture. Further, in many, but not all cases, it involves differing interpretations of how persons experience their sexuality and how this relates to their personal identity. Even where there is significant agreement on interpreting human sexuality, there

---

3   I owe this formulation of the problem to a conversation with Sam McBratney.

is hermeneutical diversity—that is, differences of understanding about how to relate the interpretation of the biblical texts concerning sexuality in the contemporary context. In this sense, regardless of one's viewpoint, however one interprets the scripture, there is the certainty that human finitude and fallenness will impact human knowledge and ethical decision making. In both the traditional and the affirmative approaches, interpretation is shaped by the contextual bodily character of human knowledge and as a consequence of influence by social, political, cultural, and personal factors.

Given the human propensity for fallible interpretation, then it is imperative for people on all sides to recognize that no matter how convinced they are of the correctness of their positions, it is always possible that they are wrong. Hence we all should approach the issue not only with a willingness to learn from others but also with a preparedness to question their own viewpoint. Further, people involved in discussing the issue need to seek the truth and not merely try to persuade or, worse, condemn others. All forms of selective use, distortion, and deliberate misuse of data are to be rejected. In addition, an attempt must be made to account for all data from scripture and human knowledge and not only that which serves one's own opinion. Wesley affirmed both the authority of scripture, the validity of human knowledge and learning, and the use of reason in interpreting scripture, forming knowledge, and relating them to each other.[4]

The recognition that faithful Christians may come to different interpretations of the moral law and are conscience-bound to act on such different interpretations has significant repercussions for the way one evaluates a person's views and actions. Wesley's understanding of sin and the law of love was that if a person is genuinely convinced of their position, whether it is affirming or traditional, they are not sinning (properly so-called) if they act in accordance with their convictions. This is because they are not acting contrary to what they know to be God's law, as long as they are acting out of genuine love for God and neighbor. In my discussion of Wesley's theology, I propose that the motif of righteousness, as covenant faithfulness in the context of diverse relationships, includes Wesley's concerns but goes beyond it to include the aspect of the consequences of one's actions. Hence a righteous position is one that takes cognizance not only of motive and intention but also the concrete consequences of one's actions. As a consequence, I would argue that an ethical viewpoint and consequent action is not sinful when a person is genuinely convinced that it is in accordance with God's will, when motivated by love, and when due consideration has been given to the concrete consequences of one's ethical position. Nor

---

4   See for example "Cautions and Directions Given to the Greatest Professors in the Methodist Societies" (1762), *Works of Wesley*, 13:84.

are proponents advocating that people commit sin by promoting their particular position. Ultimately people on both sides are responsible to God for their opinions and the actions that flow from them. As Wesley argues, it is wrong to compel people to act against their consciences even when the conscience was wrong; hence when seeking to change a person's approach to this issue, the goal is to demonstrate that the opinion one represents is truthful, just, compassionate, and an expression of a deep commitment to the comprehensive well-being of others that has the concrete consequence of improving the actual well-being of persons and does not contribute to harming them spiritually, physically, or psychologically.

Given that as a result of human fallibility people may and do hold different opinions with regard to homosexual relationships, and that these different opinions are held in good faith, it does not mean that the differences are insignificant or of no consequence. Wrong opinions and wrong behavior have serious consequences, even if one is convinced (wrongly) that one is acting according to the moral law. For the traditional position, those who hold to the affirming position are advocating an approach that violates biblical commands and God's revealed purpose for sexuality and marriage. They argue that affirming such relationships is detrimental to people's well-being and, more significantly, has serious and possibly ultimate spiritual consequences. For those holding an affirmative position, the traditional view misinterprets the biblical passages and is contrary to the overarching biblical message of God's welcoming grace. This misinterpretation is driving people away from Christian faith, is psychologically damaging, contributes to suicide, and legitimates the rejection of people, resulting in bodily harm. Both traditional and affirming groups see their opponents' views as legitimating sinful behavior with serious consequences. Ultimately both approaches cannot be right, yet both are sincerely held by Christians committed to following Christ and loving their neighbors. Thus, Christians who genuinely hold to their diverse opinions are obliged, out of love for others, to promote them. This is not to deny that other factors do play a role and that not all people who hold to and advocate a particular position are genuinely motivated by loyalty to Christ and love for their neighbors. Very often people's behavior demonstrates the opposite of love.

I have argued that it is possible that faithful Christians might, as a result of human fallibility, come to different understandings of the moral law in relation to homosexuality. These differences, even when acted upon, do not necessarily constitute unrighteousness, yet wrong opinions do have significant consequences. Recognizing this, the substantial question remains: Are these differences of such a character that they should lead to the division of churches? This can only be determined by examining the relationship of the differing positions to the core of the Christian faith; that is, to God's gracious action in Christ by the Spirit to transform the human person, enabling people to genuinely love God and their neighbors. Representatives of both sides claim that their position is an expression of genuine love for one's neighbors—

the difference lies in the interpretation of biblical texts and human sexuality, resulting in what one approach regards as a loving action, the other understands as deeply damaging. If this is to be a church-dividing issue, it must be demonstrated positively that one's position flows out from the central core of the Christian faith and negatively that the views of one's opponents cannot be held without contradicting the central core of the gospel.

The question that churches need to answer is whether, after sincere, intense, loving conferencing, people who hold contradictory opinions are attempting to be faithful to the core of the gospel message and can sustain this same loving stance with others when they disagree. This coherence entails both theological and practical dimensions. Theologically does it cohere with, from a Wesleyan perspective, the central doctrines of sin, justification, regeneration, and sanctification? Practically, are their approaches to and positions on human sexuality compatible with seeking the comprehensive well-being of others? Answering this question entails examining the actual consequences of one's positions on the lives of real people yet recognizing that people will differ on how to determine the characteristics of comprehensive well-being. If this is so, can significant numbers of people on both sides of the debate recognize that they share a common faith and a common mission despite their differences?

If people recognize a common faith, a common mission, a genuine desire to act out of love for God and neighbor, and a broad agreement on core theological issues (recognizing the complexity of defining core issues), then churches have the obligation to develop structures that ensure that people are not required to act contrary to their conscience or be prevented from acting according to their consciences. This is both a rejection of a persecuting spirit and the attempt to fully embody the transforming love of God. What this means in practice is more complicated and will require considerable creative thinking. The following are put forward as proposals for consideration.

1. If there is a common faith, a common mission, and a common desire to act out of love for God and neighbor then, even when there is substantial theological disagreement, these are to be understood not as corrupt churches with "mitred infidels" and "heathenish priests," but as visible expressions of the body of Christ with siblings in Christ who disagree with each other.

2. If, in the context of sanctified conferencing, it is accepted that both an affirming position and a traditional position are compatible with the church's understanding of the core of the gospel and its ethical consequences, then the spiritual integrity of the people holding diverse posi-

tions must be upheld. This means that the offices of the church, including the ordained ministry and the episcopacy, should be open to people holding and practicing both traditional and affirming views. To be an active participant in a church that includes people who disagree with you is not to compromise your faithfulness to Christ. On the contrary it is to faithfully express holiness as love for God and one's siblings in Christ in the recognition that those with whom one disagrees are acting out of love for God and others and thus righteously.

3. Even when the spiritual integrity of the people holding contradictory positions is affirmed, the polity of the church needs to be shaped to provide for people holding opposing positions, so that they can be members and exercise their ministry in a way that is consistent with their consciences. Traditionalist pastors, for example, should not be required to marry same-sex couples, and affirming congregations should not be required to accept pastors who hold to and teach traditionalist views. The dynamic relationship between central and local authority that characterizes Methodist connectional structures will need to be adapted without being transformed into congregationalism.

Even in the context of sanctified conferencing, some people believe that while there is a common faith, a common mission, and a common desire to act out of love for God and neighbor, the disagreement over homosexuality is so serious that it is not possible for members of one group to ordain or offer leadership positions to members of the other group. If this is the case, a more substantial restructuring of church polity will be required. Given Wesley's understanding of sin and holiness, the focus should be not on people's ways of life, when this is consistent with their own theological ethical positions, but on the contradictory character of the content of the theological positions that underlay their ways of life.

If the three "commons" enumerated above are present, then the spiritual integrity of persons must be affirmed even when their ethical views are rejected. Such a church restructuring could include not only separate congregations but also Conferences and bishops (where a church has them) within the context of an overarching structure. Yet, even here the spiritual integrity and faithfulness of the different groups ought to be respected in terms of Wesley's understanding of sin and holiness. Again in this context, to be an active participant in a church structure that includes people who disagree is not to compromise one's position; it is rather to faithfully express holiness as love for God and one's siblings in Christ.

Is it possible to remain a united church when there is no common recognition of each other's faith, mission, and love for God and neighbor; that is, when some members of the church do not regard other members, particularly leaders, as siblings in Christ or view them as deeply compromised in their faith and life? In Wesley's understanding, there is an obligation to remain as long as one is not forced to compromise by being obliged to act against one's conscience nor prevented from acting in accordance with one's conscience. One is not compromised by the presence of people one regards as faithless within the church and its leadership structures. The obligation to remain lies in a duty to pursue the spiritual welfare of others and hence to work for the spiritual renewal of the church. In Wesley's context, remaining was accompanied by pursuing one's own spiritual well-being through active participation in the parallel structures of the Methodist societies.

This book's discussion clearly does not resolve all the issues raised by the divide over human sexuality. To do so would go beyond the scope of this book and transgress into the area that I have argued is the responsibility of Methodist Conferences. However, this discussion also argues, and I would suggest demonstrates, that a Wesleyan theology has a very strong bias toward unity even in the context of deep disagreement and contradiction. Yet I also recognize that there are situations where love requires exclusion, because to remain in connection with holders and practices of some viewpoints would be a denial of a genuine commitment to the comprehensive well-being of others. It is this bias to unity that should fundamentally shape the orientation of the church in facing its decisions about whether to divide. It is precisely faithfulness to the core of the tradition that motivates the struggle for unity with those with whom one disagrees. By this, the church can express the love of God in contrast to the pressures of society and thus embody holiness in the world.

CPSIA information can be obtained
at www.ICGtesting.com
Printed in the USA
LVHW042003230819
628815LV00001B/47